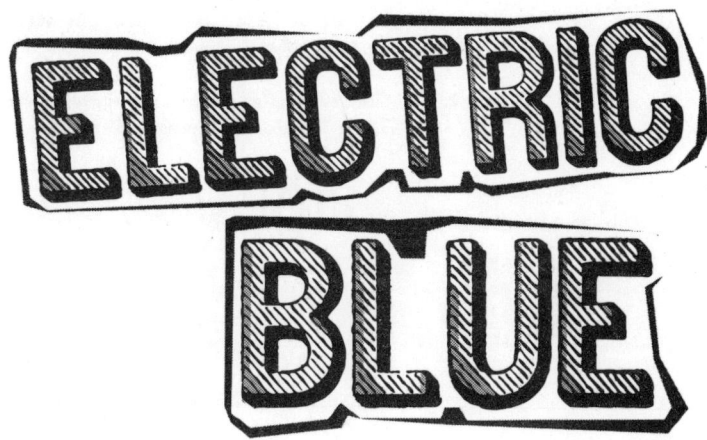

Paul F. Verhoeven

VIKING
an imprint of
PENGUIN BOOKS

The following is based on true events. In order to make this into a good read, some cases have been played with, stitched together, mashed into one another or blown apart for the sake of making them into actual tellable stories. Some names and locations have been changed to protect identities and organisations. Some stories told to the author were unfathomably threadbare, and the author was given permission to 'fill in the blanks carte blanche', which was initially vexing, especially as the author is convinced his father has no idea what 'carte blanche' means. In short, all of these events happened, but joyful, extensive and sensational liberties have been taken.

VIKING

UK | USA | Canada | Ireland | Australia
India | New Zealand | South Africa | China

Viking is part of the Penguin Random House group of companies whose addresses
can be found at global.penguinrandomhouse.com

Penguin
Random House
Australia

First published by Viking in 2020

Cover images: gun © CSA-Printstock/Getty; background texture © meiwphotographer/Shutterstock
Cover design by Alex Ross © Penguin Random House Australia Pty Ltd
Illustrations by Paul F. Verhoeven
Typeset by Midland Typesetters, Australia

Printed and bound in Australia by Griffin Press, part of Ovato, an accredited
ISO AS/NZS 14001 Environmental Management Systems printer

A catalogue record for this
book is available from the
National Library of Australia

ISBN 978 1 76089 777 2

penguin.com.au

MIX
Paper from
responsible sources
FSC® C009448

This book is dedicated to
[Deep inhale, extremely loud Borat voice]
MAH WIIIIIFE!

CONTENTS

PROLOGUE

John's hands gripped the wheel. Blood soaked his shirt. The man writhing next to him screamed and groaned through his ruined face.

This, thought John, *is shaping up to be a really shit day.*

He checked the dash. Not because he needed to glean anything from the speedometer or the fuel gauge, but to distract himself. His friend, he was certain, was going to die. He wasn't ready to admit that just yet – best not to admit defeat, even when it's nuzzling up your leg – but things weren't looking good. The car was dancing below the speed limit, skirting the very edge of it, a warm hum pulsing as the engine threatened to overheat and gutter out entirely.

Another noise, this one more of a bloody burble, yanked John from his trance. *Focus,* he thought. *Focus. You're not far from the hospital. You can fix this. You can make this work. You can get the shit back into the horse, John.* A confused, wet, garbled scream drew John's eye. He looked over at his friend, doubled up, utterly soaked through with his own blood, clenched hands holding his face in place.

John flashed back, somewhat inappropriately, to himself as a child, holding stolen apples in his shirt and sneaking into his house round the back. Just as he was about to make it to his bedroom, the buttons popped and the shirt burst open, unable to bear the burden of his stolen goods. The apples tumbled forth. His dad yelled at him for an hour. *Why am I remembering this?* John thought in a daze, foot stamped down on the accelerator. *Oh. He looks like he's about to let go, too. He can't carry any more.*

They were, John realised, snapping back to the present, still a long way from the hospital. They were in the backstreets now, burning up and down long roads, coursing along winding avenues, and into the kind of dips and troughs you only really saw on the Northern Beaches of Sydney. *We aren't going to make it,* John thought. *He's collapsing. I'm going into shock. I'm—*

And with a rather pleasant *FLOOMP*, the car mounted the gutter at high speed.

And everything went dark.

I

COP TO IT

There's blood everywhere. A murder has been carried out, and only I can solve it.

This, I think, *is shaping up to be a really good book.*

I'm eleven. I'm in a cavernous bookstore at Warringah Mall with my dad, John. He's an ex-cop, and he's over by the thriller section, but before he wandered off to busy himself, he guided me to a shelf, this shelf right here. Then he reached up and handed me a book.

The book is called *Who Killed Harlowe Thrombey?* and, much like me, it weighs almost nothing. I'm tall, and lean, and very bored. And I'm sad. I'm very sad, and I don't know why. Maybe Dad knows. Maybe that's why he's brought me shopping.

The book isn't a normal book, not like the one you're holding. Huge, delirious letters proclaim that it's a Choose Your Own Adventure story. The cover is a brazen late-seventies-style mishmash of tropes: the sinister gardener lurking in the corner, the big-chinned hero detective floating up near the title. It's like a movie poster, I think to myself, turning it over in my hand. A movie poster on a book. What a world.

Dad is eyeing me from across the store. He's wearing an expression one wears when hoping not to startle a deer. I open the book, that heady new-book smell reaching my nose almost instantly, and I'm worried that after years of completely bouncing off the written word, this book will offer me nothing.

I have ADHD, you see. My brain just sort of wanders off after a few pages whenever I try to read. I enjoy the first few pages, the promise the books hold, but then I fear that the ADHD will take control yet again. ADHD: Attention Deficit Hyperactivity Disorder. Ever tried to wrestle with ADHD? Imagine your brain, your focus, your drive, your attention, as a plume of smoke. Got it? Thick, cloying, sweet smoke, swirling churlishly around your head.

Now, imagine someone standing in front of you. They're waving. You should probably wave back. There we go! Now you're both waving.

And what's that he's holding? A big glass bottle. He's handing it to you. He's . . . right, he's seen something shiny and run off after it. Just you and the bottle now, kid.

Now, do me a favour, would you? Try to get the smoke back into the bottle. No, I'm serious. That's what having ADHD is like.

Eleven-year-old me – god, I'm adorable – looks up at Dad again. See how hopeful he is? He wants me to read the book, I can tell. He wants me to make an effort.

When I was a kid, my dad was a cop. He's not a cop at this point, mind you, he's a firefighter. And as I stand there in the bookstore, walls of great works towering around me, and my dad's great works practically wafting off him like a highway mirage, I wonder what it must be like for a person like him to have a kid like me. Because it's bizarre growing up with a larger-than-life father, let me tell you. Dad spent years in General Duties, which just means he was a regular beat cop, in uniform, patrolling the streets and relent-lessly pursuing leads. Then he headed to Forensics. You know, all the really gory stuff: corpses, fingerprints, trace evidence. Digging up bodies. Autopsies. Snappy one-liners. A weird career path, to be sure, but Dad's a weird guy.

He's walked over now, trying to act casual. So I humour him, and begin to lazily peruse the book he handed me. And there, right there, on the second page, is . . . wait.

A choice.

This book is going to let me choose. If my idiot brain wants to run away with itself and pursue leads, pursue what-ifs, run down forgotten alleyways, the book will actually encourage it. Unlike regular books – and real life – this story in my hands encourages do-overs. I look up at Dad, wonder in my eyes.

'Is real police work like this?' I ask, holding the tiny paperback aloft. Dad looks down at me, smiles – a smile which, upon reflec-tion, is a little too sad to burden a kid with – and says, 'No, mate. If I made a mistake when I was a policeman . . . I had to live with it.'

Dad takes the book from me and kind of tunes out for a moment, clearly thinking something over. I just sort of watch the guy, holding the book in his hands, thinking. He looks around the store, smiles at me, and heads to the counter. He pulls out a huge leather wallet, distended from a thousand compressed business cards crammed inside, draws out a crinkled note, smooths it, and hands it to the cashier. She rings up the purchase, and Dad hands me the book in a brown paper bag. Then we head home.

Because of the unique yet exhausting way my brain works, you're going to have to keep up with my ricocheting between the present and the past. Now it's twenty-six years later, and my folks live somewhere else. But it's okay, we're still home. Their home. We're currently standing outside my parents' cosy little apartment. They've lived here for a touch over a year, and it's so immaculate, so carefully curated and stacked with artisanal, minimalist pieces of design and art that you'd be forgiven for thinking you're standing in a film set.

Let's head on in. You can leave your shoes on, just don't drag any mud in. We'll just head down these stairs and knock.

It's okay. Don't be nervous. Dad is lovely. Weird, but lovely. Those two things aren't mutually exclusive, at least not in my family. What we're about to do, friends, is sit down with Dad and find out where I went astray, if indeed that's what I did. Why wasn't I capable of doing what he did? And why are we so different? He's a man of focus, of drive, of grit. I'm the exact opposite, and that point of difference has been eating me up, as much as I hate to admit it. So I'm here for answers. I want to find out how Dad made the hard choices, and why I struggled to make even the simplest of choices. Was it the ADHD? Was it cowardice? And why did the apple fall so far from the tree?

Shh! Here he comes.

It's actually Mum who opens the door. Mum, actual name Christine, beams at me and envelops me in a hug. She makes an elongated, delighted 'ohhhh!' sound, as if she's surprised to see me, which is impossible because I called ahead. I think what I'm discovering as I get older is that Mum is perpetually stoked to see me, which is the kind of ambient affection that really keeps the emotional engine running on low days. She ushers me into the living room.

'Your father is driving me insane, Paul.'

Dad looks up. Currently, the hero cop (ex–hero cop) is leaning over, refusing to bend his legs, combing the tassels on a lavish Persian rug . . . with a hairbrush. He looks up at me with an expression that says, *I know you want me to look ashamed about this. But I'm not ashamed about this. These tassels were out of alignment, Paul.*

'This had better not go in the fucking book, mate,' Dad says aloud.

'Why would I put it in the book?' I reply calmly, making a mental note to put it not just in the book, but right near the start of the book so it sticks in everyone's memory.

Dad places the hairbrush on a sideboard, asks me if I want anything to drink, ignores me when I tell him I'd like a whiskey sour, then sits. He picks up a leather-bound Moleskine, carefully unwinding the elastic that binds the pages in place. I told Dad to take lots of notes on cases from his Forensics years, because they're the years he never talked about. I knew it would take him months to dredge this stuff up. And if I'm honest, his notebook is practically creaking. The damn thing is fit to burst, and I realise he's done to it what most men do to their wallets: overstuffed it to the point where storing it in his jeans pocket would give him a herniated disc.

It's at this point that Dad notices the book I bought. It's gift-wrapped, carefully swaddled in coarse brown paper and crisscrossed with frayed twine. I hand it to him. He weighs the package, shaking it as if it were something other than a book.

'Did you wrap this?' he asks, eyeing the small rectangular parcel.

'Yes,' I lie. It was, in fact, wrapped by my wife, Tegan. She has the kind of dexterous hands that were born to pick locks; thank god she avoided committing larceny in the past, or her having ex-cops for parents-in-law would be a jot awkward.

Dad pulls the bow and the string cascades to either side with a soft *shfffff*. He then peels away the paper – just the top at first – and stops. Peering out from the opening is the edge of a small paperback. In a decidedly dated font, bold and hugged by a red bar, are the words *CHOOSE YOUR OWN ADVENTURE*.

Dad pauses and smiles at me. 'I think I know what this is,' he says. 'I'll get to this tonight. I . . . Is this the crime one?'

'Yes,' I answer, returning his smile. 'The crime one.'

He looks at it again, a grateful expression playing over his face. He then pops it down next to his notebook, picks the warped object up, and flicks to the first page. 'Where do you want to start?'

'Well,' I reply, 'I'm trying to figure you out, Dad. And I get why I didn't end up in uniform – I'm a tremendous physical coward. But forensics is details. It's Sherlock Holmes dusting for prints, analysing evidence. It's granular. It's . . . perfect for me. And yet, even forensics wasn't something I felt the pull to do. I need to find out why I didn't end up where you did, Dad. So let's begin at the beginning. Forensics – it's not car chases, sprinting after bad guys, arrests. It's just . . . pretty basic, right?'

He looks like I just farted into his drink.

'Buckle up, dear boy,' he says, glowering smugly. 'Buckle up.'

2

KEEPING IT CLEAN

John wanted to be a detective.

As in, past tense. Wanted. He'd spent four years ostensibly fighting crime, going above and beyond. Police in General Duties often just got on with the job. Not John. He'd been singularly focused from day one, secretly running towards his *actual* goal: making detective. Detecting. He even had his detective 'look' sorted. When John started out, he was as skinny as a rake, but he was a rake with ambition.

By the time he finished General Duties, however, he'd seen some serious shit. And it had worn him down a little. Aged him. His dark hair was still swept to one side, he still had piercing blue eyes, and he still (mostly) loved being a cop. But he'd stopped smiling quite as much as he had when he enrolled, and after witnessing a string of incidents involving detectives behaving appallingly, he'd become . . . a little scuffed. A tad worn down. John thought about all those bodies, all those cases he'd chased to curry favour with the boys upstairs, to impress people. If detectives were bent, were broken, what was he supposed to do now? The prognosis was clear. He had officially become jaded.

John spent a solid week mulling things over. He'd return home after each shift and sit there, holding his young son on his knee, staring out the window. He'd press the heels of his hands into his eyes until his vision was filled with prisms of light undulating sickeningly towards him. He even considered taking up smoking again, but was too worried about the smell seeping into the carpet. 'Maybe you could try chewing tobacco,' his colleague and occasional mentor Dunne suggested in his thick Glaswegian accent. *Maybe that could be my thing,* thought John. Then he realised he'd have to buy a spittoon, and swiftly jettisoned the idea.

In short, John was lost. Very, very lost.

If you've never been lost, it is, in the words of Oscar Wilde, rather fucked. Your brain throws a vigorous pity party to which nobody is invited, except for you, and you're in a terrible mood, so naturally the party is not a fun one to attend. And in order to alleviate this darkness, you can of course bury yourself in your work. But what if your work is mind-numbingly dark already? John could spend a whole night talking with his wife, Christine, about the job they shared; she was, after all, a hell of a cop herself. He could build up buttresses and merlons and crenels—

'Paul, what the fuck are merlons and crenels?'

'Well,' I explain, 'you know those towers on castles?' Dad nods. He is, for now, following me. 'You know the bit along the top that goes up, then across, then down? Like teeth?' Dad nods. He is still following me. 'The merlons are the top bits, the crenels are the in-between bits.'

Dad is no longer following me.

John could bolster his defences until the cows came home, but by the morning, he'd head into work, check the roster, and before lunch a domestic assault or a dead body would blast his precious defences away. Fighting off a sense of directionlessness in the face of such overwhelming adversity was like building a sandcastle in the hopes of stopping a rising tide. It also occurred to John that enduring these ordeals made a degree of sense . . . only if they were adding up to something bigger, something better. What was the point of facing such horrors if they weren't leading him to his promised land, his dream career?

John had no idea what to do. Julian, his old partner, had buggered off to another department, heading up the ziggurat of promotion after promotion, but John had sworn off being a detective. He needed something new. He needed something fresh. And he thought he knew where he was headed, he truly did. But there were things that John had seen over the years in the New South Wales Police Force that had begun to make him question everything.

John's stomping ground as a beat cop was North Sydney Police Station, a looming wedge-shaped building in the heart of the bustling suburb. But given that his ex-partner Julian had since hoofed it, John needed to get a little time away from his usual surrounds. Ever been dumped and had everything in your hometown remind you of the one that got away? North Sydney Station had become a minefield of reminders. That cell? That's the cell John was planted in when he pretended to be a prisoner to sneak intel from a crook. That interview room? Julian and John once fished inside a jewel thief's jocks and pulled out a king's ransom in warm, sweaty, priceless purloined goods. Julian had ignored the warning signs and accepted the offer to become a detective. He'd been gone for two months now. And as time marched on and John lapsed back into his routine without his partner, he got . . . well, sad. And he needed a change of scenery, if only a slight one. So he requested a temporary stint of shifts at a nearby station. Just to get away from his ghosts for a bit.

As he rocked up at the new station for his first proper shift, it struck him how odd every shift there was going to be. The building was an old Victorian home in a quiet street.

'Dad,' I chime in, 'you're describing Heartbeat. *This is literally just the show* Heartbeat.*'*

'Paul,' Dad replies, 'you and I both know that Heartbeat *took place in Ashfordly, the small town in Yorkshire. And while I cut a good figure, I'm nothing on PC Nick Rowan.'*

My dad is a weird guy.

The period home, John realised after being given his first proper tour of the place, was a legitimate period home. Fireplaces (roaring, on occasion); antique clocks thwacking away in palatial rooms; ornate wallpaper; thick, opulent curtains bound up with fat coils of velvety rope. It was, John noted as he walked from room to room, gazing with wonder in his eyes, not a place that invoked the enactment of justice. It called to mind tea and scones, perhaps, but not justice. Maybe Miss Marple's brand of justice, he amended as he traipsed through another doorway.

John was soon reminded that this station had another few curious quirks. Until recently it had no night shift, only day and evening shifts, as there were no detectives stationed there. At 11 each night, the doors would be locked and the station would be closed. It was a deeply eccentric place to work, but John began to take to it somewhat. Or, at the very least, it was different enough from North Sydney to confuse him out of his funk. This ridiculously well-appointed building was . . . well . . . it was ridiculously well-appointed.

'Why,' John asked his new desk sergeant, 'is this place so ridiculously well-appointed?' And the desk sergeant leaned in, somewhat conspiratorially, and told John why.

This station had been in a state of disrepair, if not utter decrepitude, for many years. The building was in such a bad way that the New South Wales Police Force was on the verge of shutting it down. A formerly great thing, capable of doling out justice, was utterly spent. Then a very influential pillar of the local community entered the scene. He just so happened to live across the road.

This very influential pillar of the local community was old, and fussy, and liked what he liked. And he liked living across the road from a stately home within which hot piping justice was dispensed. And so he brought to bear his considerable influence, and called in every favour he could – and he could call in quite a few. And before long, millions upon millions of taxpayer dollars were being channelled passionately and somewhat recklessly into this old, gorgeous house. And that's what John was gazing at as he paced around his new temporary workplace: a very expensive passion project. Before long, the pillar of the local community had defibrillated the husk of a station into a thriving enterprise staffed by detectives, highway patrol . . . you name it. And they made it open twenty-four hours. So when John wandered in for his tour, the place was pumping.

'Why would he go to all that effort,' John whispered to the desk sergeant, gesturing around the room at all the majesty, 'to get this place up and running to this degree? Why would he insist on having it going around the clock?'

'Because,' said the sergeant, 'two things. First off, he wanted to feel safer. To know that at any given moment there'd be a fully functioning bastion of law enforcement awake and alert literally across the road from his house. And secondly,' he said, leaning in closer, 'sometimes . . . sometimes it's nice to see something with potential and to . . . you know. Fix it.'

I'm this building, thought John. *I'm in a state of disrepair. I could be helping people. I just need to find something to . . . renovate me.*

After his leisurely tour of the building, John was led around a corner and introduced to the officer in charge of the whole place. It was rather late, which John thought might at least partially account for this officer's attire, but only a little. The man was dressed in pyjamas.

'Pyjamas?'
'Pyjamas.'

Head to toe in lovely, cushy flannelette pyjamas and a soft, downy dressing gown. The enormous senior officer had a ruddy complexion, grey hair in a military buzzcut, and jowls that made him look like a cartoon St Bernard. He held a steaming mug aloft, and John noted a hint of something sweet on the air. Chocolate? Was this platinum-grade eccentric really running a police station, even one as homely as this, in his pyjamas . . . while drinking hot chocolate?

John shook the man's huge, clammy hand, eyeballed him cautiously and let the sergeant lead him into an adjoining room to fill out some paperwork. Once he'd checked to see St Bernard had toddled off into the recesses of the building, he resumed his whispered debriefing with the sergeant. 'Was he drinking hot chocolate? Was he wearing . . .'

The desk sergeant waved John off. 'Yes. He does that. But of all the shit he pulls here, that's just about the tamest.' At which point the desk sergeant unloaded something which was at best corrupt, and at worst very corrupt, into John's lap.

St Bernard, as John discovered with increasing disgust, was an industrious man. Perhaps this quality came from being in a state of constant pre-beddy-byes-level relaxation, but regardless, the man had done something rather brazen. You see, the sergeant told John, every police station has to be cleaned. But who actually does the cleaning? External companies, cleaning companies, typically bid for the contract to be the dedicated cleaners of said facility. Because the police are taxpayer funded, this means that the cleaning bill is footed by everyday schmoes. But St Bernard, what did he do when the refurbishment finished and the bid went out? Pulled some strings of his own, he did. Made sure that he got the cleaning contract.

'But wouldn't that mean he'd have to, you know . . . clean?'

'Yep,' replied the sergeant. 'That's the implication.'

'So how does he manage to clean the place? He's just one man.'

The sergeant raised an eyebrow.

Later that night, John was scrubbing the downstairs toilet, wondering if this was the kind of distraction he'd been looking for.

'So . . . wait,' I interject. 'You cleaned? He made you clean the toilets?'

Dad shakes his head and waves his notebook around emphatically. 'Mate, he got everyone who wasn't senior to clean the place. Toilets, floors, windows . . . lawns, the whole thing. Then he'd collect the contract money himself, and put it straight into his account. A sizeable annual sum. So we'd come in on the night shift, and the constables did all the station cleaning, scrubbing away. And that, Paul, is not why I joined the police force.'

I sit up straight, eyes wide. 'No: you want to clean up crime, not poo!'

Dad pauses for a long while. Then, finally, he speaks. 'That was good, Paul.'

While the constables were cleaning, where *weren't* they? As John thought on this much later that evening, hunched over the porcelain bowl in the narrow cubicle, it finally twigged. 'We're not out there,' he muttered, panting. 'We're not out there, helping people. We're not . . . policing.'

As the week wore on, so did the cleaning. It became apparent to John that neither he nor any of his colleagues were going to receive any kickback for doing this manual labour.

'Think it's too late to ask him for your money now?' I ask.

Dad scoffs. 'He was ancient then, mate. He's long dead by now.'

Anyway, John was realising he wasn't being treated as a cop. He was a custodian. He was the groundskeeper in some corrupt little fiefdom. And as he slogged away, he racked his brain for something else he could pursue career-wise that would allow him to solve problems and fight crime but keep him away from this shit, both literally and figuratively.

Truth be told, while John was scrubbing he spent most of his time drifting back into his head, gradually building a case against becoming a detective. Which is odd, because he'd always wanted to be one. But just like someone considering leaving a long-term relationship, John felt he needed to be sure, really, truly sure, before he pulled the pin. John had already seen smatterings of corruption, obfuscation, double-dealing. He'd already seen these apparent pinnacles of the policing institution disappoint him countless times. He'd seen detectives assault witnesses, bend the rules, and even scuttle one of his investigations. But he still felt he needed just a little more certainty. He needed something potent, something final that would push him over the edge, and towards his fallback avenue of career advancement.

Forensics.

Mere days later, he was given the push of a lifetime.

Detectives were, John had discovered over his four years in General Duties, ranked unofficially among the regular cops by how intense they were. Not intense in terms of their haughty demeanour, but in terms of how willing they were to scare the shit out of everyone around them to get results. And on this particular night, John was called away from his housekeeping duties to deliver some paperwork to North Sydney Station. He pulled up some way from the station in his vehicle, yanking back the handbrake and letting the engine cool down as he sat there, staring down the alley towards the place he'd become a cop.

It was raining heavily that night. Film-noir heavy. Pissing down. One of those torrential nights that seemed to suit Sydney, all the rolling hills and crunchy, complex little backstreets turned into darkened waterfalls. John stared down at the pinpricks of light coming from the station, dancing around, peeking at him through the torrents of water that flowed over the car window. He grabbed the paperwork, opened the door . . . and was instantly drenched. Nipples completely visible through his shirt.

This is one of those details I'd generally cut out, but if Dad says 'my nipples were completely visible through my shirt', I think it's useful for him later, when this is being read out at a book launch or a panel discussion at a writers' festival, to know that he did, in fact, specify that his male nipples were standing erect and completely visible. There you go, Dad. Never say I don't pay attention to what you tell me.

Realising the manila envelope he was holding was going to get drenched in the downpour, too, John cast about for a safe place to shelter during the storm, and spotted . . .

The front entrance to the detective HQ. He'd pulled up outside the very place he'd been hoping to avoid. 'Unsubtle,' John muttered skywards as he ran for cover. 'Some pretty un-fucking-subtle symbolism.' Reaching the safety of the entrance to the building, John stood panting with his back against a large cement pillar, water pooling by his feet. He swung the file back and forth. Relatively dry, he noted.

Unlike his nipples, which stood aggressively to attention.

Is this a sign? he thought. *The department I'm trying to run from literally offering me shelter?* He looked up at the building. It was glowing, sturdy. A beacon in the storm. *Jesus,* he thought. *This is a metaphor. I'm standing in a fucking metaphor.* And because John was tired, and a little confused, and thoroughly soaked, he began to do the thing all tired, confused and soaked people do: he began to over-analyse. And he began to attribute meaning where there was none. And John didn't realise this, but he was already at something of a fork in the road. Here, he could make a choice. A choice that would change his entire life.

He looked at the entrance to the building, the lift parked patiently in the lobby. *I could walk over to that lift right now,* he thought. *I could head up to the fourth floor, shake some hands, say*

I changed my mind. Change my no to a yes. Fill out the paperwork. I could do it. Maybe this is a sign. I was looking for a push . . . maybe I was just looking to push myself in the wrong direction. John looked down at the file, at his hands, hands that still reeked of cleaning fluid. *What am I doing,* he thought, a sudden startling clarity flooding his addled brain. *I'm here. Just go in, John! Enough with the shit-kicking grunt work. It's easy. Just walk over, and choose to be a detective. Time to do some fucking policing. Time to—*

SLAM.

The sudden, violent expulsion of the stairwell door inside the lobby sent any cosmic significance zipping into the night air. Through the door came two large detectives, one frighteningly bulky and with a face like a clenched fist, who dragged a man behind them towards the sliding doors, and towards John. He stared, then realised staring would be very, very dangerous, and made himself as inconspicuous as he could, pretending to peruse the file as he leaned against the pillar. It worked; the detectives dragged the man, half walking, half stumbling, through the doors and into the rain.

The lead detective, however – the one with bulk that made the ground shake – looked at John. Looked at him with the dead eyes of a shark. And with a sinking feeling, John realised he didn't need to hide. Because these men didn't care if a shivering, confused uniformed officer was there. They were detectives. They were going to do whatever the hell they wanted to.

The larger detective let go of the prisoner, leaving the lightly battered man wobbling in the clutches of his colleague. He strode over to the nearby gutter and reached down, threading his thick, callused fingers through the grate of a stormwater drain. John watched as torrents of rainwater flowed around the detective's meaty wrist, soaking his sleeve. The man grunted through a frankly impossible display of strength: there was a metallic whine, a scraping sound, and then a kind of wet, sucking *POP* as the grate was wrenched free and laid aside. The detective, grey suit now almost black thanks to the endless rain, gestured to his colleague. The prisoner was dragged over, and the two of them lowered the man – screaming and burbling beneath the torrents of rainwater – into the storm drain.

John watched them put the grate back into place. And the man, now out of sight, screamed. He screamed and he screamed. And as the pleading turned to babbled, frightened, desperate confessions, the lead detective looked over at John. John, standing there, also frightened, transfixed by the brazenness, the injustice of what he was watching. And the detective raised a hand – a hand John now noted, with some alarm, was marked by faintly split knuckles – and shushed John.

Shushed him, and went about his business.

John watched, entranced, as the man inside the drain frantically confessed to all manner of things, things he likely didn't even do, to earn his freedom. John watched as the man's fingers clung to the bars of the grate, grasping white-knuckled, to stop himself being washed out to sea. And before John knew it, the grate was lifted off and the man hauled out and dragged back into the building. The detectives ignored John this time, heading back through the double doors and over to the lift. There was a ding, the lift doors groaned shut, and John was left staring at the dark, wet trail that marked their passage back into the building.

There was a loud ringing in his ears.

He looked down at the file. It was shaking. His hands were shaking. *Why didn't you say anything?* His hands wouldn't stop shaking.

And just like that, his choice was made for him.

Plan B.

3

AWW, SNAP

First off: readers, I hear you. I thought Dad was going to barrel headfirst from one exciting career path to the next. I didn't realise he almost relapsed, almost drifted back towards something he swore he'd never do.

But more alarming, to me at least, is something he just told me.

'Dad,' I ask, not entirely sure which approach to take here, 'why didn't you stop them?'

Dad scoffs. Well, he doesn't exactly scoff. Harrumphs? 'Mate, if I'd said anything, told them to stop . . . I'd have been put in the drain with that man.' I look at Dad. He's serious. They'd have done it. Or, at least, he believes they'd have done it.

'But why not . . . you know . . . try? Why not at least try?'

Dad looks decidedly uncomfortable. Then he squirms a little, looks at his hands, clears his throat and begins leafing through his battered notebook. 'So,' he says, signalling that this line of questioning is at an end. 'Forensics.'

John began his career in forensics at Chatswood Scientific.

It wasn't hard for him to secure a position working in Relieve and Assist, the wing of police forensics which, at that time, didn't actually require any formal scientific training. All training took place on the job, and because of John's somewhat dense and bizarre service record, one that involved his actively pursuing the most challenging cases he could, a quick perusal of his arrest rate and case history meant he was something of a shoo-in. Forensics were, as it turned out, more than happy to snap up the young constable who'd been offered a chance to become a detective and actually turned it down.

You see, there were scientists in the Scientific division, but they needed eager young minds with a thirst for the strange, the unusual. And John was . . . well, he was unusual, and he was running very hard away from one thing, and looking for something to run towards. So he'd made some calls, filed some paperwork, had a word with a friend down at the Glebe Morgue, and before long he was working in Relieve and Assist.

'Relieve and Assist,' I remark. 'Sounds like . . .'

I make a hand gesture. You know which hand gesture. I immediately regret it. Dad gives me a 'I know, I know' look and, upsettingly yet predictably, returns the gesture. Mum chooses this moment to walk into the room, seeing her husband and her son miming jerking it in her living room. Her eyes widen and she spins on her heel, heading back the way she came.

To relieve and assist meant one thing: when an actual trained forensics person was away, a regular cop with potential – and an inclination to climb the forensics ladder – would step in and fill their role. Lots of people applied, but John impressed the higher-ups, and before long, there he was.

The new position gave John the distance he needed. He was suddenly whipped away from his precinct and flung across to Chatswood, a wealthy, woody and slightly mysterious suburb. Chatswood looked vaguely suburban, but it had nooks and crannies John hadn't traversed yet. Not a world away from North Sydney, only fifteen minutes or so by car to the north, but John was going to have to learn the ins and outs of his area once again, which meant distractions. Good. More distractions were good.

Chatswood Scientific was attached to the main Chatswood Police Station building, squatting in what could charitably be called the Chatswood CBD. Well, 'attached' might have been a touch inaccurate, John noted. Chatswood Scientific resided in a free-standing cottage out the back of the station itself, and one of the great things about being there was that he could do plain-clothes work.

At long last. John was in plain clothes. Something – you guessed it – he'd been secretly looking forward to before he went off the idea of becoming a detective. You know how sometimes there's a thing you want, a small, silly thing, but you don't want to admit out loud the magnitude of its significance to you? See, John was a romantic. He'd been reading detective novels his whole life, and he was dying to build a look for himself, for his detective persona.

Now, this? This I find fascinating. I've been floundering a little, to be honest with you all, trying to find commonalities between Dad and me. He was a cop, I was a nerd. He was a man who made the hard choices, I was – and am – a man who simply cannot choose. But this is magical.

'Dad,' I ask, 'before you tell me about this look you were going for — if you were going to be a detective . . .'

'I wasn't a detective,' he responds.

'Yes, yes, I know that. But if you were, would this look you're going to tell me about have been it?'

'I don't know,' he replies, dryly. Nope. Not backing down.

'Dad, humour me. You wanted to be a detective for ages. You also just admitted you were looking forward to the plain-clothes part. So what I want to know is this: the look you built, was this the look you would have worn had you been a detective?'

He stares at me, shrugs, then nods.

'Right! That's great, Dad. So what would you have called your detective self?'

Now he's thrown. Truly thrown. 'What do you mean? John. I'd have been called John.'

'No, no no. John is boring. No offence. But John isn't a cool detective name to go with a cool detective look. Just for fun, what would your cool detective name be?'

'John.'

'No, not John!'

Dad, irritated, glances around. This isn't going anywhere.

'Right,' I say. 'Here's what I'd do, Dad, and I can't believe I'm having to walk you through how to use one's imagina-tion. See what I'm drinking?' His eye comes to rest on my drink.

I look down at the can. It's one of those hipstery canned drinks with a flexing arm on the front, below which aggressive, bold letters proudly spell out HARD SELTZER. I nod approvingly. Hard Seltzer. Good, good detective name.

'Right,' I say, smiling. 'If I was a detective, that's what I'd call myself. Hard Seltzer. See? Easy. Sure you don't want to take a spin at a cool name?'

And Dad, bless him, looks a little . . . ashamed? Maybe a touch embarrassed. So I smile at him. 'You can have the name, Dad. I'd have made a terrible detective anyway. So . . . talk me through this look of yours.'

John went to Warringah Mall, sans Christine. For the first time in a year he was excited about work. He had to look the part, though. For years he'd seen detectives spruced up in three-piece suits, but that was old school. John needed to bring something fresh to the table.

Unfortunately, police don't earn a lot, and raising kids wasn't cheap. So after perusing the price tags at Warringah Mall, which induced in John a deep, smoky depression, he hopped back in his car and made the drive over to the nearest Vinnies. John wandered in, still determined to come up with a look that suited him, that would be his personal brand as he coasted from crime scene to crime scene. He sauntered over to the nearest rack and began flicking through shirts, the smell of mothballs assailing him.

An hour later, he stood in front of Christine in their apartment, wearing his freshly assembled ensemble. John wore chartreuse corduroy slacks, an off-white shirt, suede shoes, a skinny brown tie and a mustard-coloured suede jacket. The jacket he already owned, and the shoes were a gift from Christine that he'd not yet had cause to wear, but here he was. Hard Seltzer.

'John,' Dad corrects me.

Here he was. John Verhoeven. Plain-clothes. Not a detective, but hell, Chatswood Scientific was his new beat. And he had a whole lot to learn. Why not do it with a new look?

'You look like a pimp,' Christine said, leaning against a door-frame, before she took a bite out of an apple and chewed it nonchalantly.

John looked up at her. 'What do you mean? I look hip!'

She shook her head, tutting. Christine was the kind of dry, no-bullshit second opinion John really didn't need right now. She chuckled. 'No no no no. You look like . . . Well, I think you know what you look like, John.' She padded over, kissed him on the cheek, and left the room. Christine was a uniformed officer, John thought sulkily. What would she know?

The fact is, when you're in uniform, you're aspiring to get into plain clothes. Some cops want this because they crave the informality, others because they yearn to craft their own identity. Uniforms are a way to make people . . . well, uniform. But John's whole career had been about him trying to stand up, to stand out, to exceed the constraints of his predetermined role. A uniform made him less distinct, and he'd regularly gone outside the bounds of his jurisdiction to close cases that ordinary patrol officers usually wouldn't think to pursue. Suddenly, he was able to *look* different, too. As if to illustrate this point, he'd made sure to pick up multiples of his slacks and shirt, so that he could wear his new look over and over. His new 'uniform' might look a little eccentric, and it might smell like mothballs, but it was his.

John also found out that while in plain clothes, he still got to carry a gun. Just like a detective. He still got to drive to crime scenes in unmarked cars. Just like a detective. And if he saw something horrendous, something sketchy going down, he could still barrel over and intervene. Just like a detective. *I am,* John thought, walking into Chatswood Scientific for his first day, *basically a detective. I got everything I wanted, and I didn't have to sell out. I did it. I won!*

John was halfway through congratulating himself when he walked, face-first, into a very clean glass door.

Once he'd recovered, he strolled inside to make his introductions. His new supervisor, a bookish man named Grey, was already waiting at the entrance to meet him. The reverberant *PONG* of John connecting with the glass door had apparently alerted him, and he'd shuffled to his feet and walked from his desk to usher John in.

Grey was tall, wore a velvet suit, had enormous sideburns and was, as his name would imply, grey haired. His hair, which was an absolute mess of curls, sat above two piercing eyes. His big, rubbery, droopy face was friendly enough, and the pat he gave John implied that he, too, had at one time or another *PONG*ed the door as well.

'Oh, good grief,' Grey exclaimed, eyeballing John. 'You need a coffee. Poor lad. Let's pop off to the kitchens, then we can start our work in earnest.'

Thus began a rigorous game of catch-up, with Grey as his mentor. Grey's teaching method was set to 'deluge': drown John in as much information as possible, and hope that some of it stuck. It took John about a week to get into the rhythm of his simpler duties, but in a nutshell, his job in Relieve and Assist consisted of the following.

A horrendous crime is committed. A body tumbles to the floor, someone finds said body. There's a scream, a panicked phone call. General Duties arrive and realise they're out of their depth, because the crime scene is more tangled than they're capable of untangling. No big deal. Call in Forensics! When John was in General Duties, he'd regularly discover a scene and in most cases – unless he was truly sneaky, which he often had been – he'd be told to piss off, leave it to the experts. Those experts? John was working with them now. Not even detectives were allowed into the inner sanctum of a taped-off crime scene before Scientific got a look-in. John would head along to these horrendous crime scenes – evidence, organic and inorganic, strewn about like wrapping paper after a vicious Christmas morning – and duck under the tape, ready to begin observing.

And that's what the core of the job is, Grey would tell John, watching him with a bushy, wizardly eyebrow raised. Gesturing at the bodies lying about the place, he'd ask probing questions: 'What do you see, John? Does anything about this look off to you? Tell me what you think happened.' John would venture his guesses, taking a swing at deduction, and often Grey would politely correct him. John would then take photos, always in black and white, of the grisly remains hither and thither, as a way of preserving the crime scene long after clean-up.

'Why black and white?'

'Because,' says Dad, 'the courts reached a point where lawyers defending killers were arguing that the red of blood in photos would sway juries. Too evocative. So they made us take all photos in black and white. Stupid. And do you know the worst part of that job, of photographing victims for court cases? Many of them were alive. Many of the photos I took were of women's injuries after they'd been bashed by complete pieces of shit, whose lawyers didn't want juries swayed by purple bruising or red blood. The defence counsel, defending wife-bashers, started arguing that we could have been using

different-coloured filters to make the bruising, the swelling, the
bleeding look worse. How's that?'
     My expression provides Dad with his answer.

'John,' Grey said later that day, after a tour of the facilities and a
rundown of some fundamentals, 'I truly am glad you're here. And
I suspect we'll get along like a bloody house on fire. So. You up for a
little on-the-job training? I'm heading off to an arson. If you're game?'
     John was, indeed, game.

Dad gets up to visit the bathroom, grunting slightly as he goes
from sitting to standing. He turns, heads to a dresser drawer,
opens it, and hands me something heavy. The thing is wrapped in
one of Mum's scarves, and all I can feel is a jumble of odd, indis-
cernible angles. Once he retreats into the room he's likely going
to render uninhabitable for the next hour, I gingerly unwrap the
parcel. Inside lies an old but very well-cared-for camera. The lens
is enormous, and the whole thing gleams. This, I realise, is Dad's
camera. Dad's bloody camera. For all his talk of minimalism and
getting rid of possessions to avoid being tied down by them, Dad
has swaddled his precious camera up and hidden it away. What else
is he hiding, I wonder? What other artefacts has he secreted about
the apartment? And why did he hand this to me now?
     As I probe the camera, inspecting every detail, I have a flashback.
Hah! Flash. It's a camera. I chuckle at my shitty joke.
     I'm in a darkroom at Cromer High School. Which is to say,
I'm there in the flashback; I haven't literally travelled there to tell
you this story. But the flashback feels real. Very real. I'm about
eighteen years old and it's a humid afternoon, the coarse fabric of

my uniform clinging to my gangly frame. The fabric is cerulean blue. Cerulean blue. Cerulean blue.

My art teacher, whose name escapes me but whose face is etched in my mind, is trying to tell me how to develop film. The smell of chemicals is making my eyes burn . . . or maybe my brain is adding that part. A sort of mimetic garnish, to augment the vividness of the flashback. You know, dramatic set-dressing. Maybe it was odourless? *Get back on track, Paul. Don't lose it.* I'm in the room, and the teacher is asking me why I volunteered for photography if I wasn't going to listen. I tell her sorry, I'm sorry, I'm having a flashback, I'm trying to remember this as it's happening *and* explain it in the present day. Or maybe I didn't say that . . .

Ah.

That was it.

I'm telling her that my dad has a beautiful camera at home. A beautiful old camera, one he used to take photos with at work.

'And what does he do?' the beleaguered teacher asks in the muddy red light of the darkroom, her sooty eyes burning into me, just as the fumes that may or may not be there burn into my eyes. And I say, oh, he was a cop. And she says, okay. He'd have photographed some pretty horrific stuff, huh? And I say, yes. Yes, he did. I saw the photos.

And now I'm remembering being a seven-year-old. The school uniform is gone, replaced by pyjamas, and I'm playing in our walk-in wardrobe, shimmying up the walls like an acrobat. My arm span is the exact width of the tiny space, so I plant my hands on one wall and my feet on the other, and I inch my way up until I'm almost flush with the ceiling.

Then my dad comes in, looking for me. It's dark in the wardrobe, and Dad squints, peering about the place. He seems confused. *If he's a cop,* I think, *why's he so bad at detecting me? Why can't he crack THIS case?* He makes a loud sighing sound, and I feel guilty.

That's interesting. I've looked back on this memory many times, but I've never remembered *that* detail before.

Dad turns and leaves. And then, as I'm trying to make my way back down, the suction gives out and I plummet into a stack of cardboard boxes. They burst open and spill their contents over the carpet, and as I heave myself to my feet, I come face to face with a big, glossy black-and-white photo of a crime scene. There's blood, and a scorch mark. Something terrible happened there.

But it's in black and white. Dad was right: someone, a woman, was subjected to an almost otherworldly level of trauma, and they had to photograph her injuries in black and white. I idly wonder how much more traumatised I'd have been if her blood had screamed at me from the glossy rectangle in a striking muddy crimson. But I realise now that would have probably been better. Because my brain then spent years wondering what the blood actually looked like, felt like, smelled like.

'Paul?' the art teacher says. I look up at her with a start. She's been saying my name for a while now, and I apologise. I do this sometimes. Become a little . . . unmoored.

That night, back at home, I place my backpack down and head over to Dad's camera, left sitting out on a dresser. Dad comes over and tries to find out how my day went, and I explain that I sort of drifted off during art class and am struggling to really 'get' photography. He gently takes the camera from me, in that way people do when they love you, but *really* don't want you touching their stuff. And he tries to explain just how fraught photography can be: 'Try to imagine,' he says, 'heading along to a crime scene with this camera. It's a murder scene and it's been kept pristine, preserved, for Forensics. So you step in . . . and you start taking photos. But you don't actually know what you got on film until you leave the crime scene.'

I look up at him, curious now. 'What if you leave and something went wrong, there was a light problem, or you didn't get the person in focus?'

This is clearly what Dad was hoping I'd ask. 'Good, very good! You're in real trouble, Paul. Because once Forensics leaves, the scene gets cleaned up. You have a small window to capture it, and you don't know until later whether you did it right.'

The pressure of this scenario terrifies me. 'How do you choose what to photograph? What if you do it wrong? Can you not, you know . . . just photograph everything from every angle?'

'Nah, mate. Time is a factor, and bodies decompose, and you only have a small window. You just have to . . . pick the right thing to preserve in the moment. Press the button. Lock it away.'

I think about the photograph in the wardrobe. And then—

'Paul!'

Dad is sitting back in front of me. It's the present day, and we're back in my parents' apartment. I'm in the chair opposite him, and I'm holding his camera.

Hello, ADHD. Thanks for the road trip.

See what I'm dealing with here, people? Dad can tell my attention has just grabbed me by the scruff of the neck and led me somewhere far away and then rubber-banded me right back to the present. This is something he's become accustomed to over the years. It's like daydreaming, I once told him.

'Do you want it?' he asks.

'The camera?' I reply, confused. I shake my head. I don't think I could handle the memories clinging to this thing.

4

CAN IT

John knew that learning from Grey at Chatswood Scientific was going to be fun. Grey couldn't stop rubbing his hands together, a tell which would have made him the perfect kind of enthused mark to play poker with.

It took a couple of days before Grey finally complimented John's look. 'Sharp dresser,' Grey noted as he led John into the cluttered building and showed him to his new desk.

'I have a desk?' John said, thrown by the compliment. The desk was small, but there it was. Not a shared workspace in a bullpen. A desk, with his name on it. It was empty but for a small bakelite phone and a sheaf of fresh paper.

'It's not much,' said Grey, apologetically. 'But you can spruce it up as much as you want. See? I've given mine a few personal touches.' John looked over at a desk barely visible beneath the accrued affectations of a truly weird man. A glass jar held what looked like pickled remains of something that was once human. John let his eyes drift back to his new workspace. He smiled. No, he didn't smile. He beamed.

Suddenly, he thought, *I feel like I'm where I'm meant to be. Maybe, just maybe, choosing this over detective was absolutely the right thing to do.*

The first thing Grey taught John was decidedly odd. First, he and John headed out to John's new unmarked car, one he'd requested specifically – a cream-coloured Kingswood. Grey opened the boot, put a crate of forensics gear inside, closed it and flung John the keys. 'All yours,' he said, nodding approvingly. 'The clothes. The car. Good. Good.' He headed to the passenger side. Once inside, he patted the driver's seat, leg jiggling with anticipation. John got in, turned the key, and his first unmarked vehicle rumbled awake.

They drove to the site of a suspected arson. Grey didn't talk much during the drive, and neither did John – as if he felt he might puncture the potential of this special, strange new thing by making idle chatter. Later, much later, Grey would admit he was thinking the same thing: that he didn't want to ruin the moment.

Half an hour later, Grey was placing his crate of goodies down on the floor of a burnt-out suburban home. He and John had arrived and made their way past the police cordon, under the police tape and straight into the remains of a house fire that had claimed several lives. John suppressed a glimmer of a flashback to a similar case, one involving a woman who thought she was – or actually was – a witch. She'd set herself alight, tried to purge the demons inside her, and John had stood in the room where it happened. Everything had been blackened, just like it was here. As John stood there trapped in his memories, Grey finished setting up his gear in a room away from any bodies, and re-entered to retrieve his new protégé. He looked like he was humming with energy. He stood up straight, did a little stretch to loosen up after the drive, and adjusted his rubber gloves. He then gestured about the place and waltzed over to John.

'John,' he said in a clear, declarative, perhaps even performatively booming voice. 'What do you think happened here?'

John, pulling on gloves of his own, pondered this for a moment. Finally, he responded. 'A fire?'

'Yes!' exclaimed Grey, as if John had hit upon something truly revelatory. He clapped his broad hands together, then pointed at John. 'Fire. A fire. And John, fires really only fall into one of two categories: accidental . . . or deliberate. And I happen to know which of the two this one was. Now . . . what I'd like you to do is figure out which it is. Don't feel bad if you don't nail it right out of the gate, but I'd like to see you take a guess.'

John looked around the blackened room. There was something . . . off about the whole scene, beyond the ruined personal mementoes, fused into grotesque lumps, and beyond the dull, disturbing smell of burnt pork. This realisation clearly crossed his face, because Grey's eyes lit up. 'There's . . .'

'Yes?' muttered Grey, on absolute tenterhooks, rubbing his hands together like Alfred Molina watching Indiana get ready to replace the idol with a sandbag. 'Yes?'

John exhaled carefully. 'Over the smell of the victims. Just past the smell of burnt flesh . . . I . . . Accelerant. I can smell accelerant.'

Grey's clap echoed through the gutted two-bedroom home. 'Yes! Bang on, John, bang on. Accelerant. Volatile, flammable and . . . yes, that smell . . . fragrant. You can smell it, but something about the human brain is usually so upset by the smell of the bodies, the mind filters it out.'

John sniffed again. 'But it's too strong. Right. So accelerant, at the site of a fire, in a home that has burned down. But what do we do about it? Take a note down? We can't capture the smell.' Grey was beaming at John. 'We can't. Can we?' stammered John, almost fearing the answer, but beginning to also feel some of the electricity flowing from Grey, his palpable enthusiasm revitalising John after weeks and weeks of sleepwalking through his job.

Grey strode over to his gear, charcoal and broken glass crunching beneath his feet. He reached down, yanked something out, walked up to John, and placed in his hands . . .

A paint can.

There were no labels on it. It was a gleaming silver, untouched, sparkling. A four-litre can with a round lid. 'John,' Grey said, eyes twinkling, 'I want you to go outside, and I want you to find a tap. Pop the lid off, and fill the can up with water.'

John did as he was asked, walking out and wrenching a reluctant tap back and forth. No water. *That's odd,* John thought.

'Mate,' came a voice from over his shoulder. A patrol officer, wearing the uniform John had until very recently worn himself, was calling out. 'Had to cut all the services off after the fire. Water isn't on. Give the neighbours' yard a crack if you're after some.' He jerked his thumb towards the house next door, and John gave a small nod. John carried the can over, found the tap around the side and yanked the hose free. Cold, running water poured forth. He filled the can and walked back into the burnt house, being careful not to spill any water. *This could be important,* John thought. *Don't fucking spill this while Grey is watching.*

Grey clapped his hands together again upon seeing the filled paint can. 'Right. Now, John . . . here's the fun part.' He then carefully took the paint can, held it aloft . . . and poured the contents out in front of John. Right on the floor. And then . . . he put the lid on. John, shoes soaked, looked up at Grey, who was grinning.

'Let me explain,' Grey said, cradling the can. 'The water leaves the paint can . . . and air rushes in! I then put the lid on, trapping the air. And what's in the air, John? What is in the air?'

'The smell of accelerant,' John answered, cottoning on.

'And where there's the smell of something . . . there are traces of the thing itself. Which means we now have traces of accelerant trapped in this airtight can. Ergo . . .'

'. . . We've just trapped potential proof of arson in a fucking paint can,' finished John, eyes now as wide as Grey's. Grey clapped John on the shoulder, and gestured towards the Kingswood.

'Hang on,' I say to Dad. 'This Grey guy . . . he's your Dumbledore.'
Dad looks at me as if he's going to correct me, admonish me, tut me. But then he settles back in his chair with a thoughtful look on his face. 'I guess he was Dumbledore-esque,' he admits.

Later that day, Grey had John drive the paint can forty minutes across town, all the way from Chatswood to the Division of Analytical Laboratories in Lidcombe, for analysis. As John watched, a lab tech carefully inserted a syringe through the can lid and sucked out a sliver of the preserved air which John and Grey had jubilantly captured like some kind of crime genie trapped in a cut-price lamp. John stood there, watching a scientist in a literal lab coat eyeball the can and nod approvingly, muttering 'Old school, nice. Old school' to himself. He let the scientist shake his hand and watched him head into the bowels of a lab full of whizzing, pinging machinery. John thought, *If this is what forensics is like, I'm in.*

And that was that.

*

Dad turns the camera over in his hands, perhaps realising he'd gone off-topic somewhat. 'I also learned, in detail, from Grey about how to be a crime scene photographer,' Dad says. 'Not as exciting as the paint can thing. Not as cinematic, you know. But he walked me through it, day by day: how to take photos, frame them up properly. How to move around a crime scene, taking them without disturbing evidence. Then to the darkroom at the back of Chatswood Scientific, where he taught me how the chemicals worked. How to develop them, how to hang them, how to keep them safe in the darkroom until they were ready. And because I was very precise, I found that part comforting. The system had rules. Nothing was subjective, really. If you wanted to be good at it, you had to organise, archive, pay attention. That . . . really spoke to me.'

And then Dad looks at me holding the camera. And I remember something else from that odd, distant high school memory, something that didn't quite filter down before – he told me that if I learned how to develop photos, like he did, he'd gift me the camera. He'd give me the camera he bought for himself when he started in Forensics as a gift to himself. But after we had that talk, I got distracted, didn't I? I didn't commit. Couldn't listen. But he kept the camera anyway. Just in case.

I don't quite know what to say, so I wrap up this precious relic, this monument to a path I didn't commit to, and place it next to me.

5

BATTER UP

Abe Saffron basically owned Kings Cross in the eighties.

John had come across some of Saffron's handiwork while in General Duties. In fact, it was hard to be an intuitive cop and not brush up against the collateral damage left behind by a man so prominent in Sydney's criminal underworld. If you were the kind of cop who tended to dig a little into promising leads or poke things you weren't meant to, you were sure to cross his wake. John, however, had a particular distaste for the man.

His first encounter, his first direct encounter, more or less, happened when he was in uniform, back in 1983. At this point, he was still partnered with Julian: his best mate, the definitive loose unit, a strong, quiet man with black hair and black eyes with whom John had accrued a stellar reputation. So let us whip back to a particular day when John and Julian were contacted by a senior sergeant while they were waiting around one afternoon at North Sydney Police Station.

'We've had a call,' came the gruff voice down the line, 'from a young girl in Cremorne. Scared shitless.' The sergeant, whose voice wasn't really conveying any particular sense of urgency, told John and

Julian to head over there. Sort it out. See what's what. And because John and Julian had spent years building a comfortable rhythm of solving as many difficult, dangerous crimes as possible, and were racking up arrests and cases solved like nobody's business, they looked at one another, nodded, and headed for their car. They cruised up the Pacific Highway, and eventually made their way into the opulent Cremorne backstreets, pulling up to a large apartment block.

In the apartment they'd been called to was an eight-year-old girl, who was living there with her dad. No mum on the scene. Her dad, they found out, had owed money to someone, about a hundred thousand dollars in today's money. Two men had rocked up that morning, and guess what they wanted? They wanted their money. So what they did, the girl explained in a shockingly even tone, was come to the apartment. And in front of the girl, they brought out two chairs and sat the father on one, placing his outstretched leg on the other. A sledgehammer was then brought out, raised into the air, and brought crashing down onto the man's femur. Smashed his leg in two with one blow. They then left, having told the scream-ing, writhing man, bone protruding from his pant leg, that they'd be back for the money, and that if he wanted his other leg to remain intact he'd better have it ready.

He didn't pass out, though. And all of this took place in clear view of the girl. The men gave her a look, one of them smiling at her pleasantly, her father bleeding and ruined in the far corner of the kitchen, and toddled off down the stairs. The girl, however, made a choice at this point. She calmed herself and walked out to the balcony, and watched the two men, one carrying the hammer that had sundered her father's leg, over to a white Mercedes.

And what did the young girl do at that moment? At eight years of age, she somehow had the prescience to peer down into the street, lock eyes with the vehicle and write down as much of the registration number as she could.

As the ambos wheeled her father away, John, deeply concerned, knelt down and talked with the girl. 'Is there anything you can tell us? Anything at all, love?' he asked as delicately as he could. The girl just nodded, and handed him a piece of paper. 'The number-plate started with *LM*,' she said. 'Sorry I couldn't get it all. I hope this helps.' John took the paper and looked it over. He handed it to Julian, who looked furious.

Once this remarkable girl was taken care of, John and Julian began digging, running the plates. But nothing came up. You see, John and Julian were General Duties police, and were way out of their depth. But they were angry, and angry people tend to push themselves past their limits. Julian, sensing John's blood rising, looked at him and said, 'Look, John. It's a public holiday. Let's fucking run with this.' So they did.

Because this call took place on a long weekend, and because many specialist divisions of the police were off work, there were suddenly huge gaps through which the two of them could stride. Stopgaps put in place to prevent rookies running roughshod over protocol were lax, meaning John and Julian could slide stealthily into the Bureau of Criminal Intelligence, fill out a form in tripli-cate and nervously try to get it processed before the hammer came down on them. They'd decided to play detective, and the only way to get away with it was to not bring anyone else in on it.

The results came in, giving John and Julian the intel they needed, and they spent the next few hours zipping around from lead to lead, trying to track down the driver and his associates. Finally, they dug up a photo of the driver, with a note attached to his file stating that under no circumstances were police to approach him, as he was a certified schizophrenic who would kill any cop who so much as looked at him.

After four or five hours of digging, and of waltzing into under-staffed high-security places like the fingerprint bureau, they'd done it. They had a match. This Mercedes, it turned out, belonged to a truly infamous figure in the Sydney criminal underworld: Lenny McPherson. And who did Lenny work for? Abe Saffron. The crooked businessman who ran most of the Cross. Lenny was paid muscle, willing to hobble a man while said man's eight-year-old daughter watched on.

LM.

Lenny McPherson.

John and Julian had bluffed their way to something incredible, had built a case – a completely illegal one, but a case nonetheless – against Lenny McPherson and, by extension, Abe Saffron. *Fuck the rules,* John thought, unable to get the image of the girl watching the sledgehammer come down out of his mind. But, much like the sledgehammer, everything was about to come crashing down on all of their glorious detective work.

John and Julian were sitting in a small room in North Sydney Police Station, their ill-gotten case assembled in front of them. They were giddy. They'd done it. *This is what justice feels like,* John thought. *We're going to get him. We're going to make this happen.* But the police force, like any workplace, is not a closed circuit, and gossip gets out. As Julian was typing away furiously on their brief, implicating Sydney's underworld royalty, the door burst open. In walked two absolute leviathans, no chins, sunglasses obscuring their eyes, who snatched up the files. One of them reached down, his hand engulfing the typewriter, and plucked it off the table. Then they turned around and walked out.

Later that day, John and Julian were told by their betters to cease and desist. The incident never happened, they were never to mention it, and their report disappeared without a trace. All that work, up in smoke.

John couldn't sleep that night. He couldn't stop thinking about how brave that girl had been, and how much she'd trusted him with the information she'd gleaned in a moment of overwhelming terror. How much he'd let her down. And the name Abe Saffron lodged in his young mind.

Several years later, a fortnight into John's fledgling forensics career, the name was still there, lingering. And having received a crash course in the gorgeous, granular particulars of fingerprinting from the capricious Grey, he was being sent off on his very first proper assignment for Scientific, to fingerprint a body. But not before Grey informed him that there was, in fact, a catch. 'He's still alive.'

John blinked. 'What do you mean, he's still alive?'

'Well, he won't be for long. But he's been . . . very badly done over, I'm afraid.' And Grey laid out the specifics for John.

Back in the eighties, bouncers were elemental forces. They cut no slack, brooked no trespass. They also were, quite often, eager for an excuse to turf someone out of a joint in as rough a manner as possible. And the nightclubs, specifically those situated in Kings Cross in this era, had two ways of throwing you out.

Through the front door, onto Darlinghurst Road . . .

Or out the back door.

In this case, the man John was heading to see had been found out the back of the Persian Room, an infamous nightclub right in the middle of the Cross. And on this particular occasion, two bouncers had decided to throw this guy out. They could have done just that – thrown him out the back, into the filthy alleyway, roughed him up with their fists and told him to never return. Sure, their fists were the size of smoked ham hocks and he wasn't that big a guy, so they'd have really done him some serious damage. But that would have been the end of it.

Instead, these particular bouncers, who were uniquely vicious, decided to use a baseball bat.

On this man's face.

John winced as Grey relayed all of this, and when he arrived at the hospital, rounded the corner in the ICU and walked into the room, he saw a man whose head was beyond recognition, tubes running from him in every direction. The terrible grinding of life-sustaining machinery working overtime ticked away next to the bed, and sitting there, utterly drained and tear-stained, was a woman with a couple of kids clinging to her, staring up at their dad with hollow, confused expressions on their pale faces.

John introduced himself as tactfully as he could, and set about preparing to take the man's prints. He looked at the man, and realised Grey was right. He'd nearly been murdered by the bouncers, who'd caved his skull in with their bats. John knew he was human, but everything on his face was in the wrong place. Life support pinged away valiantly.

The man had ID on him, but he was essentially unrecognisable. And as the medical staff swirled around the room, sadness emanating from their every step, John reminded himself why he was here: fingerprint the guy. So John asked for the curtains to be drawn around the man and for the family to stand back, something he did with as much gentleness as he could muster, and once he was alone with the victim he laid out his inkpad.

One of the first things Grey had imparted to John was how to fingerprint a dead body. A cadaver. John took the fingerprint form and slid it into the morgue spoon, a small curved copper scoop. He then placed this on the bed and, using a washcloth, gently cleaned the man's fingers. If the victim could feel this, he didn't respond; his even, laboured breaths continued to leak out of him, his chest a silent accordion going up and down, up and down.

John watched the man's chest rise and fall as he continued to clean. He held the limp hand for a moment, and felt a flutter of something. Rage? Probably rage. He pushed the feeling down, deep down, and carefully removed several small pieces of glass from the man's palm with tweezers, popping them into a metal dish on the bedside table. He noted the multitude of defensive wounds where the man had raised his hands above his head, likely begging the bouncers to stop, to let him go. John wiped away blood and wrung out the washcloth, repeating this process again and again until the man's hand was presentable.

Then he took the prints. One after the other, he inked the man's fingers and inserted them into the morgue spoon, pressing the finger into the curved metal. The form was then pressed back into the spoon, letting the paper curve around the finger. John slid out the form, and there, as if by magic, was a complete print. John moved the form so that the next blank space was sitting nestled against the curve. And after some time, he had his prints.

He looked at the man's arms. A few distinct tattoos, he noted with interest. But John was done here, his job for Grey almost at an end. He packed up his gear, stood up, and pulled the curtain aside. Staring up at him were the wife and kids. He gave them a kind look, and went to talk to one of the doctors standing by the respirator.

'Hey, mate,' John whispered to a bearded doctor hovering quietly nearby, 'what do you reckon his chances are?' The doctor looked up at John tiredly, and replied in a matter-of-fact voice, 'Oh, he's cactus. We were told to keep the life support going until he's been ID'd.'

John felt like he'd been slapped in the face. 'You . . . you mean he's going to get turned off?' The doctor nodded. John looked over at the family. 'Do they know?' The doctor nodded again, a glimmer of sadness behind his eyes. 'Yeah. They know. I think they're happy you were a little late; gave them a few extra minutes with him. Just call when you want him turned off.' And with that, the doctor began twiddling dials and preparing various switches on the life support machine. And John left, in a mild state of shock, but clutching what he came for.

Once he was back at Scientific, he processed the prints, cross-referenced them, and got a match. As he worked, as he filed and pored over and analysed records, he realised that the longer he took, the longer this ruined family would have with their dad, the longer this woman would have with the dying remains of her husband. And he wondered whether he should work faster, and put the poor man out of his misery . . . or maybe drag his heels a little.

Eventually, John found that he was so absorbed in his work that it was done before he had a chance to decide. He found a minor criminal record for the man, and a name, and he called the hospital. He asked the doctor to turn off life support, and hung up the phone, and stuffed everything deep down. Very, very deep, where it couldn't get him.

Grey traipsed up to John later that afternoon, gripping a sheaf of papers. 'John,' he said, placing a hand on John's slumped shoulder. 'Good work. Nasty business. The Cross . . . bit of a fucked place, really. Abe Saffron has a lot to answer for.'

This mention of the crime lord's name startled John out of his encroaching funk. He shifted and turned to face Grey. 'What did you say?'

'Oh, Saffron. Abe Saffron. The club your victim was beaten out the back of? The Persian Room. Owned by Abe Saffron.'

John thought back to the girl in the apartment, that brave eight-year-old girl. And he thought back to the hospital room, and the children brave enough to look their dying father in the eye. And he thought about his son and daughter, at home, and he felt that anger rising again. And he chose to stay the course. Because he might not be a detective, true. But he was going to keep pursuing justice.

6

LOCK-NESS

I don't know about you, but if I had to witness villainy of that magnitude, and if I had to call some bearded guy and tell him to turn off a man's life support, I'd probably begin to regret my career choices. I'd probably begin to have a crisis of faith, maybe look for a sudden career change. Something sunnier. Something less . . . grim. Actually, you know what? I'm writing this book; I can just ask Dad whether he thought the same thing!

'Dad,' I say, leaning back in my chair, 'did you ever regret your career choices? And, you know . . . wish you'd chosen something else?'

He doesn't seem blindsided, per se, but if I had to guess I'd say he's not been asked this before. 'I wanted to play trumpet.'

Well, I don't think any of us were expecting him to say *that*. 'What do you mean, you wanted to play trumpet? For a living?'

'Yes. Did you know I used to play when I was a boy? I got very good. I played on the *QE2*, when our family crossed over to England.' I'd heard about Dad and his family heading to England for a few years back in the early seventies, but never imagined Dad as a musician. This is . . . interesting. Very interesting. 'So what if

you'd chosen to pursue that, Dad? What if you could have circum-
vented all that trauma you endured—'

'I didn't endure any trauma. I'm fine.'

'Sure, sure you are. But if you'd chosen to go with, as you say,
the trumpet . . . what would your life have been like?'

Dad shakes his head. 'But I didn't do that. I was a police officer.'

'Yes,' I reply, seeing where this is headed, 'I know you were a
police officer. I'm asking you to consider, just for a moment, the
magical, wonderful potential of making choices different to those
you did in fact make.'

'But I did, in fact, *make* them. I can't unmake them. And I didn't
have . . . choices.'

This is intriguing. 'What do you mean, you didn't have choices?'

'Well,' Dad says, looking as though he's pondering how
to phrase what he's about to reveal, 'I chose things, true. I chose to
be a cop. Chose to do forensics. Chose to marry your mother. But
I didn't see . . . other choices. There was just the one door in front
of me, and I went through it. I chose to go through it. But there
was only ever the one door, the one choice.' He nods, pleased with
himself, like he's finished inspecting a boat before pushing it out.
It's seaworthy, his face says. *The thing I just said? It's true, and I back
it all the way.*

One door. Can you imagine one door? Just one? I sure as
shit can't. The ADHD means basically every moment in my life
is strewn with doors. My mind is perpetually playing host to a
fucking door clearance sale, a factory floor drowning in doors.
Every moment has multiple unseen pathways exploding out
behind it like a fractal hellscape, slender threads blossoming into
the distance. Maybe we've just found another way in which I'd have
made a terrible cop, the exact opposite of Dad. Can you imagine

a car chase? What if I was driving after a criminal and I had to decide whether to take a shortcut or stick to their tail? Or, worse, what about interviewing a suspect? According to this revelation from Dad, he'd just ask question after question, all leading down a single, inexorable path. I'd be paralysed by all the forks in the road, all the permutations, the potential for screwing up.

I relay all of this to Dad, and he looks confused. Kind, but confused. 'Paul . . . you're a gentle soul.' Which, dear reader, is his way of saying he loves me, even though I'm what he once referred to as an 'artsy weirdo'. He smiles at me, clears his throat. 'But I can't imagine what it's like to think the way you do. It sounds . . . fun, but I can't even imagine what it's like.'

We sit there in silence, both having just learned something new, something rather big, about one another. And ourselves, for that matter. Then, Dad does something rather lovely.

He throws me a bone.

'Actually,' he says, 'I did almost become a locksmith.'

Now I'm intrigued. 'What do you mean, you almost became a locksmith?'

'Well, I trained to work with locks. Before I enrolled in the force, I was a toolmaker, yes?' I nod. Dad has told me about this before. 'That was just *part* of what I did. We worked with locks. Safes. I loved the attention to detail involved. Loved how . . . precise it all was.'

'Aha! But by your rationale, Dad, you never would have become a locksmith, or a safecracker, or whatever, because by your reasoning, the second you were presented with the choice to go and apply to be a cop, *the only thing you could have done would be to apply to be a cop*.'

'That's . . . probably true,' he concedes. 'But I'd have made a fucking good thief, let me tell you that much for free.' And so I ask him to tell me what he learned working with locks and safes, partly to see if he would have made a good thief. But also because I want to see if he gets my point. If he can sit there in front of me – of us – with wonder in his eyes as he ponders a big what-if.

One of the things that made John a good cop, or at the very least an interesting one, was how willing he was to test the limits of what was allowed. Or what wasn't allowed. Or what was allowed, but shouldn't have been. He never strayed too far from the path, but his time as a patrol officer in General Duties was rife with almost-but-not-quite rule-breaking.

Perhaps this impulse came from the fact that he was an absolute ratbag in school. Mucking up and thumbing his nose at authority was part of his DNA, so perhaps he was always going to be a fairly unconventional cop. Once, when he was in Year Seven in high school, he joined the shooting club. Yes, readers. A shooting club. Standing proud at the back of the playground, tiny shorts clinging to his pale legs, and arms unerringly steady, he held his air rifle aloft as his classmates watched, rapt. Then, for a laugh, he turned his gun left, left, left . . . and there, in his crosshairs, was one of the senior boys. A prefect, in fact. With his back turned. 'I don't like prefects,' John muttered, the butt of the weapon resting against his bony shoulder.

'You'll never make it,' a boy behind him said, sounding pretty sure of himself. 'And what's wrong with prefects?'

John held his breath, lined up his shot . . . and pulled the trigger. *CRACK.*

The prefect whipped forward, grabbing his behind, and made a coarse grunting sound as he fell to his knees.

John picked this moment to turn to his detractor. 'What's wrong with them? They're a pain—' he paused for effect '—in the arse.' There was a gasp, followed by laughter. Followed by silence. Followed by looks of abject terror. John watched the faces of his classmates staring, dumbstruck, at something behind him. John turned. There, wincing and furious, was the prefect. He plucked the rifle from John's hands, inspecting the weapon.

'Never . . .' he said, pulling the hammer back, then gently pressing the barrel against the top of John's foot. John didn't dare move. 'Never turn your back on your target.' Now it was the prefect's turn to pull the trigger. There was a muffled *CRACK*, and John felt the pellet dig into *his* skin. Nerve endings screamed, but he didn't. He didn't dare. The prefect looked John over, raised an eyebrow at the lack of reaction, and hobbled off.

As we've established, after high school John's choice of trade was toolmaking, but he really only did this so he'd have a legitimate excuse to regularly pick locks and break into places. He liked puzzles, and he liked solving problems, and he adored the clean precision of tumblers falling into place, but he also innately knew that if he kept on down this road, he'd likely use his skills for nefarious purposes. Not because he wanted to steal, or hurt people, but because he got bored. He wanted a thrill. He didn't yet know that he'd end up a cop, but he spent a good year before he enrolled in the force learning how to break into all manner of places.

It was about two years through his time in General Duties when he let slip his past vocation. Julian was gobsmacked. 'You mean you can break into . . . anything?'

John sipped his thickshake and nodded. 'Almost anything.'

Julian looked awed but unconvinced. You see, it's not like police didn't ever break into things. Every police officer's hat had a metre of packing tape, rigid and blue, rolled up and hidden beneath the band. If someone was locked out of a car, John would draw the tape out, pry the offending door open a crack, then slide the looped tape through. He'd draw back the side closest to him, which would tighten the loop and pull it into position, then he'd lower it over the pin, tighten it further, carefully draw it up . . . and voila! The pin would pop up, and the car was unlocked. Not larceny, but thrilling nonetheless.

Part of what appealed to John about picking locks was getting into places you weren't meant to be. And what was police work if not the pursuit of secrets, of knowledge, of peering beneath the polite facade of society to see those grubby places you weren't meant to be? But Julian had a big mouth. A kind mouth, but a big one. And one day, John got a call from ██████████.

>'Dad, why have you redacted someone in my book?'
>
>'Because,' Dad says, 'I know it's your book. I know it's your story, based on things I lived through, which I love. But if I dropped ██████████'s name, there wouldn't be any book. Every country has spooks, Paul, or the equivalent of spooks. Australia has their own, and ██████████ was pretty high up. And he found out – thanks to Julian – that yes, I knew how to break into places.'
>
>'Would it,' I ask, 'be a fair assumption to say that they guessed, correctly, that due to your junior status on the force . . . and your need to seek thrills . . . that you'd be a very compliant lock-picker?'
>
>Dad just nods.

John sat at his desk in the bullpen at the station, dumbfounded as ██████████ spoke down the line. Julian watched, rapt at first, then increasingly worried as John's eyes darted around. John fumbled for a pen and began scribbling directions, then hung up. 'Julian,' he said, glaring at his partner, '. . . what the fuck have you got me into, mate?'

An hour later, John was arriving at a fairly nondescript building in the Sydney CBD. To be fair, it was extraordinarily ordinary, its entrance set back in a filthy, darkened alley. Several men in black suits waited by the top of the alley, and as John pulled up, one of them approached him. The man had ███████████ eyes, ███████████ hair and was ███████████.

'You must be ███████████,' said John, trying to sound more composed than he felt, carrying his tiny leather bag of tools.

The man gave John a ███████████ handshake and smiled. 'Good to have you here, John. I hear you're quite good with locks?'

'Dad, why did you have me redact the description of the guy's handshake?'

'Because if people know how firm ███████████'s handshake is, there's not going to be a book.'

███████████ led John through the huddle of other agents, all looking about the place calmly yet furtively. He pointed to the door – a fairly harmless-looking door set into a brick wall – and looked at John. 'Think you can get this open?'

John nodded. He thought he could, sure. And being sur-rounded by spooks was certainly incentive to not fuck it up royally. He got down on one knee and unfolded his bag, an array of tools gleaming in the faint light. Sorting through them one by one, he attempted to make small talk. 'So . . .' he began. 'What are . . .'

'Can't tell you, mate. Need-to-know basis.'

'Ahh,' John said. *For all you know,* he thought to himself sulkily, *I could have been asking about anything, not just what's inside this building. I mean, I was going to ask that, but you shouldn't just assume.* He found what he was after – a device that looked like a small gun, with a spike on the end – and raised it to the lock. And that's when he saw it.

'███████████,' John said over his shoulder.

The agent knelt down beside John. 'You right, mate? Problem?' he asked with surprising warmth.

John pointed at the lock. 'Run your finger over that spot there,' he said.

'Where? Here?' replied ███████████. The man was way off. So John, hopped up on adrenaline – he was working on a covert operation with actual secret agents, after all – panicked. He tenderly grasped ██████████'s extended finger, directed it a centimetre to the right, and ran it up and down along an invisible groove. 'Feel that?' he asked, not entirely sure whether what he was doing was weird or not.

'It was weird,' I tell Dad, matter-of-factly. 'It was weird.'

John continued to direct the spook's finger along the indentation. 'Feel that?' he asked again.

████████████ looked at John calmly. 'Yes, I can feel it, John. This is nice.'

'The groove?' John replied, still moving the man's finger up and down, up and down.

'No, this. What we have between us. It's nice.'

John, suddenly aware of what he was doing, dropped the man's finger. ████████████ laughed, clapping John on the back.

John cleared his throat. 'Look at your finger. You'll see residue.'

███████████ lifted his finger, and then his eyebrows. 'You're right,' he said. 'Someone been in this way before?'

'Yep,' said John. 'More than likely. Residue from a previous attempt at jimmying this lock, probably using the same method I'm about to use.'

███████████ looked at John approvingly. 'Nice bloody work. Tell you what, you go hammer and tongs on that, get us inside, and I'll see if "Careless Whisper" is playing on the radio. Bit of background music.'

John grinned. This guy was weird. Weird in a good way, but weird. He began pumping away at the lock, and finally, several tumblers untangled, there was a soft, distant, metallic *SHLUNK*, and the lock breezed open. John went to turn the handle, but another agent placed his hand over it. John stood up.

'Thanks for your help, mate,' said ███████████, shaking John's hand. 'We'll take it from here. Oh, and . . .'

'I was never here,' finished John.

'You were never here.'

As John drove away, he reflected upon the fact that this might be an interesting avenue of career progression. Maybe he'd just made inroads with the right spooks to give him a leg-up. Or, he realised even further down the road, perhaps he'd just helped the Australian Government violate someone's civil rights. *Maybe I should just keep going the way I'm going,* he thought. *Maybe I need to keep working towards detective.*

But as we've established, that's not where John ended up.

And John doesn't wonder what-if.

Does he?

Locks are precise. Locks are detailed, complex, and you can't open them unless you're willing to embrace the details, explore every nook and cranny of an unseen space. So the moment John began taking people's prints, the moment Grey threw him into the deep end of Scientific, the dusty wing of his brain that craved precision, that longed to unlock doors, sprang to life again.

But he still kept his lock-picking kit in the back of the car. Just in case.

7

ANAL THERMOMETERS

Dad gets up to grab a glass of water, and I stretch out like a cat on the armchair I'm hunched over in. 'So,' I say through a yawn, 'Dad. When are we going to get to a proper case?'

Just to clarify, between you and me, I know we've been dealing with 'real' cases. But I also know Dad sometimes needs a nudge, and I already know which case I'm hoping he'll dish the dirt on. You see, growing up with a cop for a parent means hearing snippets of stories told to captive audiences – in Dad's case, dinner parties filled with frightened guests. And the stories always stop short once you enter the room, because you're a kid, right? But you manage to catch a little. Just a few key words. And one I happened to almost hear over and over was the story about the anal thermometers.

Anal thermometers. There's a tie-in merch idea. We could package them with lube!

Lube Units.

Anyway, it works. Not the lube, the provocation. Dad turns to me, water half drunk, and looks mock-appalled. 'Proper case?'

I nod. I smile.

'What do you mean, proper case?'

I stand up and waltz breezily over to the kitchen counter opposite him, like it's the Old West and I'm about to order three fingers of sippin' whiskey. 'A proper case,' I reiterate. 'I want something with a beginning, middle and end. We keep giving them small cuts of a bigger animal: just the ribs, the thigh, the rump.'

'The only rump here is you,' he replies.

I continue, undeterred. 'I want to give the readers the whole animal. I want a case that starts when you get the call and ends when you wrap the case up. I want a proper case, with a capital C.'

Dad glares at me. He swallows and leaves the kitchen, heading for his notebook.

Guess I ain't gettin' that sippin' whiskey.

I watch as he flumps down into his chair and, as he flicks through the pages, gives me an occasional look to indicate that I've shown quite some nerve. 'No,' he mutters, turning page after page. 'No . . . no . . . nope . . . AHA!' He holds the book up, pointing smugly at the name of a case. I squint and lean forward, trying to read Dad's utterly nightmarish handwriting.

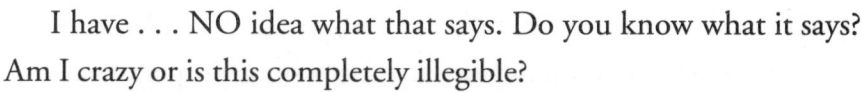

I have . . . NO idea what that says. Do you know what it says? Am I crazy or is this completely illegible?

Dad glares at me – at us, I guess – and taps the book emphatically. 'Anal thermometers! Anal! Thermometers!'

'Easy, easy,' I say, in a placating voice. 'Keep yelling that and you're not gonna get your bond back. Fine. We'll do . . . anal thermometers.'

And if 'we'll do anal thermometers' isn't a wild way to start a story, I don't know what is.

John was loving his time in Forensics.

Sure, he'd not been there very long, but he'd had an eventful few weeks. He and Grey were getting along famously, his on-the-job training was rocketing along, and he'd realised he had something of a knack for the most detail-oriented work. Grey had clearly picked up on this, too, assigning John crunchier and crunchier tasks. John began to feel at home at his small desk, opposite a huge glass cabinet bustling with forensics ephemera. This evening he cast an eye around the office, crammed with tools of the trade, and leafed through his paperwork. *There's always paperwork,* he noted. *Upward mobility may have its perks, but there's always bloody paperwork.*

He looked over at his reflection in the glass cabinet. He'd begun taking more and more care with his appearance in the Hard Seltzer guise, and was beginning to enjoy not just playing the part, but also looking the part. It was starting to feel like his look was bang on. And his delicate suede shoes, he thought while inspecting them, might not be practical, but he doubted he'd be diving into anything particularly messy today.

And as that thought was exiting through the gift shop of John's sleepy mid-afternoon brain, Grey finished a phone call and walked up, rapping briskly on John's desk. 'John!' he said. 'Job. We've got a good one.'

And so John grabbed his case of gear and hauled it to the Kingswood, and they began their drive to Greenwich, a particularly affluent area a couple of suburbs to the south of Chatswood. Grey let John drive. The Lower North Shore, which they were winding their way through, was leafy, hilly and enigmatic, full of darkened gardens and fenced-off private schools.

As they drove, Grey asked John if he'd noticed anything. And John, being unusually perceptive, began glancing into people's living rooms. As he cast his eye into house after house, he looked over at Grey and took a stab in the dark, in the dark. 'Where's the power?'

'Where's the power!' yelled Grey, sounding more than a little like Emmett Brown, clapping his voluminous hands together. 'Well spotted. No power. Well, almost no power. Most of the suburb has lost power, John, and the call I got was interesting . . . well, for one reason in particular. Guess where we're headed?'

John took a guess. 'The . . . source of the outage?'

Another sharp, fricative clap split the air. 'YES! Shit, John. Shit. You are doing very well this evening. That's where we're going, my boy. Right to the source of the problem.' And he drummed the dashboard in time with the music; 'Under the Milky Way Tonight' built to a crescendo, and Grey was lost to the song. John sped up towards their destination.

They soon pulled into what could only be described as a mansion. Patrol cars were idling near the house, and vans bearing council workers in high-vis uniforms who milled about. The driveway was a long one, and looming, motionless Moreton Bay figs dotted the palatial grounds of the property. The Kingswood approached the other vehicles, and John stopped, pulled on the handbrake and turned the car off.

Grey turned to face him, expression suddenly serious. 'John,' he said. 'Here's what you need to know.' He looked less jubilant now. All business. 'For the past hour, the local boys and the council have been dealing with the outage. Well, trying to deal with it – not much you can do until you've located the source of the problem, which, as I stated earlier, is why we're here. But this problem was traced, very cleverly I might add, to this particular street. And to this particular house.'

He pointed out the window at the house, a 1920s sandstone property with views looking out onto the magnificent Sydney Harbour. One of the officers outside gave John a look which, later on, he would realise was the tail end of nausea. 'Looks pristine, yes?'

'Actually, no . . . he looks sick as a dog.'

Grey looked at the cop, and chuckled. 'No, John, no. The house. Looks gorgeous. Quiet. Calm. Inside, it is anything but. I want you to prepare yourself – can you do that?'

John nodded, thinking back to one of his most traumatic cases back in General Duties: a woman shorn in half, dying in his arms under an idling train. He shivered involuntarily, and looked back at Grey. Grey had the presence of mind to let this slide unquestioned. 'So, John. Time to get the gear. Time to get to work.'

They hopped out of the car and headed to the boot. John flung it open and looked down at his case of gadgets, with which he'd turn a grisly crime scene into a litany of accurate, revelatory facts.

'What was in the case?'
  'Ahh,' Dad says. 'Supplies.'
  'Supplies?' I ask.

'Supplies,' Dad replies.

'I guess what I'm getting at, Dad, is . . . what supplies, specifically?'

Dad stares right at me. I've got him now. 'You know, brushes. Fingerprint powder. Ahh . . . brushes.'

I raise an eyebrow quizzically. 'Surely someone in the Scientific Division has more than just that. It's a case! Lots of room, right? What else was in there?'

Dad looks a little uncomfortable. 'You know . . .'

I tell him I do not, in fact, know. And he groans. He mumbles something indecipherable.

'What's that?' I prompt sweetly.

'Anal thermometers!' he yells. 'Anal thermometers!'

'How many?'

'Too many! I packed too many. I didn't know exactly what to pack for a field job so I grabbed too many. I wanted to look impressive, so I grabbed a whole lot of them . . . What? I thought I was grabbing lab equipment!'

'You were!' I exclaim. 'But you only need one, maybe two, anal thermometers. Not every anal thermometer in Chatswood Scientific. That's a whole lot of arses.'

Dad is laughing now. In fact, he's laughing so hard his eyes are tearing up. 'We should . . .' he manages to squeeze out through guffaws, 'we . . . we should sell them. Merchandise.'

We spend the next half-hour brainstorming, and subsequently scrapping, the idea of 'Lube Units'.

Grey followed John to the front of the house, and while Grey got caught up with the attending officers, John gathered up some

supplies from his case, leaving behind most of the anal thermometers. Not all of them, mind you. But most of them. Maybe he
had too many in the first place? Yes. Definitely too many.

As John busied himself, he looked around and noticed a mass
of thick electrical cables winding their way from a large, rumbling
generator on the lawn and converging in slick coils disappearing
into the darkness of the house. *That's odd,* he thought to himself.
Emergency lighting. Couldn't they have just . . . cracked a window?
An odd feeling flickered across the back of John's neck. This was
getting weird.

Another thing John noticed, and something Grey had clearly
noticed, too: there were a lot of cops here. A lot more than normal.
Grey approached, looking wary. 'John, mate,' he said. 'Time to
head on in. Let's have a recce, see what we're looking at. All these
blokes did was set up the lights for us so we could see what we're
doing. Vicks?' John was offered an extended finger, the end thick
with viscous goo. Before John could offer an answer, said finger
whipped forward and smeared a strip of the burning menthol crud
under his nose. The fumes filled his sinuses and his lungs, but he
gathered this measure would be necessary deeper inside the house.
'After you,' Grey said, gesturing towards the door.

And in they went.

The first thing John noticed was the garbage. It was everywhere. Walls, literal walls of hoarded refuse – takeaway cartons,
newspapers, moving boxes full to bursting – teetered around
head height. It was like negotiating a maze. Even with the Vicks
tearing its way through his skull, John could still smell decay,
the residual heat of decomposing matter burning his eyes a little.
With dismay, he realised he was barely touching the ground; every
step was met with crunching and cracking, like he was treading

through an above-ground graveyard. Plastic bric-a-brac popped and rotten food squelched, and with a sigh John realised he'd been an absolute fucking spanner and worn his favourite suede shoes. He looked down. Already, stains crept across the fuzzy surface, but he pressed onwards.

Finally, he broke free of the garbage maze, and found himself in the hub of this awful place: the kitchen. The enormous room smelled and looked even worse than the rest of the house, and the emergency lighting, placed in each corner, brought the space into a kind of dreadful, stark relief. The floor in here was flooded to ankle height with viscous brownish water, scum floating on the surface in frothy little islands. Grey, John noted, had stopped just beyond the entrance and was standing safely atop a mound of pizza boxes. 'Off you go, John,' he said politely. 'Age before wisdom.'

John nodded, reminding himself to buy some gumboots the second he had a day off work, and turned to reappraise the room.

Every shelf, every spare surface, was filled with an unfathomable number of empty wine bottles. There must have been well over a thousand of them, arranged with the kind of fastidiousness that hints at oceans of trauma. In the right-hand corner of the room, a mountain of garbage rose to meet the ceiling, and right in the middle was a filthy rollaway bed, tilted at a nauseating angle, the lower end of the bed almost engulfed by the stagnant stew of detritus coating the floor.

And there, up the back near the kitchen bench, was the body.

It was a woman, lying on her back, hands gripped tightly shut, neck bent backwards. John approached carefully, wondering what in this room constituted evidence and what was just garbage. *Normally there's one thing,* he thought. *One stand-out thing which doesn't belong at the scene. What the hell am I supposed to do when nothing here belongs?*

As he reached the body and looked down, he noticed the cord. He followed it to a blackened wall socket, and traced it from the wall to the woman's waist, then past the woman and to an iron, also blackened, sitting in the six inches of slop that lapped around the woman's corpse. The cord was frayed, burnt, and . . .

And there it was. 'The cause of death?' asked Grey from the doorway, one of his wizard eyebrows arched. John saw a dreadful burn running around the body, and turned to face Grey from his crouching position. 'Well,' he ventured, 'this poor woman has clearly become entangled in the cord connecting this iron to the wall. Then, something's gone wrong.' He spied a fried washcloth plastered to the counter near the cord, and guessed that the cloth had been wet, and had sent a lethal current through the cord. He looked back at the wound. 'It . . . Shit,' he said, half thinking out loud. 'It's shorn right through her. The cord, I mean. Garrotted through her midsection. The heat it would take to . . . ahh.' John sighed, looking back at the wall. 'She got tangled up, and the iron fell into the water. The current hit like a bolt of lightning. She'd have locked up, bones almost breaking from pressure, and she'd have fallen . . . and the pressure from her weight, pulling into the lasso of the cord, would have slowly carved through her like a hot knife through butter . . . Yep. Stopping only when it reached her spine.' He peered closer. Sure enough, what was left of the cord disappeared into her ruined midsection.

'Very good, John. Really good. But you missed something, I think.'

John looked over the body, then he spotted it. To one side of the woman's skull was what looked like a monstrous exit wound, a clutch of wet brain matter sitting there like bubbles atop a fleshy milkshake. John was suddenly glad for the Vicks coating his upper lip, though he did have to suppress an almighty retch and look away. 'Brain,' he said, fighting off nausea. 'Brain matter.'

'Yes,' said Grey. 'Brain *does* matter.' He stared at John, waiting for appreciative laughter. When he got none, he smiled. 'I'd rather not come over, given the state of the floors. Where do you think she got that wound?'

John cast his eye about, truly grateful for a chance to look at something other than exploded brains for even a second. The bench? Maybe she hit her head on the way down. But that wouldn't make sense . . . She fell away from the bench, he knew that much. He looked around more carefully, becoming agitated, wanting to leave. The fluid beneath him had filled his shoes, and his socks clung to his feet. *How much of her blood is in my fucking shoes?* he thought. *How much of this poor woman am I standing in?*

Just as Grey was about to come over and assist, John laughed out loud, then stopped himself. The sound felt alien in such a place, and he quickly reached behind the body. He picked up a small piece of the brain matter from the woman's skull, stood up, and approached Grey, a look of pure revelation on his face.

'So,' Grey said. 'Where'd she get the injury?'

'Nowhere,' replied John, eyes ablaze.

'Nowhere?' said Grey, eyebrow almost reaching the ceiling now.

'Nowhere. Because this—' John proffered the brain on his finger, and this time held it right under Grey's enormous nose '—is not brain.'

Grey sniffed, then sniffed again . . . then it was his turn to light up like a firecracker.

'Sweet and sour pork,' they both exclaimed, in unison. John raised his other hand to reveal a takeaway container, half full of Chinese food.

The two men cackled like absolute ghouls.

John's forensics career was officially off to the races.

'So what actually happened to the woman?' I asked. 'What was she doing there?'

'Well, I was right. It was obvious to us both from the moment we went inside . . . She was a hoarder, and had been living in her kitchen for decades, hence the bed. She was drunk – she was always drunk – and got caught in the cable. The iron fell, she got cooked, and as she fell back, almost in slow motion, the cord cut through her and cauterised her at the same time, meaning she'd have been alive for quite a while. And at some stage, she reached for the counter and grabbed the sweet and sour pork, pulling it towards her.' Dad sits back, satisfied.

'But . . . who was she?'

He looks a little more sombre now. 'Well, she was very wealthy, in her sixties, but many decades earlier she'd been very high up at a psychiatric hospital. And she'd seen too much, confronted too much, then had a breakdown. Had a terrible breakdown. Started hoarding, started drinking, wouldn't leave the kitchen. She always took care of her gardens, though. The grounds were immaculate.'

I sighed. 'Guess you can have some parts of your life in perfect order on the outside, while on the inside . . . things are an absolute mess.'

If I were a lesser man, I'd have said that house was a metaphor.

'So,' I ask as Dad places his notebook down, looking a little winded by the story, 'if I'd been there . . .'

'Right, right,' he says, looking a little irritated. 'You'd have done things differently, chosen to do things another way. I know, I know.'

'No, no,' I say. 'I'd have just worn anything other than suede shoes, to be honest. Because yours got covered in shit.'

He stares at me blankly.

'Poo suede shoes.'

He places his head in his hands.

8

BIKIES

'Right,' I exclaim, clapping my hands together just like Grey did. 'Blood spatter!'

'Blood spatter,' parrots Dad.

'Blood spatter!' I repeat. 'I like that we're getting a bit of a step-by-step through some of the tasks you were given while at Forensics. Taking prints, heading to crime scenes, getting up close and personal with really gruesome stuff. But if we're following along with all the TV tropes, all the trappings of shows and movies that I associate with forensics, blood spatter is the next logical step. You know. Looking at where the blood came from, tracing paths with red string back to an impact point. That stuff. Is that . . . you know. Real?'

He rolls his eyes. 'Nah, mate. Red string? No. That's fucking stupid.'

'But did you analyse blood spatter?'

'I don't know about analyse,' he says, 'but we certainly dealt with it. It's true; you can absolutely use blood spatter to deduce things, but you're often more concerned with the body, at least I was – fingerprints, you know. But I can think of one case . . .'

Then Dad does the strangest thing. He drifts off.

I drift off all the time. Like a cartoon dog following the smell of food into a neighbour's kitchen, I'm drawn away from the moment. But Dad isn't like me; he doesn't get distracted, indecisive. Which means he's clearly not wandering. Maybe he's . . . running? Running from a memory? I place my hand on his knee, gently, so as not to startle him.

'Dad. You okay?'

He looks at me vaguely, then nods. 'Sorry. Yes.'

He grabs his book and begins riffling through it. Something crosses his face. Embarrassment? Hell, knowing Dad, it could just be indigestion. He's taken to fasting outside the hours of 5 pm and 9 pm each day. Outside of those hours, his stomach is clenched, making frightening gurgling noises. Inside those hours, it's the culinary equivalent of The Purge. He could strip a cow of its flesh in twenty seconds flat. So maybe he's just struggling because his body is literally eating itself as a result of his new diet. Or maybe, like I said . . . trauma. Maybe it's trauma.

'Right,' he says finally. 'Blood spatter.'

And off we go.

Things were going well in Forensics. John still hadn't been there that long, really, but Grey had already forced him into a litany of abominable situations. 'Learn by doing', he called it. John was seeing things he'd never be able to unsee, sure . . . but he was learning.

One day John was driving with Grey to the suburb of Kingswood, near Penrith in Western Sydney.

'I don't want people to write in saying, why are you bagging out Kingswood,' says Dad, looking concerned.

'Okay,' I reply. 'So don't say anything bad about Kingswood!'

'But Kingswood was depressing and shit,' Dad says, steam-rolling past his previous point.

Welcome to my life.

Driving his Kingswood through Kingswood felt like a mildly cosmic connection to John. It was summer at this point, and it was hot. And something about this particular summer felt weird. There was a kind of energy building around him; John had, over the years, become convinced he could sense when he was about to enter a crime scene that was significant. Uniquely awful. The girl under the train. The witch. The cases that change you. *Or maybe,* John thought, *I'm just thinking of all the preceding moments as monumental in retrospect. Maybe I'm revising history.*

As he pulled up to the address he'd been given, though, he thought, *No. This isn't revisionist history. Something is definitely off.*

Grey cleared his throat, gesturing to the driveway of the property. 'Look,' he said, nodding in the other direction. 'Perfect location for a crime like this one.' John followed his eyeline. Sure enough, directly across the road from the house they'd been called to . . . the hospital. Nepean Hospital, a foreboding clutch of slate-coloured buildings behind a half-full car park. John spotted an ancient man in a terry towelling robe, holding on to his IV drip for support, trying to escape down the driveway. An orderly strode over to him and placed a hand on the man's arm. *This place,* thought John, *is wrong.*

This story, however, didn't really take place in the house John was pulling up to. It took place in the granny flat out the back.

John and Grey picked up their gear and made their way past a handful of General Duties officers, down the driveway to the small fibro one-bedroom building, and under a gently flapping ribbon of police tape.

Once inside, they immediately saw the blood.

The blood was everywhere.

John carefully crossed the room, and made his way over to the body. A young woman. Her head was completely caved in, and as John looked around he saw evidence of the killing everywhere. Spraying out from the body like a crimson corona, plumes and flecks of blood and gore decorated the walls and the ceiling, all radiating away from the point of impact: her skull. Her hands were raised, fingers clenched. The sheets were drenched with still more blood. John blinked, trying to process what he was seeing.

He looked around the small apartment. Spartan. Not much in the way of possessions, but the place was lovingly kept – or at least it had been, until now. John swept the room with his eyes, taking in several key details.

First of all, the small, high window on the left-hand wall was open. The frame was slightly warped, and scuff-marks marred the wall beneath it. Clearly, the killer had jimmied his way in, and had likely left in a hurry. John would have to get photos of this, and check outside to see if the marks inside matched any impressions outside.

Secondly, and more upsettingly . . . there was a cot next to the bed. A few old toys lay in there, grim reminders. *No blood,* John thought. *Did the dad take the kid? Did he kill the mum, then lose his nerve, the monster? Did he . . .* John flinched, thinking of his own kids. His daughter, Anne, was a newborn. He shoved down the impulse to run outside, forcing himself to look back at the woman's body, lying distended on the bed. *Men hurting women,* he thought. *It's always men hurting women.*

Voices drifted over and John turned to see who was talking. A patrol officer stood outside, talking with Grey, whose name was seeming more suitable than ever.

'John,' he declared across the room, beckoning with his hand. 'Here.' John, grateful for an excuse to look away from the carnage, headed over to his supervisor. 'John, this is Constable George Simons. George, tell my friend John here what you just told me.'

Simons looked nervous, and a little sick, but he kept it together as he relayed what he knew. 'So,' he began, 'the victim, young mum, lives here . . . lived here . . . with her baby. Single mum in her early twenties, alone. Fell asleep last night in her bed next to her baby. Now . . . she'd had an on-again off-again relationship with a particularly bad person.'

'How bad?' John asked.

'As bad as you can get,' Constable Simons replied, rubbing his palm with his thumb. 'Last night, when this happened, their relationship sat firmly in the off-again category. She had told him the relationship was over, and that she didn't ever want to see him again. Ever.'

'Smart girl,' Grey said.

'Yes. Smart girl. But the nasty piece of shit didn't take to this news very well. So he came over, and climbed in through a window.' The officer gestured towards the side of the granny flat, and John checked a box in his head. *Point of entry confirmed. Good.* 'Then, while she slept, he . . . attacked the victim with a hammer.'

Grey exhaled, staring wordlessly into the flat. John did the same. From his current position, he could see the viscera showering the scene, and he realised what the thicker, more clotted remains were. Brains.

Brain matter, Grey had told him over lunch a week back – Grey often talked shop over lunch, which without fail ruined lunch – is pressurised. The skull carries an organ in a pool of fluid, and if enough pressure is applied, the brain seeks an exit. Needs somewhere to go. A hammer, when brought down with enough force, would have busted through the bone and into the skull cavity, meaning the brain would have been smashed, too. And sprayed out, and upwards. Painting the walls.

'John?' said Grey. John drifted back to the conversation.

'Right,' continued the constable. 'Once he'd killed her, he left the kid behind. It was his kid, you see. Didn't take the poor thing, mind, just left it there, crying. Screaming.' A flicker of anger crossed the constable's face, and he let it pass before barrelling on. 'Then, he climbs back out the window . . . not sure why he didn't take the door. Panic, maybe? Not sure. Anyway, he shimmies back here, heads to his car . . . and, racked with guilt, pulls out a knife and tries to off himself.'

John and Grey were now both visibly confused, and cast their eyes back along the driveway. 'Where is he now, then?' Grey remarked.

'And how do you know he used a hammer, that he didn't take the kid? Were there witnesses?' John chimed in.

Constable Simons shook his head. 'No, no witnesses. Well, just the one, technically.' He pointed at the empty driveway.

'Son, there's nothing there,' Grey said, dryly.

'No,' Constable Simons repeated, pointing even more emphatically. 'Not the driveway. The hospital. He sat in his car and tried to kill himself. Then he chickened out, called for help. The paramedics grab him, stitch him up, and as they're working on him, trying to get him fixed up, he appears to have felt a touch of guilt. So he spills his guts. Tells the paramedics everything he's done, and to their credit, they don't let the fucker – sorry.' Grey waved for him to continue. 'They didn't let him die. They saved him, and he's currently in the ICU over the road. He told them how he killed her with a hammer. Child Services have the kid, she's gonna be okay, but we can't find the weapon.'

Grey nodded, thanked the man and led John back to the door of the granny flat. He sighed thoughtfully, then leaned in to whisper to John. 'John. If you were a murderer, and if you'd just killed someone with a hammer—'

'I'm not, though.'

'Yes,' muttered Grey, patiently. 'But try and use your imagination, John. If you'd done what that shitbag did . . . and if you had a hammer. What would you do next?'

John furrowed his brow. He wasn't big on imagining he'd done things that he hadn't, in fact, done. But he cast his mind back, remembering his first walk-through of the flat. He walked over to the gap between the flat and the fence surrounding the ratty property. A foot-wide strip of wild, parched lawn lay between. John could see the window, high up on the wall, still half open. He'd have pressed his hands against the wall and the fence and shimmied up, swung in . . . and then come out that way, too.

He squeezed himself between the fence and the building, and walked the length of the darkened trench. Cicadas trilled in the distance, and dry grass crunched underfoot. After a full sweep of the walkway, with no hammer to show for it, he stopped, looking about. Slightly above head height on his right was the window. *I'm standing where he stood*, John thought. *He'd have hopped out, right here, having killed her. Holding the weapon. But it wasn't in the car, clearly, so he had to have disposed of it.*

John tried to imagine holding the hammer. He'd held a hammer recently, repairing a pipe beneath the sink at home. He'd broken the pipe in the process, and Christine had to call a plumber as a result. Christine. He thought about her, about the smell of her, and his idiot brain flung him momentarily back inside the granny flat. To the young mum with her brains decorating the walls. *Get a grip,* he chided himself. *Focus.*

Where could he have thrown it? John imagined the weight of a hammer in his hand, and lifted his arm to enact hurling it away. His hand almost immediately made contact with the wall behind him. The space was narrow, he realised, so narrow that only the meekest of flings would have been possible. So if he did land on his feet and immediately think to dispose of it, the only place it could have been hurled was . . .

He stared at the fence to his left. *Of course.* Standing up on his tiptoes, he glanced over.

A huge, almost vacant lot, tall grass everywhere. The perfect place for a murderer to fling evidence. John's eyes worked their way across the expanse of grass. It could be anywhere in there, but he couldn't just hike his pants up, leap over and have a cheeky look for it. At least, that's what he told himself at first. He was about to throw caution to the wind and dive over anyway, solve it here and now . . . when he saw the house at the very back of the property. Where the grass ended, a busted porch began, with rotten timber and a canvas awning. And on that porch, people.

Bikies.

A swarm of overweight bikies, all wearing road leathers and wraparound sunnies, standing idle at the back of an unassuming suburban home. Guns? John couldn't see any, but there were plenty of concealed bulges. Were they just happy to see him? *No,* John thought. *They haven't seen me, so they couldn't be happy to see me.*

'OI!' came a gravelly bellow.

They'd seen him now.

And they weren't happy.

John ducked back down, and scampered back towards Grey. 'Grey!' he whispered as loud as he could, shushing madly. 'Grey!'

'What is it?' he answered at full volume, totally missing the sign John had given him.

'Shhhh! Bikies!'

Grey stood up straight, like an owl about to be flung a dead mouse to eat. 'Bikies? Where?'

'Over the fucking fence!'

Grey hunched over to hide his gigantic frame and loped over to the fence. He stared through a knothole, gasped comically, then ran back to John. 'You are correct. Bikies.'

'What do we do?' rasped John. 'We need to sweep that lawn for the hammer. And they're not going to let us just pop on over and look.'

Grey shook his head at John. 'There's only one thing to do, John.' He paused for effect. 'Our jobs. Get your dust jacket from the car. We're going to work.'

As John headed to the Kingswood to gather up his gear and get ready for the sweep, Grey did a sweep of his own, gathering up the congress of assembled patrol officers. John walked back to the crime scene and as he was finishing setting up, Grey approached with five police in tow. 'I've called for a little extra,' he said, 'but we can get started whenever you're ready. We're just gonna hop the fence and get started. Do the sweep.' John swallowed. This case was veering wildly from tragic to foolhardy.

He looked at Grey. Grey looked at John. The other police didn't look as worried, which either meant they were very brave or very stupid. Possibly both, thought John.

The line of cops, following Grey, headed to the fence and hopped over, one by one. John watched them go, like Lemmings in blue, vaulting the rickety fence effortlessly. Grey went last, grunting a little, though John suspected that his mentor, given his height, could have stepped over the fence if he'd felt inclined. John passed the gear over the fence and held it aloft; Grey's huge, gentle hands appeared, seized the goods and took them out of sight. John sighed, gripped the fence, and over he went.

He landed with a crunch. The grass at the back of the property was dryer than the rest, and John could see bindies nestled in the scrub like hateful little landmines. At Grey's behest, the rest of the cops were already spreading out, snapping on gloves he'd provided them with. Grey was issuing instructions when John tapped him on the shoulder. 'Sir?'

Grey turned, smiling pleasantly, as if this whole scenario was perfectly normal. It wasn't normal, clearly, but people who are eccentric have their notions of normal bent slightly out of align-ment, and Grey was, most assuredly, eccentric. 'So,' he stated in a voice which caught the eye of a waddling bikie in the distance. 'This, John, is called an emu parade. We form a line, you, me, and these fine young men. We walk very slowly up the property, looking for the hammer. Once we have it, we leave, hopefully without having upset these fine gentlemen.' He gestured towards the house with a flourish; the waddling bikie waddled over to a group of other bikies, who looked the type not to waddle but to stomp. John realised he was sweating, and not from the heat.

'So what happens if we don't find the hammer and make it all the way to the house?'

'Ah,' replied Grey, checking his gloves. 'That wouldn't be ideal. Because then we'd have to question said gentlemen, and if I'm to be candid, John, I think the less time spent in here, the better. Looks like the natives are getting restless.' Grey was right. More bikies had emerged from the compound and onto the balcony, and they did not look pleased.

'All right!' Grey barked down the line. 'Here we go! Eyes open, eyes open.' And with that, the line of police, hunched over and sifting through the dense lawn, began walking laboriously forward. Every step bringing them closer and closer to . . . an altercation, John thought. A brawl? He thought again about the bulges. A shoot-out? Surely not. Surely they wouldn't attack police.

And that's when the yelling started.

Indistinct at first, but soon, roars of 'FUCK OFF, COPPERS' and 'GET THE FUCK OFF OUR LAWN, YOU CUNTS' came thick and fast, thicker than the grass, and certainly faster than the speed at which this line of police were conducting their fastidious search for a bloodied hammer. John saw one of the officers – possibly Simons, he couldn't quite tell – rest a hand on his holster. The veins on Grey's forehead bulged with exertion as he leaned over, focusing as hard as he could on his search. More yells from the bikies, more screams of pure, liquid hatred. Then, the yells pivoted towards threats.

'DON'T COME ANY FUCKIN' CLOSER,' came one gravelly bellow. John looked up. The waddler was beetroot red, fists white-knuckled. Then, a bark. John watched as yet another bikie, this one blanketed in tattoos, emerged from a recess bearing a German shepherd the size of a horse. At least, that's how it looked to John. One of the other cops saw this, too, yelling for the man to send the dog back. The bikies bellowed with laughter. Not mirthful laughter, mind you. Threatening, jagged laughs from large, dangerous men. Grey had stopped in his tracks, and was telling the line of police to do the same. The leash strained. Simons drew his gun. John thought, over the ringing in his ears and the sudden peal of chaotic exchanges, that he heard Simons yelling 'Stand down!', but he wasn't entirely sure. All he could see was the dog, black eyes fixed on his.

Everyone was yelling now, screaming. Something was about to break. The sun bore down on John, and his heart rate quickened. *That dog,* he thought. *That dog is going to come for me.* And then . . . the bikie holding the leash bellowed something indecipherable, and let slip the dog of war. He heard the dry, rasping *shffffff* of the leash sliding through the man's glove, watched it flail in the air, and then snap taut as the forty kilograms of beast leapt from the deck. Suspended in the air for a moment, John could see the muscles beneath the fur, coiled like pistons, paws ready to hit the ground running. *Yes,* John thought. *Paranoia aside, fear aside, it is coming right for me. It's still a way off, but it'll be here in seconds flat.*

John turned and ran.

A cacophony of screams and barked orders, and barked barks, crisscrossed in the hot, fuggy air. The cicadas had stopped dead.

John had never run from anything in his life, at least nothing he could recall. He'd almost made it to the fence, lungs burning and legs pumping, when he tripped. Looking down at his feet, he reached down and . . . the hammer. He'd tripped over the hammer. *God knows who missed it on the sweep,* he thought, but as he held it up and went to alert Grey to his find, he saw the chaos that had erupted. Guns were drawn, yells drowning out yells . . . and the dog was still coming. Scrambling to his feet, John dared to turn his back on the animal, and as he vaulted the fence back into the driveway and to safety, he heard a sound. A terrible sound that rang out and almost stopped his heart.

A shot.

There was silence, and John, sweating and flushed, peered through a gap in the fence. The German shepherd lay dead, foam on its lips. And whatever sense of restraint had held the bikies back before this moment snapped. They charged. The cops charged. And John, holding crucial evidence, sprinted for his radio as Grey's promised backup arrived. They exploded out of their vehicles, grabbed their batons and charged into the fray.

'Why did you run?'

Dad looks startled. He does that thing people do when they're shaken from a particularly deep recollection: shakes his head to free himself from the memory he's immersed in. It's like time travel, remembering things. You have to suspend your brain and body for a while, then send your consciousness spinning back into the past. And Dad, as he pops back into the present, looks . . . shaken? He doesn't look shaken very often. I hand him his water, which he holds idle.

'Sorry, mate. What did you say?'

'I was asking why you ran,' I say gently.

'Big fucking dog,' he answers, with distant eyes.

It's more than that, I can tell. But I'll get to that later. Don't worry. I'll get to that later.

9

IT SEEMS THE CAT HAS BEEN CAUGHT BY THE VERY PERSON THAT WAS TRYING TO CATCH HIM

One thing I've learned from having ADHD is the power of a distraction.

Dad loves magic tricks. His midlife crisis was an odd one; about ten years ago, rather than dumping his wife and buying a Bugatti, he became mildly obsessed with card tricks, coin tricks, anything that would baffle and delight people at a dinner party. Fun fact: he has a few legitimately good tricks quite literally up his sleeve. If you ever meet him, harangue him until he pulls a Copperfield for you. Well worth the effort.

But magic is all about misdirection: getting your mark to look one way while you do something devious in the other. Once you can guide and control someone's gaze, you can get away with almost anything. ADHD is all about distractions; if I see something I like, my brain will hyper-fixate on it for a matter of months, so I'm an excellent person to pull magic tricks on, because my brain is, frankly, ready and willing to enjoy being fooled. Maybe that's why I enjoy fiction so much – when I'm in an imagined world, for all intents and purposes I'm there; the outside world ceases to exist. Experts call this kind of laser-beam focus a 'disregulated attention system', which basically means my brain is drawn to things that give instant feedback. Like stories. But where was I? Oh, right. Magic tricks. Misdirection.

And right now, I'm about to pull a little misdirection of my own on Dad.

'Dad,' I say, 'you know what struck me earlier?'

He still looks a little vacant, but he answers. 'What?'

'That you're excellent at magic tricks, right?'

He shrugs. He doesn't say no, mind you. He's nothing if not humble.

'Well, magic tricks are about deception, misdirection. Cheating, playing people. And you've told me how adept you were at picking locks. Now . . . I know you bounced off the idea of imagining what-ifs – what if you'd become a thief, for example.'

He nods.

'But,' I continue, 'during that last case, I don't know if you know you said this out loud . . . but for a moment, you actually tried to imagine you were the killer. And you basically said, what if I was him, and what if I had to dispose of the weapon?'

Dad gives me a look. The kind of look that indicates someone wants the conversation to change topics, fast.

'Look, all I'm saying,' I continue, 'is that I am truly fascinated by what kind of a thief you'd have been. But I'll settle for talking about the kind of thief you wouldn't have been. By which

I mean . . . disastrous. Skills-wise, I think you'd have been an amazing thief, I really do . . . but what's the most insane case you dealt with in forensics involving thievery?'

'Thievery?' he says, mulling this over.

'Yeah. I know you didn't deal with burglars in forensics, not really, but what's a case you lived through in Scientific that had you brushing up against the lives of proper thieves?'

I know what case he's going to talk about. He's told me this story before, you see. And just like a willing mark during a magic trick, Dad knows he's being played, but he's willing. He's up for it. But even so, he pretends not to know what's going on, and delightedly ploughs into one of his favourite stories to tell. It's comfort food, and I just tricked him into eating it. Because it's good for him. And because he seems outrageously hungry.

There's a building in Manly called Carillon. It looks like a complex, towering array of intersecting, blindingly white triangles, and it has commanding views of Sydney Harbour. John was about to inspect a body that had been found there.

He and Grey stood side by side in the cavernous Glebe Morgue. Grey had insisted on coming with John for this one. It had been a week since the hammer case, since John ran. John claimed he'd seen a glint of something in the grass and made a beeline for it before it became lost in what shortly turned into an all-out brawl between bikies and cops, resulting in several arrests. Grey made a show of nodding and exalting John's rigour and attention to detail, especially in the face of such anarchy, but they both wordlessly agreed to pretend John hadn't almost fled the scene out of . . . fear? Was it fear? John knew Grey knew, and Grey knew John knew he knew. And so on and so forth in that fashion. John chuckled to himself. Either way, he'd found the murder weapon, and that's what mattered.

In the week since, however, Grey had ramped up his mentorship, and had been sticking by John's side more than usual. Now, he stood next to John, eyeballing the body laid out before them. 'What does this look like to you?'

'A body,' John replied, casting his eyes across the cadaver.

'Yes, a body. Could you be more specific?'

'A pizza supreme,' replied John, transfixed by the face, which was flattened, pocked and smashed beyond recognition.

Grey harrumphed. 'Lovely. No, John. Give him a once-over, tell me what you think happened.'

John looked at Grey, concerned. 'Sorry, mate. Insensitive.'

Grey waved him off. 'Gallows humour, John. Only way to cope sometimes.'

John began his inspection, gently probing the body with gloved hands. 'Look, he's been through a severe trauma. Who is he? Sorry. *Was* he.'

Grey turned to John, folding his arms and speaking quietly. 'The Carillon is a very, very tall building, John. Very tall. And what else would you say defines the building?'

John stewed over this. 'Expensive. Costs a lot to live there. High-income tenants. Lots of linen, chardonnay. Doobie Brothers. Cocaine. Bad hair.'

'Accurate, but cruel,' replied Grey. 'But yes, John, very well off! Which makes them prime targets for . . . well. Anyway. I'm jumping ahead. Tenants on the ground floor have a bit of a rare advantage at Carillon. They have access to a private balcony garden . . . thing. Lovely, enclosed space. Accessible via glass doors. At around four this morning, a tenant heard a thump.'

'A thump?'

'A thump. Very loud one, too. And they think nothing of it, go back to sleep.' Grey was more animated now, hands moving excitedly about the place, swishing through the air to punctuate his story. 'A few hours later, this tenant wakes up and gets her coffee. She toddles around the kitchen, and while sipping on her beverage, she happens to idly glance out into the rock garden, where she sees a maintenance worker, busy adjusting something. He's got an arm out of sight, and he's clearly reaching into a pipe or something. She doesn't think much of it, so she finishes her coffee and goes to have a shower.'

Something twigged in John's brain, but he let Grey continue.

'When the woman comes back, the maintenance worker, clad in white denim overalls and a white cap, is still there! So maybe there's a problem with the plumbing, the old girl thinks. Maybe the works are gummed up. *Tell you what,* she thinks. *I'll be a good Samaritan, take him a coffee.* She pours the chap a mug of Blend 43 – which is scarcely coffee, but anyway – and opens the sliding door. She walks over to him, and that's when she notices he's still.'

'Still what?'

'You're a funny one, John. He's still, inert, motionless. Hasn't moved. Maybe he's stuck, she thinks, and she pops the coffee down and leans over to give him a friendly nudge. He doesn't move. And then she rolls him over, and what she finds will likely have put her off her knitting for the next decade.'

Grey gestured towards the body, and John finally realised why he'd felt uneasy. The man's clothes were filthy, true, and bloody, but they were definitely white overalls. And his face . . . to think that some old woman confronted that face first thing in the morning.

'This rock garden,' John murmured, beginning to feel a little nauseous himself. 'White pebbles? Smooth? About a centimetre in diameter?'

Grey smiled sadly. 'How'd you guess?'

The face was flattened and spread out, and riddled with what looked at first like polka dots. Every inch of skin was peppered with the tiny rocks, which had become embedded in the flesh and looked immovable. The kind of impact it would take to slam that many rocks into someone's face . . .

'He fell,' John said, turning to face Grey. The revelation and the strangeness of the case had suddenly yanked him out of his funk. 'The Carillon. Big money, expensive apartments, full of valuables. He posed as a maintenance worker, or at least dressed like one in case he was caught. Look at his build.' John pointed at dead muscles, still tensed and bulging. 'The guy is built like a brick shithouse, but he's kind of lean, too. He's a climber. He . . . yes. He scaled the building. Scaled a lot of buildings. But . . .'

'Go on,' prompted Grey, hands clasped together.

'But he fell. I dealt with B&Es in General Duties. Crims climb apartments, and have no trouble getting into the places because people high up never think to lock their balcony doors. Who's gonna break in that high up, right? And as these people living at the Carillon are well off, they don't think anything can touch them. Grey, did anyone in the building report anything stolen?'

'Yes,' Grey said, fingers dancing on invisible strings.

'Did anyone find anything on him?'

'No,' replied Grey. 'Nothing.'

'I'm guessing the person who reported stolen goods locks their door from the inside with a deadbolt.'

'Yes, they did tell that to the police.'

'Right. See, normally these crims climb up, walk on in, and then they leave via the front door. But this guy . . . this guy had to climb back down, which is much, much harder, especially after the climb up. And something's gone wrong, he's slipped . . . and fallen into the rock garden, face-first. His arm has landed under his body, making it look like he was reaching down into a hole, and your witness has headed out to offer a dead man a cup of coffee.'

John looked at Grey, a 'How'd I do?' kind of look. Grey looked at John with a 'You did beautifully' look in return. 'John,' he said warmly, 'it says a lot about you as a person that in order to cheer you up, after something you perceive as a failing but which I saw as a deeply human and perfectly normal moment, you had to be shown a dead body and told to figure out how the man died. That—' Grey placed a hand on John's shoulder '—that is why you're so good at this job.'

'Why?' asked John, guiltily. 'Because I like dead bodies?'

'No!' replied Grey. 'No! You don't *like* dead bodies. You like solving problems. And these bodies? These bodies are doors through which lie answers. And you're brave enough to step through them. John . . . John, I know you think you fucked up last week.'

John looked at the floor.

'You didn't. You'd just seen something utterly inhuman inside that granny flat. And I know you're not going to want to hear this, but each person, however remarkable, is a container. You follow? And every time they see something like that, that container is filled up a little. Now . . . most people? Most people have a thimble's worth of tolerance for the trauma, and it'll overflow easily. And that's fine. That's normal. But you . . . you have a tanker. And do you want to know how to know you've got fluid spilling out?' He raised an eyebrow and leaned closer. 'You'll know you're full to bursting if these things *don't* affect you anymore. The second you lose your ability to feel, to get hurt, is the second you need to stop.'

He stood back up. 'So you see, John? You running away from the dog, from the bikies, was the only healthy thing to do. The only sane thing to do. At least . . . it was to me. So forgive me for the . . . misdirection. But I thought the best way to cheer you was to get you back to work. And you figured it out. Because of course you did.'

'Well,' John murmured, half to himself. 'I had you helping me out. You . . . god, remember the bikies? They had concealed weapons. Bulges in their pants. Remember?'

Grey nodded.

'Well, unless this guy carried a gun to B&Es, or unless this stiff has a stiff, then there's something right there. He's packing something.' John pointed at the dead man's crotch, and Grey's eyes went wide. He clapped loudly.

'I do believe you're right, John.'

Grey and John, working in tandem, carefully worked their way into the dead cat-burglar's pants . . . and withdrew a small jewellery box. With his gloved hands shaking, John opened the velvet-lined lid to reveal a ring with a circular face. And stamped into the golden circle? Hundreds of tiny diamonds. He looked at the stones in the face below him, the dead face, the face of a man who'd chosen a life of crime.

And he didn't for a minute wonder what his life would have been like if he'd gone on to become a thief. He didn't dwell on the what-if, *the path not chosen*. Because that's not how John viewed the world.

10

THE CARVERY

The past has a way of catching up with us.

In the late seventies, back when John was still a teenager, disco was huge. When he was in forensics, in the eighties, it was deader than . . . well, disco. But back in the late seventies there was still some life in the old girl.

Disco was big. Really big. John would head along to discos in platform shoes, hair permed and sprayed to within an inch of its life. Floors were illuminated, even if gender politics were not. John would get dressed up, douse himself in some unpronounce-able Italian scent, and swagger his way over to the city with his friends. Some weekends, however, they'd stay local, which in his case meant Manly. The bustling beach suburb was unbear-ably beautiful. Natural beauty. There was nothing natural about the Hotel Steyne, though, and that's where John was headed one fateful night.

He was wearing a safari suit, his hair was a mile high, and his feet were ready for dancing in two-tone Florsheim platforms. Given that John was six feet tall, he was on the verge of suffering an attack of vertigo, but he soldiered on regardless. Entering the Steyne, his eyes straining from the pulsing lights and stinging from hairspray fumes, he set about finding himself a good time.

The Steyne had a carvery: a bistro with a cafeteria-style bar covered in bain-maries. John, bleary-eyed, wobbled up to the bar, grabbed a plate, and joined the queue. No sense partying on an empty stomach, even if that stomach was in danger of succumbing to little other than altitude sickness. And as he made it to the server, he made eye contact with the man, who was wearing an apron and holding a carving knife.

'What can I get you?' the man, swarthy and blond but otherwise fairly featureless, asked in a thick German accent. John asked for the lamb. He always, every time he came here of a weekend, grabbed the lamb, and he always seemed to be served by the same German.

'Why are we talking about a German man who served you at a carvery before you became a cop?' I ask.
Dad brandishes his Moleskine at me. 'Trust me.'

A few years later, when John was settling in nicely to Forensics, he'd left his disco days behind – mercifully – and Grey had apparently been talking him up around the station. In backrooms, down corridors, there was some gentle buzz building about the cop who'd turned down being a detective to pursue a career in Scientific, and this meant that people were asking for John on occasion . . . and not just to have him pick locks.

One quiet Saturday evening, Grey got a call for John to head over to Babcock House, detective HQ. John nodded, grabbed his gear and trotted out to the Kingswood. Just John, the detectives had said. Alone.

I suppose, he thought as he drove towards his destination, *I've proven myself now.*

John, as has been established, did not adore detectives. He still pined for the potential of the office, of what good, motivated people with their station and powers could achieve, but he'd seen things that had driven him away from that particular career path. Terrible things. He was ruminating on this as he pulled up out the front of the towering, ashen building and made his way over to the two detectives who were outside waiting for him. Waiting. For him. Odd. This whole thing was a little odd.

John shook their hands and introduced himself, and they led him to their impound lot, down a ramp and into a badly lit car park. John let his eyes adjust to the light, and found himself standing in front of a white Holden Commodore, a fairly nondescript sedan.

'John,' said the lead detective. 'Grey says you're hot shit, so listen up. We have a bloke upstairs, and he's being questioned. Vigorously. He's not giving us much, but this . . . this is his car. Bloody hard to find. And we need you to sweep through the contents of the entire thing. Fair warning – there's a lot of shit in this car. Fella wasn't exactly a clean freak.'

John peered inside and began slipping his gloves on. 'Sure,' he said, facing the detectives. 'What are you looking for? Fingerprints? Circumstantial evidence?'

The lead detective nodded grimly. 'All of the above.'

Once the men had left, tramping up the stairwell that led to the circuitous insides of the building, John looked around at the car park. Most of the spaces were taken, he noted, by what looked like cars belonging to detectives: an array of eccentric, flashy cars favoured by the Ds. *Which is strange,* John thought, *because on*

Saturdays, not all detectives would normally be at work. There'd be a skeleton crew instead. So what could have brought so many of them here, all to the one place, on a Saturday?

John looked back at the car he'd been told to analyse, cracked his neck, and got to work. And what he found was bizarre.

Pornography. John had never seen quite so much pornography in his life. All magazines, but thousands of the damned things, piled high and well cared for. After an initial assessment, he pulled out his camera and began photographing. The boot was worse than the back seat, absolutely crammed with *Penthouse* and *Hustler*, and once he'd done his pass with the camera, he began dusting for prints. Hunched over in the dim light of the car park, he reflected on his career trajectory. He'd wanted to be up there, floors above, solving cases as a detective. Instead, he was in the basement, running a fine, dewy brush across a litany of well-oiled centrefolds.

'Can you imagine what life would have been like if you—'
    But I'm cut off mid-sentence by an impatient look from
Dad.

Once John was done, he collected his camera, his prints and what was left of his dignity, and walked back up the ramp and out onto the street. As his eyes adjusted to the sudden wash of light, he got his bearings and decided to head up via the lift and deliver the results of his search to the detectives. He headed into the foyer through large glass doors, got into the small metal box, shifted uneasily on the squares of orange carpet inside, and before long was deposited on the fourth floor. Across the way, he immediately saw one of the two detectives from the car park standing out the front of an open door. John trotted over, and was suddenly struck by an odd smell.

The detective, looking more dishevelled than John had remembered, nodded hello and extended a hand to take the files.

As John passed them over, he caught a glimpse of the suspect, just a brief glimpse, sitting in a metal-backed chair, eyes hollow, tears streaming down his cheeks. Someone inside slammed the door shut. The detective gave John a flash of an apologetic look, took the files and John's film, and leafed through the pages. As the detective read, John couldn't help but notice a faint brown smudge on the man's untucked shirt. He caught John looking, and gave John a truly odd glare. And John thought . . . *You know what? Fuck it. I've earned my way. These people don't scare me.*

'So what's the story?' John asked, bold as brass. And while the detective seemed almost taken aback, he began to answer. He answered openly and honestly. And very soon, John wished he hadn't prodded the bear.

'The bloke in there? You just did a sweep of his car. Pervert, yeah?'

John nodded back, conceding this point.

'Right. Well, your job here is done. But I'm happy to fill you in. Least we can do to thank you for your help.'

John gulped.

'That bloke, in there, is bad. Real fucking bad. He worked for years on a work permit over on the Northern Beaches. And what he'd do was pick up hitchhikers. Regularly. And what he used to do . . . Are you sure you wanna hear this, mate?'

John looked deep inside himself. He could have said no, of course. Perhaps he even should have said no. But to someone who digs, who seeks the truth, being given the facts is like a drug. *So I really don't have a choice, do I?* he thought. *I've come this far.* 'Shoot,' he said.

'Well, let me give you a specific example of the stuff this animal did. One we've been chasing for a while. He picked up this nurse, and he took her to a quiet spot in a fairly prominent park up near Lane Cove. And what he did was . . . he has a scat fetish. He likes shit. And he'd get the girl to remove shit from her own . . . you know. Then he'd rape her, do all sorts of horrible stuff to the poor girl. Then he'd throw her out of the car, run her over, and set fire to the body. And . . .'

The detective's facade shifted, and just for a moment, John saw a scared, furious young man. Only for a moment, though. The detective ploughed on, almost as if moving past the horror at high speed would leave it in his emotional rear-view. 'So we found out he was also wanted in Germany. This is after we caught the cunt, mind. We finally track him down and get told he's gonna be extradited, pulled out of our hands. He killed so many women, mate. So many. So me and the lads—' the detective jerked his thumb back at the door '—so me and the fellas decided to do a whip around. Get him a farewell gift. One we thought . . . poetic.'

John pointed to the brown smear. The detective followed his finger, looked back at John's face, and nodded. 'We all took turns. Filled a bowl all the way to the top. And that fuckhead isn't leaving until he's done eating.'

A long, terrible pause. The sound of sobbing eked out from under the door.

The detective thanked John and turned to leave. And that's when something struck John, something he should have cottoned on to sooner. 'Mate,' John said, voice shaky. 'Where . . . where did you say those extradition orders were coming from?'

'Oh,' replied the detective over his shoulder. 'Germany. He's German.' And with that, the man returned to the interrogation room, and John stumbled to the lift in shock. He finally knew where that face was from, the face he'd glimpsed, tearful and hollowed out, inside the room.

A German.

The German man who worked at the carvery.

Over and over, weekend after weekend, during the period in which those women had been killed, John had been standing in front of a murderer. Worse than a murderer, in fact.

John stamped down any desire he might have had to wonder what he could have done to stop the murders. What would have happened if he'd known? Would he have reached across the carvery bar and grabbed the knife, plucking it from the man's hands? Would he have called the cops then and there?

'No,' he muttered madly. 'No. Nothing you could have done.' Some people are just broken.

11

RICE BUBBLES

John was struggling a little. Not with his job – which was humming along beautifully – but struggling to process some of what he was seeing on the job in Forensics. You can't unsee some things. You can't, as Grey would say, 'get the shit back into the horse'. But Grey also said that the best way to deal with these occupational horrors was the 'stubbed toe method'.

'What do you mean?' John asked, sitting across from Grey at his desk, leaning back on his chair.

'Simple,' said Grey. He stood up. 'John, imagine I have a pain in my knee.'

'Do you? Have a pain in your knee?'

'No,' said Grey. 'But imagine I do have a pain in my knee.'

'Just imagine it?'

'Just . . . imagine it, John.'

'Okay.' A pause. 'Did you hit it on your desk?'

'No, John. It's a metaphor. Let's say my sore knee is trauma from, for example, having headed over to the detectives' office and seen a man you met years ago being force-fed a bucket of excrement. Trauma. Traumatised. This knee—' he pointed at his knee again '—ouchie. So, what's the quickest way to stop having to think about the pain, John?'

John shrugged.

Grey clapped, beamed, and brought his leg back like a pendulum. 'Observe!' he bellowed gregariously, and swung his enormous foot down, his toes crashing into the leg of his enormous oak desk. Immediately, his face was a tapestry of agony, eyes twitching, mouth pulling up into a grimace. 'Now,' he squeaked through gritted teeth, 'what am I *not* thinking about, John?'

John, shocked by the sudden display, cast about the room. 'Are you okay? Jesus Christ! Why did you do that?'

Grey hopped on the spot, breathing heavily. 'John! What am I not thinking about?' John shrugged. 'My knee! I'm not thinking about my fucking knee!'

'Was there not an easier way to illustrate your point?'

'Yes! Yes there was. But it wouldn't have stuck with you, John. Fuck. Fuckety fuck fuck fuckington, this hurts.' Grey sat down, tears beginning to stream down his face. 'I think I broke something. John! The point is this: if you can't stop thinking about a case, a horrible case . . . busy yourself immediately with a case of equal or greater horribleness.'

John stared, agog, at his wincing mentor. 'Do you . . . do you have something for me? Of equal or greater horribleness?'

'I do. Yes, I do. And this one sounds like it's going to be greater.'

John looked at Grey and shook his head. He had silently prayed for a wise, weird and wizened mentor; this looming, brilliant ex-hippy was all of those things, and he sure as hell kept John on his toes . . . even if he did insist upon potentially breaking his own in the process.

*

One of the odd things about dealing with crime, John had learned in his time at General Duties, was the timing. You almost always arrived after the nightmare had unfolded, and it was your job not to prevent crime, but to figure out how it had happened – and then to clean it up. It was reactive. John noticed that the feeling of sudden immersion in a terrifying tableau had become heightened in Forensics; upon arriving at a crime scene, everyone cleared the area. Tape cordoned off the field of play, and John had to stare at bodies head-on and confront the horror of what had occurred, far too late to do anything to stop it.

John, on this particular afternoon, was sent – alone – to deal with the single most upsetting thing he'd seen working in the scientific division. *Scratch that,* he thought. *The worst thing I've seen, period.*

In the interest of giving you a leg-up, a bird's-eye view of the atrocity the twenty-something-year-old man was about to try to make sense of, let's skip back a few hours.

A cavernous, bustling factory chugs and steams away in the inner-city suburbs just outside the Sydney CBD. This factory, for the sake of specificity, makes gargantuan quantities of a beloved cereal. And in this factory, there's a sixteen-year-old boy. He's an apprentice engineer, and his job? His job is to inspect the vats which form the backbone of the production process for this particular beloved cereal. Tons of grain fill these vats, and the grain is then superheated by steam, practically volcanic in temperature, and once the stuff in the vats is successfully steamed and aerated, it gets doled out, boxed up and sold off. All good so far.

Now, because inspecting these vats is so monumentally dangerous, there are checks and balances in place. And on this particular morning, our sixteen-year-old is inside one of these towering stainless steel tubes. Further up the assembly line, someone has done what they're meant to do: mark the line so that no steam enters the vat and causes irreparable harm to anyone inside. But this morning, someone has made a mistake. They haven't done their job properly. Something, somewhere along the line has been overlooked. And in an instant, an ocean of incandescent, molten steam billows and furls with the speed of a roaring wave through the pipes. It cascades into the vat, surrounding the boy. Boiling him alive.

The paramedics arrive eventually, but by this point, it's far too late. All the fluid in the boy's body – and the human body is mostly made of fluid – has superheated. He's turned highlighter pink. The paramedics try to save him, but it's no good. The kid dies. Staff members can't stop thinking about their friend who died, for no other reason than because someone forgot to check a box. Forgot to pull a tiny lever. A life is snuffed out; countless others are scarred forever.

John, alone, was confronted with this boy's body. He'd been told exactly what had happened, and was making a preliminary inspection. The paramedics had sheared all the cannulas off flush with the taut, blistered skin, leaving themselves a kind of paper trail so the senior coroner could trace exactly what steps were taken to try to stave off the boy's demise. John swept his eyes across the lad. It was shocking. Utterly shocking. Grey was right; he wasn't thinking about his prior trauma anymore. All he could think about was what it must have felt like. How it would have felt to have your body boil and distend and inflate. How it must have felt to be screaming for help, knowing nobody would get to you in time.

But most of all, he felt sick. Sick at how unfair it all was. And he thought about the fact that he, prior to joining the force, not even twenty years old, had been an apprentice, too, on a worksite brimming with dangerous, heavy equipment.

'Stop it,' he chided himself, reaching for his gloves. 'Fucking stop it, John. This isn't helping.' And he realised that, unlike this kid, he could ask for help. All he had to do was pick up the phone. He did so, and a little while later, Grey entered with his finger-printing gear. He sighed sadly upon seeing the body, gave John a gentle pat upon the shoulder, and motioned for the two of them to get to work. 'Now, John. I've been told that because of how unrec-ognisable this kid is, the chief coroner can't accept a facial ID.'

John shot Grey a baffled look. 'But . . . we found his wallet in his jeans. We have witnesses. His staff ID. It's . . . it's him.'

'I know,' Grey replied softly. 'But we need to get prints. And I'm not . . . Look, I'm not entirely sure what to do here, but I'm open to suggestions.'

The body was doing what John felt inclined to do: it was weeping. Every pore was oozing liquid, giving the corpse an almost alien look, a glistening, sickly hue. 'Grey,' John said, steel in his voice. 'I . . . Hmm. I don't quite know how to say this . . . but I have an idea.'

And John told Grey his idea.

And here is what they did.

Taking his scalpel, John got Grey to hold the boy's hand still. It was shiny and taut, twice the size of a normal hand. Starting at the wrist, John began to cut a fine line along the skin. Grey had men-tioned this method to him in passing, weeks and weeks ago during a particularly grisly anecdote. It was called 'de-gloving', and in Grey's version, it never worked. But it was working now. Somehow, after a series of smooth yet terrifyingly tentative incisions, John gripped the boy's skin, gently pulled . . . and with a wet sound, the skin slipped off. Muscle and bone lay inert on the slab, and John, too deep in shock to feel sick, held aloft a human glove. He could see the whites all the way around Grey's eyes.

'Right,' Grey said. 'Now for the bad part.'

John just stared at his mentor. 'Do I have to do it?'

Grey just stared back. 'I'd really rather if you did, John. Yes.'

And so that morning, after one of the worst half-hours of his life, John held his own gloved hand up. Grey carefully held the dead boy's hand, and without so much as breathing, slipped it over John's. Grey ran across the room, leaving John standing there, staring at the hand, complete with fingernails, and briefly considered having a cry. Nothing came. How do you even begin to process something so unreal?

Grey came back, holding paper towels, reverently dabbing the skin dry. He laid out a fingerprint form and inkpad, and John did what he'd done countless times before. Countless times, but never quite like this.

He took another person's prints.

He and Grey then sombrely repeated the process with the boy's other hand. They removed the improvised gloves; Grey was kind enough to take care of them once they'd been taken off, leaving John standing in the centre of the room, skin tingling, eyes burning. John, not a religious man, said a silent prayer. He'd always been told that to understand someone else's suffering, you needed to walk a mile in their shoes. *I get it,* John thought, tears welling in his eyes. *I finally get it.*

And all he'd had to do was walk for five minutes in another man's skin.

*

'Then we had to go to the kid's house,' Dad said to me. 'And we had to fingerprint his belongings to get confirmation of who he was.'

Clearly an appalled look crosses my face, and Dad shakes his head. 'No, no. Look. We have to confirm. Have to. It's not pleasant, but what if someone stole the kid's wallet, snuck in? The parents have to know.'

'But . . .' I stammer, 'how do you do that? How do you look at a parent and tell them their kid has died? How the hell do you talk to someone about a death that just occurred? I have no idea how you could have done that.'

'Well,' Dad says, 'it wasn't easy. But I had to do it a lot more at Kinsella.'

Kinsella. Something twigs. I think maybe my eye twitches. 'Kinsella?'

'Yeah,' Dad says, matter-of-factly. 'You know. Kinsella Funeral Homes.'

And that's when it all comes flooding back.

12

DEAD SERIOUS

I'm going to level with you: I forgot that any of what you're about to read ever happened. But as I'm sitting there, talking with Dad, the merest mention of Kinsella plucks me out of my body and hurls me back in time. Ever suppress a memory? Me too. But have you ever suppressed several years of your life? That's what I appear to have done. So, as long as you're here, let me fill you in on the deluge of memories freed from the confines of my amygdala.

See that kid over there, hunched over on that small patch of lawn, playing with a large plastic car? Look behind him. You'll see a row of hearses. Now cast your eye at the building across the lawn from him, the one he's refusing to lock eyes with. See that? That's where they keep the bodies.

That kid is me. And this building?

It's a funeral home.

I grew up here. Well, I sort of grew up here. I certainly spent enough time here for it to feel somewhat like home. When I was about ten years old, my parents announced that they had a new job (Dad called it a 'business opportunity'), and that because they couldn't afford a babysitter, we got to come to work with them.

By this point it was me, my sister Anne, and my baby brother Mark. And Mum and Dad, obviously.

Ever look at what your parents do and think, huh. Weird job. Well, apparently my parents worked with dead people for a living.

Mum and Dad had met on the police force of all places, and had done so in their early twenties. After a brief dalliance – two weeks – they hooked up, and before long they promptly had me. Then, two years later, my sister. The problem was, however, that, being cops, Mum and Dad were basically bombarded with maimed bodies, dead kids and horrific abuses carried out against fellow humans on a daily basis. Mum was effectively driven out of the force because she'd dared to ask for some time to take care of her kids, meaning she went from working in Romeo Squad – investigating sex crimes – and Internal Affairs to being a housewife. I'm going to focus on Mum later – she's an incredible woman, but she's notoriously skittish about discussing her career. Which is a damn shame, to be perfectly frank.

Dad stayed in the force, and got into forensics. You know that by now, of course. We'll get back to forensics shortly, but I feel like this thread is too tantalisingly strange to not tug. We watched as Dad went from a whip-thin young man with bright eyes and high hopes to a slightly more tired, heavier, wearier version of himself. After a number of years on the force, he barrelled at Mum, and told her he needed a change. Something with less darkness.

He chose the fire brigade.

I remember noticing the change in his demeanour at once. We were living in a little fibro house in North Manly, full of second-hand furniture. I had to share a room with my sister on account of poor finances, which was fine because we both adored hanging out, but we drove my mum crazy. I used to string up booby traps around the house to ward off 'bad guys', which frequently meant Mum would find herself caught in a crisscross of interlocking ropes that I'd tied at horrifying angles across every available doorframe. For Mum, it must have felt like being trapped in the lair of a serial killer, which, as you can imagine, did her post-police brain a world of good.

Somewhere, though, somehow, as time passed I papered over that time. I looked back and just sort of gestured vaguely in the direction of my pre-teen years, remembering little more than being incredibly bored all the time. My ADHD meant I was running around like a dervish on mescaline 99 per cent of the time, and I ended up at a child shrink when I was fourteen to deal with my psychological proclivities, which in turn had me prescribed various medications. Hell, maybe they're the reason I blocked off those memories?

But then, Dad went and mentioned the funeral home in passing.

What funeral home, I asked again. And Dad repeated, Kinsella. Kinsella Funeral Homes. 'Paul,' he said, looking a little perturbed, 'we practically lived there for four years. How do you not remember this?'

A funeral home? We lived at a funeral home?

Maybe this explains why I'm so skittish, why I'm so . . . all over the place. Maybe something happened during that period. But by all accounts, forgetting four of what my parents now admitted were frighteningly eventful years isn't normal. So what happened? What really happened at Kinsella Funeral Homes all those years ago?

'I remember you used to play on the lawn,' Dad says.

And suddenly . . . I'm there. I'm looking at myself, playing on a lawn that until this very moment I had no recollection of. But I remember it now.

And I ask Dad to start at the beginning. I ask him to explain what happened.

CAR WASHER NEEDED
CALL BARRY

John couldn't tell you why he answered the ad.

He'd been sitting there all morning, perched precariously on a second-hand stool in his kitchen. *I'm too big for this stool,* he thought. The chair creaked in agreement. But he continued to sit there before the scuffed Formica table, the sound of his tiny children ricocheting around outside drifting in through the window. He'd been sitting there, squinting in the dusty morning light, leafing through the *Sydney Morning Herald*'s Help Wanted section, just letting his eyes stray from one request to another. He couldn't have told you why he felt an odd twinge upon seeing the almost comically unhelpful ad, tiny copperplate block letters being almost crushed by the box around them. It was, he thought, like one of those fake ads put in by a sleeper agent, signalling a hit carried out with nary a complication. It was cryptic in its lack of details. It was a little bit creepy.

But he needed the money.

Dad was about to hit thirty, and was feeling lost. He still had a full head of hair, but the slowing of his youthful metabolism, coupled with years of stressful work, had begun to round him out a little. He narrowed his piercing blue eyes. His huge, callused hands toyed with the paper. He sighed, turning the page.

Dad was long gone from the confines of the police force, of forensics. Like I said, we'll rubber-band back there shortly, but by now, he'd seen too many ruined lives, too many decaying corpses. By the time he was twenty-five, he'd seen so much carnage and darkness he may as well have gone to war.

So what did Dad do then? How did he leapfrog into a career that was lighter, frothier, more carefree? Well, as he was hollowed out emotionally, he'd looked at the myriad of options available . . . and jumped across to the New South Wales Fire Brigade. And he did so just as a spate of arson cases and bushfires came roaring across the state, meaning, you guessed it . . . more bodies. And burnt ones, at that.

The thing about the fire brigade, though, apart from the surprising level of death John was facing, and the mediocre pay, was the free time. Two nights on, two days on, then four days and nights off. Meaning most of his time was spent . . . waiting around. Idle. And John couldn't do idle. His pathological need to fill his time, as well as his . . . let's say unique way of thinking, meant he was going gradually insane.

And so he'd found himself of a morning, toast in one hand, paper in the other, perusing a litany of odd cries for help, looking for a job that would lighten his emotional, and financial, load. Something fun. Something brainless and utterly inane. He would look around at the second-hand furniture, the yellowed blinds that their landlord insisted they keep. Felt the slight rock as the stool, one leg bolstered up by a dull wad of folded paper, groaned beneath his increasingly sedentary behind. Thought about how much fun it would be to work outdoors, get moving again.

And that's when, after a week of browsing for a second job, he spotted the least communicative ad he'd ever seen. Car washer needed. Call Barry. *I can wash cars,* he thought. *Barry. Good, honest name,* he mused. And, almost as if drawn by an unseen force, he stood, leaving the stool rocking in place on the tiled floor behind him, picked up the phone, and began dialling. A gruff voice gave him an address, he scribbled it down, and after mumbling an excuse to his wife and the kids, who continued running laps outside around their completely shot Hills hoist, he got in the car and started driving.

A half-hour later, after skimming along in his car wondering why he was doing this and whether he should bail, he approached the address he'd been given. A looming building, red brick, 1920s, rose to meet him. Two storeys tall, its facade was beautiful and complex, cracked, the occasional vine winding across it. Countless ornate windows peppered its surface. He goggled at the scope of the thing, wondering how he'd never noticed it before. He drove up the driveway behind it and pulled his sedan into the large open courtyard. He turned the car off, pocketed his keys, stretched and stepped out.

He blinked, wordlessly.

There, weathered with age but no less striking, was an enormous sign.

KINSELLA FUNERAL HOMES

He cast an eye to his left, where a vast garage housed a clutch of immaculate hearses, sitting there flush against one another like sleek black eels. He looked to his right. An odd-looking building, fans whirring, lay there purring ominously. In front of him, a house that the Addams Family would have deemed 'a bit of a giveaway' stood, huge and dark and foreboding.

A funeral home.

A fucking funeral home.

Having had a gutful of death, John had picked the most harmless ad in the entire paper, and unwittingly answered a call to clean hearses. Not just cars, but hearses. Vehicles built specifically to house dead bodies. *I am,* John thought, *an idiot.*

But before he could get back into his decidedly non-hearse-like vehicle and reverse out the driveway, the front door of the main building creaked open, and a tiny old woman peeked out.

'John?' She smiled, not waiting for an answer, and gestured for him to come in. And John, reeling from the cosmic fuckery on show, thought, *You know what? Why not. Why the hell not.*

So he entered the building. It took a moment for his eyes to adjust, and when they did, all he saw was polished mahogany, ornate burgundy carpet, the occasional crucifix mounted to a wall, and a rather startled-looking taxidermied stag. Leadlight windows sent feeble shafts of light down at bizarre angles, chubby motes of dust swimming about lazily in the air. The old woman shuffled ahead of him, wordlessly leading him through an open door into an office. She patted John on the arm and disappeared back into the murky labyrinth, and he stood awkwardly before a desk, behind which sat an enormous man.

He had a head shaped like a padlock and a body like a muscle-bound orb. Every finger was festooned with jewellery, every inch of skin tanned like leather. He was completely bald, and he had a sharply honed goatee. He was, John estimated, in his late fifties.

John looked around the office, noting a garish blend of old – oil paintings, more stuffed animals, a ceremonial dagger mounted on the wall – and new: one of those glass orbs coursing with electricity, the kind that dads in the nineties couldn't stop blowing their money on. The kind of thing Bill Gates would covet. The padlock-headed man – Barry, presumably – registered John in his office, stood, crossed the room with surprising speed and shook his hand enthusiastically.

'John, mate. Thanks for coming. Drink?'

John politely refused and, prompted by Barry, sat down. *This chair,* he thought to himself, *has never needed to be chocked up a day in its evidently cushy life.* Barry poured himself what looked to be six inches of Drambuie from a decanter the size of a small chandelier, crossed back to his chair and sat with a creak. 'So,' Barry said as he sipped, unwincing. 'Tell me about yourself.'

'Well,' John said, 'living over in Manly at the moment. I'm currently a firefighter, out in Frenchs Forest.'

Barry looked confused. 'Firefighter.'

'Yeah,' John replied, now convinced this odd morning may as well get wrapped up quick smart. 'Firefighter, and before that, I was a cop.'

Barry looked even more baffled now. 'A cop?'

'Yeah,' John said. 'General duties, forensics, air wing, fingerprint division.'

Barry didn't blink. 'Right.'

John didn't blink either. 'So.'

'So.'

Barry, John realised, clearly didn't believe him. And why should he? Who hadn't added some special skills to their résumé to make themselves look good? And what about John was meant to indicate to Barry that he was in fact a decorated, seasoned member of the police force or the fire brigade? He'd left the house, he realised with mild dismay, in worn-out shorts, a grubby t-shirt and thongs.

Barry ruminated on this for a moment before standing up. He stared at John. 'Well,' he said, a hint of gleeful sarcasm eking into his voice, 'you've seen lots of dead bodies, hey? I mean, you'd have seen loads of them in your line of work.'

'Yes,' John replied, not biting.

'Well, seeing as how you've just been falling over dead bodies left and right, you're obviously vastly overqualified for the car-washing. That'd be kids' stuff for you. But if you're so okay with the deceased, I reckon you'd be perfect for something else I have in mind. Just making sure . . . you are well familiar with dead bodies?'

'Yes,' John replied again, still not biting.

Barry made a grand gesture, stoked beyond belief that this man was playing into his hands. 'Of course you have, John! Of course. Why don't you come with me, mate?'

Dad followed Barry, who was practically skipping at this point, back out through the winding corridors, into the courtyard, and over to the room with the large metal door. Barry grasped the handle with his enormous hand, pulled, and a small sucking sound, like a fridge being opened, sang out in the otherwise silent courtyard. John followed Barry inside.

The room was empty, he noted, and clean. An unoccupied gurney stood over a grey floor marked by a series of drains. To his left were four fridges. Barry crossed the floor, grasped a fridge door and called John over.

'Obviously,' he stated with mirth in his voice, 'you're used to seeing stuff like . . . this!' And on 'this', he stared across at John with an ecstatic look on his big, red face, yanking open the fridge and sliding out the trolley. On it was the body of a woman, in her sixties, skin sallow and pale blue. As the trolley hit the limit of its rails, the body shuddered briefly like a particularly firm jelly.

John, unflinching, stared back at Barry. Barry watched expectantly for John to break, or to run out of the room nauseated. For the shoe to drop.

John let the moment sit there in the air between them . . . then he snapped into action. He proceeded to run through how the woman died, pointing out specific points of lividity, noting that based on her hands she was a smoker, and estimating how long she'd been there. He moved around the body, scanning her hands, her arms, her face, pointing out detail after detail. And after rattling off his effortless whirlwind of an assessment, he stood up and smiled politely at Barry.

Barry cleared his throat awkwardly. Suitably cowed, and floored by John's explosive barrage of forensic acumen, he meekly rolled the body away, shut the fridge, and shook John's hand again. He began to laugh.

'Look, John, not gonna lie. I thought you were pulling my leg with those qualifications.'

'I gathered.'

'So you're the real deal! Shit.' He thought for a moment. 'When can you start, mate?'

Now it was John's turn to look confused. 'Cleaning cars?'

'No, no, no, mate. No. Helping run the place.'

Another long pause from John. 'You want me to help run the place?'

An hour later, my exhausted father stumbled through his front door in a daze. His kids pelted up to him and threw themselves around his legs. 'Where'd you run off to?' my mum asked, walking up and giving him a kiss on the cheek, wiping what looked like homemade playdough off her hands onto a ratty tea towel.

Dad blinked at her. 'I think we run a funeral home now.'

Mum was about to hit thirty-one. She was five-and-a-half feet tall with short, wavy brown hair and dark brown eyes. Although she'd never admit it aloud, she too was feeling lost. And though it's something Mum wouldn't tell you – because she 'wouldn't want to make a big deal out of it' – she used to be a cop, too. A very good one.

Mum had grown up supporting her entire family financially after her mother ran out on them. From there, she'd battled her way into the police academy. Showing a wild amount of grit, she'd become one of the first women in the New South Wales Police Force, and she fought to have female officers' uniforms changed from short skirts to pants. She had also once rushed a man with a shotgun to save a life, but, again, she 'wouldn't want to make a big deal out of it'.

Mum had seen things. Horrible things. People who worked as cops, ambulance officers, firefighters . . . Mum knew all too well there were things they confronted that would obliterate the psyches of normal people. Ever open a door and see someone you know dead? Ever drive past a car crash? 'People die,' Mum would say. 'Every day. And someone has to deal with it. Someone has to help pick up the pieces, solve it, make sense of it.' When I asked her how she coped as a cop, she just sort of shrugged, and said, 'Well, like I said, someone had to do it, and I wanted to help.' And when I asked her why she and Dad sometimes seemed so flippant talking about such dark stuff, she told me, 'What else are we going to do? Crying won't help. And we're there to help.'

So she'd served her time, made a brief foray into Internal Affairs, then was muscled out when she had the gall to have children and ask to keep working. And while she said she was glad to have left it all behind, unbeknownst to my father she never really shook the urge to deal with big, terrible things.

Maybe it was because she was forced out before she could get sick of the emergency services. Maybe it was because she was made of sterner stuff than Dad. But that day after Dad returned from his job interview at Kinsella Funeral Homes, she looked at her kids, and at the toys scattered around the house. And she thought back to rushing that man with the shotgun. And she began to spool through her greatest hits as a cop. *It was exciting,* she thought to herself. *It was horrible . . . but it was exciting. And I helped.* So she looked at Dad, stood up straight, and smiled right at him.

And with a twinkle in her eye, she asked him a question.

'When do we start?'

13

WHAT'S IN THE BOX?

I'm reeling. I'd forgotten all of this. All of it. But I manage to steer Dad back on track, and ask him what I asked him initially.

'Dad,' I mumble, as new memories start to battle for supremacy over old ones, 'we were talking about how hard it is to talk to families about dead kids. I assume you had a specific story from this funeral home period that . . .'

I trail off, and Dad nods. And he begins his story.

It was a simple request: they just needed someone to pick their son up from the airport.

When a tiny disputed country in Eastern Europe entered perhaps its darkest phase of sectarian violence, Bill Clinton was embroiled in a particularly newsworthy scandal. Having a silver-haired Southern saxophonist with a penchant for womanising at the driver's seat of relief efforts struck Dad as strange, but this was a strange time. What started as a group of rebels making small strikes against opposing forces in response to horrific treatment led to mass war crimes: terror, murder, rape, arson. Nothing was off the table.

Then NATO stepped in, and without a binding resolution, bombed this nascent country into dust. Thousands of civilians died.

It was a shitstorm. An unimaginable litany of successive tragedies.

My parents had already spent years with death, but there was something so . . . abstract about death on this scale. If one person dies, it's personal. Understandable. You can wrap your head around a single death. Like a black dot on a white canvas, it stands out. It draws the eye. And if someone commits a murder, that one death feels singularly cruel.

If someone kills five people, ten people? Earth-shaking. It's a spree. Look at all those lives, snuffed out. You can see a photo of the victims on the news, scan their faces, know that the light is now gone from their eyes, understand – at least a little – the scope of what has happened.

But if someone kills tens of thousands? The mind can't comprehend that much death. It can't compute, can't relate, can't interface with that much grief. So what does it do? Turns it into a number. Tries to find a way to quantify, to sterilise the trauma. When death strays towards that kind of grandeur of scope, everyone becomes suddenly practical. They shift from bereaved to accountant. But everyone, said Mum to Dad as we talked, every one of those tens of thousands is a one to someone. Everyone is a dot in that canvas to someone.

There were concentration camps during the conflict, and people in Australia whose families were from that country did see these lives as more than numbers. Many of them headed over to fight for their country, to try to make a difference, even a small one.

My parents got the call one morning. A middle-aged woman with a thick accent explained, tearfully, that her son had gone over to fight and had been shot. He'd died on foreign soil. And his mother, getting more emotional now, explained what they'd had to do to get their boy back onto Australian soil, so that they could take care of the remains properly. To bring a body between countries, it had to be embalmed. She explained that they couldn't afford this – the chemicals required to turn a body into a lifelike effigy of its former self were, as Dad knew, not cheap. The authorities, however, had proposed an alternative.

Dad sympathetically ventured a guess: 'Cremation.'

The woman said yes, they cremated him. Cheaper. Easier. International airline law would indeed allow cremated remains to be transported. Problem solved.

If we're talking about the cold practicality of our approach to death, cremation is the summit. Cremation ovens are surprisingly complex beasts. Built and designed in Switzerland, they are master-pieces of engineering, and Dad often reflected that the pinpoint, granular, precise technological know-how that makes Swiss watches so perfect may have played a part in Switzerland's monopoly on this grisly industry. The ovens themselves use a series of high-powered jets of flame to reduce the body from loved one to ash in twenty minutes. Skin, organs, bone . . . all seared away by the humming, efficient Swiss craftsmanship.

Well, not really ash. More like fine sand, the kind you could stain and put in a little bottle, sell by the seaside. You never would, obviously, although Dad had seen some strange things done with cremated remains. Once the white-hot flames retreated and the furnace cooled, you'd reach into the oven with a large flat spade, and bring out the powder in big heaps. Imagine a pizza oven. Got it? Now imagine never wanting to eat pizza again.

Now, the remains, some of which are still thick, hard or bony, are scooped into a tiny box. The whole process is unbelievably delicate, so that not a jot, not a skerrick of the remains scatter, lest they dissipate like a fine mist. The handler, likely wearing rubber gloves, calmly, kindly seals the box shut, then pours in a healthy serve of ball bearings and seals it all in a strange metal contraption.

A fat, thick rubber switch is depressed, a dull click is heard, and the machine spins it all up. The ball bearings build in speed, whizzing around and turning into tiny bullets that pulverise the box, the ashes and the harder remains into an even finer powder. It's like an immaculate digestion process. Not a single mote escapes, not a speck of the dearly departed is wasted. The machine stops. The remains are funnelled into a fresh box, about six inches squared, and there it is: the whole person, packed down into a box the size of a Chinese takeaway carton.

And that box is what the grieving woman's son was in, sitting in the hold of a plane bound from a war zone towards Sydney. And she needed Mum and Dad to pick up their son, put him in an urn, and deliver him to them in an appropriately funerary fashion. They needed closure.

They just needed someone to pick their son up from the airport.

Later, Dad stood on the tarmac, leaning against the hearse, watching the cargo ramp deploying slowly. Now this might all seem weirdly formal, but a body was a body, regardless of what state it was in. And if your son had been killed overseas and packed up and flown back to you, wouldn't you want his remains treated the same whether they'd been embalmed, cremated, or laid out for a Tibetan sky burial? *A body is a body,* Dad reminded himself. *And a grieving mother wants her son back.* This was her black dot. One of thousands, but it was hers.

Shaken from his reverie, Dad saw the approaching customs agent holding . . . a slightly bigger box than he'd expected, and a clipboard. Dad signed warily as the customs agent dumped the box on the ground.

'Mate,' Dad ventured, 'I was picking up a cremation?'

The agent looked down, suddenly registering what he'd been carrying. 'Shit. This was . . .? Oh, shit. Right! Sorry about that.' He picked the box up, placing it gingerly on top of the hearse. He made some bumbling apologies, took his now-signed paperwork, and hurried off, leaving Dad to look at the box.

This box was not six inches by six inches. This was a boilerplate cardboard box. This was two feet by one foot. This was the kind of box you'd use to move house.

Crisscrossed with masking tape and worn down in places, the box looked fit to burst. It had clearly been banged about during transit, and were Dad not at the airport and standing on a terrifically windy runway, he'd have cracked it open then and there, completely confident that someone had fucked up and that the box bore some tourists' misplaced laundry. But then he spotted it. In a corner of the box, near a slight tear in the battered cardboard, there was a smudge. A smudge of fine, pale dirt.

Of ash.

Dad carefully lowered the box, feeling a lurch in the pit of his stomach. Very softly, he shook it. A hard, tumbling noise issued forth, the sound you'd hear if you put a stapler in a shoebox and gave it a big shake. He placed the box on the seat beside him, and belted it in place. Patting the box nervously, he turned the car over, did a U-turn and peeled away.

Once back at the funeral home, Dad stared down at the box. He cleared his throat, a cold film of sweat forming on his forehead. The halogen light above him pinged gently. He shuffled from foot to foot.

How the hell am I going to fix this?

He'd driven into the parking bay outside the funeral home as the sun was setting. Most of the staff had checked out for the day, and Christine was back at home, so John decided to carry the box into the prep area. It sat on the cold, clean workbench, a box cutter and a heap of crumpled masking tape beside it. John took a steadying breath and ventured another look.

There, in the almost ruined cardboard box, was an entirely intact jawbone. Teeth and all.

A strange green film lined its underside. It lay atop a jumble of assorted half-burnt bones: part of a femur here, a knuckle there, all coated with the same green, mossy residue. The base of the box was lined with cremation ash of sorts, but it was full of grit. Human detritus. *Like the gravel in the Kinsella driveway,* Dad thought. *It's fucking human gravel.*

The words of the grieving mother rang in John's ears. 'Everything,' she'd said. 'Put everything they send you in your urn. I want all of him with us.' John tentatively picked up the jawbone in a gloved hand. *Mildew,* he realised. *It's mildew.*

John looked over the rest of the remains, at the box of bones. Bones that had clearly been allowed to sit in some warehouse among countless remains of the nameless dead. *This isn't a cremation,* he thought. He looked over at the urn the family had chosen, the urn that would sit on their mantel for decades to come. In a last-ditch moment of panic, he slowly placed the jawbone flush with the opening of the urn. *It's like a puzzle,* Dad thought. *A terrible puzzle: how to get a fucking skeleton into a fucking urn.* The jawbone wouldn't fit. No go.

And that's when Dad made his decision. Maybe it was hysteria. Maybe it was the fact that wartime cremation in this particular country was likely nothing more than a blowtorch and a sledge-hammer. Maybe it was the thought of the grieving mother seeing what horrific treatment her son had been given after his death, having fought for his country half a world away. He picked up the box, removed the bones, and began to carefully pour the finest remains into the urn. He'd pour a little, shake the box to clear away the grittier parts, then pour again. He stood there, under the harsh lighting, pour pour pour, shake shake shake. And finally, the urn was mostly full. He wiped it clean, then closed it. *There it is,* he thought. *I did it.*

And there, on the workbench, the bones. So many goddamn bones, left to rot. Dad carefully lifted them back into the box, taped it shut . . .

. . . and carried it out to the bin room. He put the box into the hazardous waste bin, and closed it.

The next day, he delivered the family their urn, containing probably a quarter of their son. And they wept, and wailed, and smiled. And they thanked Dad for bringing their son home. And John soon forgot about the time he threw a box full of human bones into the garbage, to be taken to hazardous waste disposal, where they'd be burned away to oblivion along with all the other hazardous waste, seared to powder in an instant with the kind of heat and clean, sterile focus that should have rendered them into ash in the first place. And years later, he'd reflect back on the fact that it was best that the family didn't know at the time. And maybe this second cremation meant the job had been finished.

And this, he eventually realised, might be why he hated picking people up from airports as much as he did.

*

I've tried, in untold ways, to get Dad to explain how he actually feels about all of this as I've chronicled and re-interpreted all of his police stories. I've tried to get him to talk openly about what it's like to confront death, talk about it, process it. He's not flippant, but he's not not flippant, if that makes sense. There's an ease to the way he and Mum converse about death or violence. And without fail, Dad waves off my concerns, citing practicality, saying that death is just a thing that happens.

Until, that is, he finishes recounting the airport story. I take another swing, and ask him how he actually feels about it. Something passes across his eyes, just for a moment, and I realise he's about to open up to me.

'It was a nightmare,' he mutters. 'Look, it's not something I'm proud of. But . . . you know. You can't give someone a body in two boxes. Imagine saying, "All of this? It's an illusion! It was a fuck-up from the beginning! And I had to decant three quarters of a skeleton into the rubbish!"'

I perk up a little. 'Illusion? What do you mean, illusion?'

'Well, people want something.'

'But why do they need anything?' I ask.

Without a pause, Dad shoots back: 'Well, do they?'

There's a loaded pause. I don't quite know how to answer this.

After a moment, Dad continues. 'When we went for coffee this morning, we drove past the cemetery over at Bronte. That stretch of land has to be some of the most expensive real estate in the world. It's sitting there, on a cliff, and it's billion-dollar real estate. And people go through this whole debate internally, you know, "Is there a god?", and I think religion is a bit . . . fucked. Sorry. Rambling.'

This is the point in the conversation where my job is usually to reel Dad in a little, but I simply make a gesture for him to continue.

He's like a sleepwalker at this point – it'd be a bad idea to wake him. So I let him carry on.

'When Christine and I were at Kinsella, we had to dress an aunt of mine. Did I tell you that story?'

Now it's my turn to let my mind wander. Do I remember any of my relatives dying, even in recent memory? I seem to recall hearing about a few great-grandparents, but this is one death I can't pull up a mental file on.

'I had to dress an aunt,' Dad continues. 'A relative. A dead relative. I was given her clothes, and I had to put her in her fucking dress. And I had to use this process – which is fucked – to seal up my aunt's mouth. For a viewing. That's a whole other very trippy story.'

'Right,' I interject. 'But what's it actually like, dressing the body of someone you know? I guess I'm trying to establish this drive people have to see their relatives in some form, even if it is cremated, like with that poor woman whose son came back on the plane. What was it like for you?'

'Well,' Dad says, 'You have to kind of be . . . hmm. Well, it's a great privilege to be asked. And I guess I'd have much preferred I do it than some stranger. But looking at someone, you know, dead . . . it does your head in. You have to be . . . gracious, but disassociate as well. You have to compartmentalise the experience, pack it away, not dwell on it.'

I take a breath. Tentatively, I venture another line of enquiry. 'Is talking about it now—'

Dad cuts me off, not unkindly. 'Yeah, it's weird.'

We sit in silence for a moment before Dad speaks up again, his hands fidgeting in his lap.

'Look, mate. I . . . I don't think you're supposed to do it. But I worked with a guy who embalmed Marilyn Monroe. Anyway, the worst thing he ever did? Embalmed his own son. I watched him do an embalming, and it's one hundred times worse than the worst post-mortem. It is fucked beyond belief. And the toll it takes to do that to someone you know is . . . But it's also incredible. They transform a ruined body into something almost alive.'

I make a note to come back to the Marilyn Monroe story later on. Dad continues.

'Paul, sometimes people just need closure. Did you know that they used to take stillborn babies away from their mothers? Just whisk them away. There's a huge unmarked grave behind Royal North Shore Hospital full of stillborn babies. Nobody knows who's who. But now they have a process where they wrap the baby up and bring it to you. Because that contact helps with the grieving process. Can you imagine what it would do to a mother to just have her baby taken away? You need closure. You need to shut that door in your mind, make peace with what's happened. For some, that's what a funeral can do.'

I shift in my seat, looking straight at my dad. I don't think I've ever seen him open up quite like this. He goes on.

'And maybe that's why that mother, who asked me to go to the airport, needed her son's remains. Maybe, in a way, she needed to hold him one last time.'

14

YOU'RE
MUM-BELIEVABLE

Speaking of mums, mine is amazing. I know I mentioned earlier that she and Dad met on the force, but she's been sort of a fringe character up until now, which doesn't seem entirely fair. Actually, forget fair. It's not accurate.

Mum doesn't like to make a fuss. Dad, as you've learned, is a show-off, a brave, weird, straightforward guy who steadfastly believes he's been barrelling down a straight road his entire life. He's sure of what he's done, perhaps in part because wondering what he *could* have done would drive him mad, so he's created a single path to sprint down headfirst.

Mum doesn't think that way. She's pragmatic. Being on the force was a job. No cosmic significance. No stars aligning. Just, you know: a job. *Stop making a song and dance about it,* Mum would say. *You just went to work and did what you were told, no big deal.*

But you and I both know the truth, don't we? It *was* a big deal.

Dad takes a call on his mobile mid-anecdote, pats me on the leg, tells me he'll be back. He's an antiques dealer now, a far cry from his prior occupations, meaning he occasionally has to hop in his ute and drive out to god-knows-where, often returning laden with all manner of exotic treasures, like a fisherman pulling into a bay with nets full to bursting. But he's buggered off. And we're in the middle of our story. I sit there, at something of a loss . . . and then Mum comes in, checking her phone.

I take a swing.

'Mum!' I exclaim, playing it as cool as I can. 'Don't suppose you'd . . .'

She looks up at me. She knows. Goddamn it, she knows. And she's going to get spooked. I've never been able to lie to Mum. But then, inconceivably, she smiles, comes over and sits down.

'Sure,' she says. 'Why not.'

Christine wasn't an extrovert. Never was. She was low-key.

She was eighteen years old when she joined the academy and nineteen when she graduated, stepping into a police force that, at the beginning of the eighties, was still systemically misogynistic. Regardless, she thought it was terrifying, and exciting, and a little bit magical. The magic dissipated, of course, but for a few years there, she was having what could – at a stretch – be referred to as adventures. But more than that, she reminded herself, she was helping people. Real people.

Christine didn't get to go to uni. Life had trampled on both her and her ambitions; although she'd been naturally quick-witted and athletic in high school, she'd often had to stay at home and take care of her siblings. But once school was in the rear-view, she cast about for some kind of qualification she could grab onto, and the only place that would take her was a secretarial school. Frankly, the idea of being some man's secretary clashed with her gender politics, to go into a field that would lead to her answering to lesser men. But with no other options available, she did it anyway.

And then, one day on her lunch break, Christine sat leafing through a newspaper in the break room. And her eye came to rest on a small ad that seemed desperate, almost embarrassed, pleading for female recruits to join the New South Wales Police Force. She looked up from her Big Mac and thickshake, her razor-sharp mind winnowing down to a point. *This,* she thought, *is what I'm going to do. I've been here six months, getting coffee for human zeppelins, typing up inane nothings and getting a sore back. I could be doing more than this. Fuck secretary work. And fuck this fucking lunchroom.*

'Is that what you really thought? "Fuck this fucking lunchroom"?'
Mum looks at me, shockingly deadpan. 'Yes. Fuck that fucking lunchroom.'

As the seventies were cresting into the eighties, there was a smattering of female officers in the New South Wales Police Force, true. But they were plain-clothes cops. Not plain-clothes in a cool way, the sort John would strive to emulate later in his career, the kind who got cool cars and could wear cool holsters and say cool things like 'No, *you're* out of order.' These women were the kind of plain-clothes cops who were treated as strictly ornamental. They'd go to schools and talk to kids as a form of token community outreach. But they didn't actually do any real policing, and they didn't get any of the duties, or responsibilities, or terrible burdens that other cops got.

Realising this, and having their hand at last forced by the glacier-slow approach of societal progress, the New South Wales Police Force decided it was time to recruit. They put out a call for female cops, actual female cops, despite not having really thought through the logistics of this move. They filed an ad in the papers. And Christine, at her wit's end, saw this ad and thought, *Yes. I'm going to apply.* And, as we've previously established, *Fuck this fucking lunchroom.*

After months of forms being filled out in triplicate and being flung back and forth, her application was accepted. She didn't quite know it at the time, and she never voiced this certainty out loud, but years later, she'd realise that she'd been a shoo-in, given her skill set. When she finally got given the green light to head to the academy for her first day, she walked through the entrance, made her way to orientation, and introduced herself to twelve other women. They were, herself included, very young and very green, and their instructor made a point of telling them that they were the first class of women to be trained as police officers on an equal footing with men. Christine briefly considered freaking out, then remembered the men she'd taken dictation from as a secretary, and that fucking lunchroom. That was the last time she questioned her choice to enrol.

She made an absolute meal out of primary training, breezing through her courses and setting several records on the track where cadets ran every morning. She made friends, too, and when the time came to get assigned to a station, she stood there with her mate Angela, fists clenched with nerves. North Sydney. They landed North Sydney.

'Can you imagine if you'd been assigned somewhere else?' I ask Mum. And, unlike Dad, she perks up at this hypothetical.

'Oh, gosh! Can you imagine? If they'd sent me to Chatswood, or even up to the Northern Beaches, I'd probably have met

someone else entirely. Maybe no one! Maybe I'd have actually been able to focus on my job. I wouldn't have got pregnant, maybe . . . Maybe I'd be senior management now, still on the force.' She looks off into the distance, something akin to wonder in her eyes. 'I wonder what I'd be like. I'd not have you, or Anne, or Mark, of course . . . but I bet I'd be completely *different.'*

'Mum, have you noticed . . . Dad doesn't think this way? Doesn't wonder what if?'

Mum looks at me, a hint of an eye roll on the horizon. 'That's how he processes what he went through, I think.'

'You should see the looks I get when I ask him to imagine what might have happened if things had gone differently. I just . . . I don't think he understands how I view the world sometimes. How I struggle with even the simplest of decisions.'

She smiles. 'Maybe you get that from me.'

From day dot, Christine realised that the police force wasn't prepared for this fresh, 'experimental' batch of police. For one, she swiftly discovered, there weren't any women's toilets. Nor were there separate locker rooms, and the cops at North Sydney didn't seem to know how to handle having two women suddenly thrust into their almost primally masculine workspace. Christine and Angela were the first two women to be stationed there in uniform, and they had their work cut out for them.

Angela was far bigger than Christine, and found herself taking point when they were forced to confront dinosaurs on the force, quite literally stepping between Christine and trouble whenever a male cop decided to say something particularly inappropriate. But it was men's versus women's gear where the differences, and disparities, really began to stand out.

First off: guns. 'Regular' (read: male) cops got to tote around standard-issue police specials, with a speedloader for extra ammo. Women, however, got a more petite, more womanly firearm: a Smith & Wesson five-shot. It wasn't quite a Derringer – so small they've been called a 'purse' or a 'stocking gun' – but it wasn't far off, and Christine was appalled that men got a bigger gun with an extra shot. Surely if women were the more delicate, fairer sex, she complained to Angela one day, they should get *bigger* guns? 'What, like a Tommy gun?' Angela joked. They both laughed, their guffaws trailing off.

Christine looked up at Angela, deadpan. 'You know what? Yes. A Tommy gun.'

Batons were also feminised. One of the first pieces of kit this brave new class of police officer were provided with, these batons were . . . small. Christine took the tiny police-issue handbag she'd been given and turned it over, unzipped it and removed the baton, which was barely longer than her hand. She turned to Angela, holding the idiotic thing aloft between thumb and forefinger with distaste. 'How the hell are we supposed to stop anyone with these? By the time the perp gets close enough to get whacked with it, they'll be practically on top of us!' Angela laughed, nodded, sighed, and snatched Christine's dainty batonette. She threw it, and hers, on top of their new lockers, where they stayed.

Pencil skirts were also forced upon Christine and Angela, and the rest of their class, too. The skirts were so short that more than once, while attempting to put her sprinting skills to good use in pursuit of a suspect, Christine had to ask her male buddy to look away as she climbed a fence to continue the chase. Once she was on the other side, he could jump the fence after her. 'We don't ride cop cars side-saddle,' Angela growled as they changed one day. 'Why the hell can't we wear pants?'

Christine agreed. Being demure and objectified was basically what she'd been fighting to escape as a secretary; she had no intention of putting up with this shit on the force. She'd fought hard to get here, and she intended to keep on fighting. She and Angela hatched a plan, made some calls to their ex-classmates, and began petitioning. Two years later, they didn't have pants . . . but they did have culottes. Not a stellar piece of progress, but it was something.

It was, all things considered, a miracle they weren't given police-issue smelling salts.

The top halves of their uniforms were akin to bolero jackets, but for women, guns and handcuffs – referred to on the force as 'appointments' – couldn't be seen in public. Or rather, as Christine learned, they couldn't be seen hanging out there visibly; they had to be concealed, which also made them harder to grab in a crisis.

Christine's first stint at North Sydney Police Station was a tough one. Seven night shifts in a row. The week was a blur of orientation and deftly sidestepping colleagues' propositions aimed her way, but the first night . . . the first night was a doozy, and what Christine would later consider one of her formative cases. She and her buddy – a senior cop and a huge man who miraculously wasn't a complete Neanderthal – got a call to a 'person on premises' at a large gymnasium. It was very late, and when they arrived they were joined by several other patrol cars. As she stepped out of the car, skirt pinching awkwardly and gun decidedly hard to reach, she made a mental note to smash the patriarchy later. For now, she had policing to do.

There were armed men on the premises, and apparently – as Christine and her buddy were told by a constable who was ducking down just outside, holding his radio, eyes wide – the men inside had been busted robbing a bottle-o and had made a break for it. After sprinting down several side streets, the armed men had holed up in this closed gym. And now, the brigands in question had decided to pull a manoeuvre that almost never worked: a siege. A stand-off. Christine felt . . . was this excitement? She knew she was in danger, but having never been around gunfire, or even impending gunfire, she was keenly aware of how fast her heart was racing. *Maybe I should have brought my idiotic baton,* she thought dryly. *Perhaps if we ran out of ammo, I could have piffed the fucking thing.*

Her buddy issued orders. The group of police were to surround the building and head inside. *Thank god I'm new,* Christine thought. *It's pitch black and god knows how many men there are inside. Maybe I could wait in the car?*

'Christine,' her buddy said quietly, approaching her with his gun drawn, 'you're with me. We'll go round back.' *Shit,* Christine thought to herself. *Shitty shit shit.*

She drew her gun, suddenly cognisant of having five shots rather than six. *I know what you're thinking,* she thought, imagining herself as Dirty Harry, standing over a bleeding suspect. *Did I fire five shots, or six? Well, I'm a lady cop, see. So either way I'm out of ammo, as the police force didn't think I'd be foiling robberies on account of being at home, with a hot water bottle on my stomach, surfing the crimson wave. But I have this tiny baton, and I can throw it pretty hard. So do you feel lucky? Well . . . do ya? PUNK?*

She shook herself from her snarky little daydream. She and her buddy had reached a back door. 'Wait,' rasped Christine urgently. 'What do I do if we open this door and they come at us?'

The senior man turned to face her. 'You pull your gun out, point it at them, and shoot them. And don't miss.' He reached his hand around the handle . . .

Turned it . . .

And it creaked open, loudly. Very loudly.

Christine and the grizzled officer both winced at each other. They paused, and after a few moments of nothing happening, headed inside, going as close to the ground as they could.

Then, a yell. Several yells. Threats. The slam of the front door rupturing inwards, practically flying off its hinges. More chaos, more crashing noises, then the lights pinged on sleepily, and Christine stood, gun held aloft. She looked across at her partner, and he gestured towards the front door, where the other police had two armed men in handcuffs. Her buddy turned and faced her, smiling grimly.

'Hell of a first shift. Nicely done.'

The following six night shifts were relatively uneventful. Mostly, Christine just watched, sitting in the back seat as her buddy and their driver ferried them from crime to crime. Mostly, she dealt with car accidents, taking statements and helping people calm down after terrible traumas. But she also became conscious of how she was perceived by the public. Some people stared, confused to see a woman in uniform. Some men ogled her, confusion inter-mingling with arousal. But on the whole, she noticed that people seemed . . . grateful, perhaps? Whenever they collared some roided-up alpha male, said male always seemed to cast about for a weak spot in her armour. But she'd just busted into a warehouse holding a gun. *Deadshits can't do anything to me, five shots or no. And besides,* she thought to herself, *if push came to shove, I wouldn't need five. I'd only need one.*

I gaze at Mum with a newfound respect, and a little bit of fear, in my eyes. 'Did you really think that?'

'Of course not,' she says. 'But it'll make me sound cool. So please leave it in.'

15

MAXI-MUM CARNAGE

After several weeks of policing, honest-to-god policing, Christine
and her buddy got a truly odd call. They'd been on the road for
about an hour when Dispatch radioed through, and as the driver
made his way through traffic, Christine's buddy took the call.

Here is what was going down.

A young man, frightened out of his wits, had called the police.
Apparently, he and his girlfriend had been tied up in their apartment by someone who lived in their building. This man had
managed to escape and sounded utterly bewildered, said Dispatch.
Mid-call, Christine's buddy handed her the radio, giving her a
look that was part encouragement, part goading. She took the tiny
plastic square, hand betraying a slight tremor, and told Dispatch to
tell this man to stay where he was, and to hide if he had to. 'We're
on our way,' she said, endeavouring to sound braver than she felt.
'We're on our way.' She handed the radio back, received an appreciative glance, and sat back in her seat. The car surged forward. The
siren blared to life. They were off.

They pulled up outside the two-storey block of flats, and made
their way in through the front door. The foyer was oddly quiet,

Christine noted. They walked past a ground-floor unit near the foot of the stairs, which were an unusual design: floating wooden slats with a yawning, stygian cavity underneath. Christine noted flecks of debris on the upper stairs. They made their way up, slowly and carefully, guns drawn.

Once on the landing, they came to the door of the apartment they were there to visit. Silence. The door was busted, hanging slightly ajar; Christine nudged it and it swung open laboriously. Inside was a still-unfolding nightmare. The boyfriend who'd called looked manic, kneeling with two crying young women in the corner. He stood to meet Christine and her buddy, and began explaining what was going on.

A young man, very young, had barged into the apartment where this distraught boyfriend lived with his girlfriend and her best mate. The home invader had come in, tied the couple up and sexually assaulted the friend, then left to check on something downstairs. 'What do you mean, downstairs?' Christine asked, noting with a degree of foreboding his hushed, urgent tone.

'Downstairs!' the frantic, bruised man replied. 'He lives downstairs! And he has a shotgun!'

Christine's stomach sank. She turned to tell her buddy, but he was standing right there. He'd heard it too. His eyes went wide, and his jaw clenched as he walked over to the phone and began dialling.

'You would have passed his place on the way in,' continued the boyfriend. 'He's just a teenager, he lives there with his mum. He's got a shotgun . . .' Then the adrenaline began to wear off and the young man collapsed, inconsolable. The driver ran over, trying to keep him quiet.

Christine's buddy, gun still drawn, hung up the phone and beckoned Christine over. 'Right, I've called for backup and an ambulance. Meantime, come with me. We've got to try and shut this guy down. Stay behind me, you'll be right.' And for the second time in a week – her first week as one of Australia's first uniformed female police officers – Christine headed off with her gun drawn to try to apprehend an armed and violent assailant.

They made their way back onto the landing together, and inch by painful inch headed down the stairs towards the ground-floor apartment door they'd passed on the way in. And then, as Christine watched, the barrel of a shotgun eased the door open and was trained on them both. Instinctively, Christine's buddy raised his gun, yelled something garbled, and fired two rounds. There was an instant suffocating ringing, Christine's eyes stinging from the impact. Both shots ricocheted off the door and the doorframe, and the door blew open. And out came . . .

A kid. Well, a fifteen-year-old young man, with a round, cruel, stupid face, his eyelids lolling hatefully. He yelped and aimed the shotgun right at them. *He has acne,* Christine thought. *He's just a kid. And he has acne.*

And he raped that girl, replied another, far angrier voice in her head. For a moment, this voice seemed to regret that those two shots had gone wide.

Christine's buddy had also clearly noted how frighteningly young this criminal was. And acting almost on instinct, he lowered his gun . . .

And leapt into the air.

We're halfway up a storey-high stairwell, Christine thought, distantly. *We're very, very high up.*

It was too late, though. Her buddy had propelled himself over the railing, and was now soaring down, down, down towards the teenager, who looked to be shitting himself, too confused and awed to fire a shot. And with a bone-crunching impact, the ninety-kilo cop came down on the rapist, dropping him like an absolute sack of shit. Christine's partner got to his feet and jammed his knee in the cretin's back. *It's a miracle he didn't break anything, the idiot,* Christine thought as she ran down the stairs, gun at the ready. As her buddy held the shooter in place, Christine calmly cuffed him and read him his rights.

Later that day, while she was filling out reams of paperwork at the station, her buddy would explain three things to her. First off, he'd felt sorry for the kid for a moment, and didn't want a dead teenager on his conscience. Second, he'd been genuinely concerned that Christine was going to get shot, and that he was sorry if his worrying about her safety to the point of making such a macho gesture was taken as his not having faith in her abilities. And third, he whispered with a look of dead calm on his face, the kid had later admitted that as they made their way up the stairs to the apartment upon entering the building . . .

He'd been in the darkness under those stairs. Gun trained at them.

'And I reckon he didn't fire because . . . well. Because he saw a woman in uniform.' He nodded at Christine, gave her desk a rap with his knuckles, and headed off further into the station.

'Were you always so lucky?' I ask.

'You mean with men I was partnered with? Look, the force was sexist and backwards, but for the most part these cops were trying. But the majority of the men I was buddied up with were like big older brothers, always keeping an eye out for me. If we went to do an arrest, they'd ask if I was comfortable making the arrest myself, and if I was, they'd let me go ahead.

But if I didn't feel up to it I would stand back while they ran point. It was less because they thought I couldn't do it, and more because they were . . . well, protective. In a nice way. Mostly.'

'Does that mean you didn't get to run in and take charge?'

Mum smiles. 'Yes. Most of the time, men's urge to help would mean I became a background player. The thing is, though, whenever I did push I was . . . well, as good as they were. Better, even.'

I smile right back. 'Right, so you arrested people.'

'Heaps.'

'And you got high test scores?'

'Top of the class,' she shoots back cheerfully.

'And you were a good shot?'

'Great shot,' she corrects me.

'Okay. How about driving? Were you a good driver?'

She grimaces, dredging up another memory.

As with all police, Christine was soon buddied up with someone different. General Duties functioned like much shiftwork does; you'd head into work, and before long you'd find yourself tethered to a new offsider. In Christine's case, this was a blunt-headed macho man named Alan. Alan was huge, wide, muscular, and looked at Christine warily at all times, as if he thought she might, at any moment, burn her bra in front of him. He remained polite and stoic, most of the time, but he never let her actually *do* much.

Until a certain fateful Thursday.

It was an afternoon shift. Christine was driving, with pinpoint precision, and a call came in about an assault-in-progress. She flipped on the siren, and the patrol car promptly doubled its speed, becoming a blur that flitted deftly from lane to lane. Updates flew from the radio, with Alan responding and issuing directions.

As they neared the address, a small house in a small street, the decidedly not-small car bearing the attackers jolted to life and pulled away in front of them. Christine matched their speed, eyes never leaving the car before her. Unblinking, her hands acted almost of their own accord. It was shit-hot driving, and Alan knew it.

But Alan was a proud man, with a head like a slab of beer and an ego the size of Belgium. So after several superb blocks of pursuit driving, he turned to Christine. 'Love,' he said. 'Pull over. I'll take it.'

Christine couldn't believe what she was hearing. What was this bridge troll of a man thinking? She had them. She was gaining on them! But Christine, for all her ability and determination, was still in his eyes just a nineteen-year-old woman. She'd escaped a truly shitty home life, and survived an endless cavalcade of failures and thwarted dreams. She knew she was in the right here, and she knew she shouldn't pull over. But she was, at heart, a gentle soul, not built for conflict. She hadn't yet figured out who she was, and here was this overbearing, mountainous cretin, pulling rank mid-chase. What choice did she have? She sadly pulled over, opened the door and ran around to the passenger side, switching places with him.

Alan's hairy-knuckled hands almost engulfed the wheel entirely. 'Buckle up,' he said, clearly proud of how cool he sounded. He sounded like a dickhead, but Christine didn't say this. She simply nodded, and off they shot. The attackers' car was still, miraculously, within eyeshot, and Christine and Alan watched as it pinged around a corner and down a laneway. Alan gave chase, Christine gripping her seat with a mixture of nausea and suppressed frustration. *I'd have had them by now,* she thought, regretting giving in to the man.

Alan span the wheel; the car drifted, and then righted itself. They were burning down the laneway towards . . .

Shit, Christine thought. *Shit shit Shitty McShittington.* About twenty metres down the laneway was a huge, odd roundabout. Massive. Beyond it, the other car was making its way into the distance. The roundabout had several bollards punctuating its breadth, to stop cars trying to fang it over said roundabout, thus gaining sick air. The gap between the bollards had somehow not been too narrow for their quarry, but as Alan slammed his foot down on the accelerator, Christine realised that, once again, a male cop was about to play action hero to . . . what – impress her? *Even if it works,* she thought, *I'll still be mad about this.*

The car sped up . . . the bollards rushed towards them . . .

SHUNK.

With a gut-wrenching scrape, their car became perfectly, instantly, irrevocably wedged between the two iron poles. And because they'd been mid-jump at the time, it was wedged between them several inches above the ground. It was as if they'd been frozen in the air, Alan's absolute dickheadedness immortalised forever in some idiotic tableau. Alan just sat there, hands still gripping the wheel, staring dead ahead. He swallowed, and for the longest time, he refused to look over at Christine. She folded her arms, cleared her throat, and radioed for help.

'Does that not piss you off, Mum?' I say, still reeling a little with laughter. She's laughing, too, but she does betray a flicker of weariness.

'Of course! Of course it pisses me off. We lost them because of him. I guess what's interesting . . . Look, I put off telling these stories, and I don't know if I'll ever sit down and tell them all. But one thing I'm noticing telling them is that, yes, the men seemed to step in front of me and stop me achieving what I could have achieved. So these are my stories, yes. But . . .' She trails off.

'But?'

'I feel powerless over my own stories. I was always there, but never in control.'

I've never heard Mum say any of this before. Maybe that's why she didn't feel comfortable bragging about her adventures like Dad has over the years – she feels, and has felt for some time, that men always made themselves the hero of her stories without her permission. Maybe they saw it as their right as male cops.

'But you were, by all accounts, an amazing cop. I knew you were good at a lot of things but now I know we can add "pursuit driving" to your long list of skills.'

'And I was fast!' she says suddenly, and with eyes wide. 'All of these big, slow men . . . I was faster than them!'

'You mean in the car? Intellectually?'

'I mean physically – I was a faster runner! Every time we had to give a foot chase, I was off in a flash, and they'd be a block behind me, out of breath. I was fast, Paul. One of the first times John saw me was on the track, running. Just running, running as fast as I could. My mum left us when I was ten, and I had to take care of my siblings while my dad drank and was never around. I ran away from that as hard as I could. I became a secretary, and I ran away from that. But with the police force, I finally felt like I was running *towards* something. And I helped people, I really did. But there was often someone there, waiting to take the baton from me and cross the finish line, and get the credit themselves.'

We sit in silence for a moment. Finally, a look crosses her face, a beautiful, strange look. 'Here's a fun story, though,' she begins. 'About eight years ago, I was working for Centrelink, doing work with Indigenous communities up north, right there in the desert. And I became friends with an Indigenous Elder and activist named Bunny. She basically became my interpreter with the local community, and we became good friends. Good friends. I lived up there for close to four months, working with her community, working hard. Very hard. And I was helping people, and making a difference. And there were no men in the way. It was just me and Bunny. And one day, she sat me down and told me that she knew what I'd done for her community. And because of what I'd done, because of how much I'd managed to do, she gave me a skin name.'

'A skin name?'

'A name to indicate she considered me family. She called me Nabarula.'

The weight of this sits with me, with both of us, for some time. Finally, Mum speaks again, already sounding younger and brighter than she had been while talking about the police. 'One day, she told me to run around Uluru, if I had it in me. And I did. I ran the ten or so kilometres around it – *not* over it – and as I came to the finish line, it was me, just me, running. And there was John, waiting to surprise me at the end. Watching me run, again, all these years later. Only this time, I'd figured out who I was. I wasn't scared anymore.'

Mum gets a slightly dreamy look, the kind you wear when you're deep inside a memory, usually a very good one. She blinks the memory away and smiles pleasantly at me.

'How was that? Was any of that good?'

16

QUITE A PAIR

You get it now, right? You get the powerhouse couple that is John and Christine Verhoeven. They were both incredible people in their own right; they're twice as potent when they're paired up. Of course, they were smitten from the moment they met.

The truth, however, is that Dad noticed Mum. Not the other way around.

I think that's the way it is with remarkable people; they're noticed. Because Mum was so doggedly running at her goals, and because she was simultaneously sidestepping the advances of other officers, she didn't see Dad right away. Didn't twig that he was there on the periphery, trying to impress her. Once they fell into each other's orbit, however, it was never going to end any other way. They were always going to end up together.

As Mum said, at first Dad saw her running on the track at the academy. Not that she remembers; she has no recollection of the gangly young man staring at her from the raised seating, though he recalls that same moment clear as day. Later, when they were both working at North Sydney, he saw her in the dispatch room at the station. He remembers that moment vividly, too, but

Mum doesn't remember a thing. Every time John saw her, the image of this woman was stamped deep into him. Christine didn't really notice John until much later. They were rostered on together, tackling a handful of cases and bantering while driving around on the job, and after a very short amount of time, she caught up. They were smitten. Totally smitten.

I can relate.

There's a Melbourne-based actor and comedian who goes by the name Tegan Higginbotham. Her last name might read like someone sneezed, slamming their wincing, snotty head into their keyboard, true. But Tegan was doing improv comedy at the age of eighteen when I wandered in, aged twenty-three, fresh from moving to Melbourne. I was studying film at UNSW, and after a particularly bad breakup, I threatened to move to Melbourne. My ex called my bluff, and I had to move. I was lost, depressed, confused, and had a film degree. I was, in a word, insufferable, so naturally I headed along to see some improv comedy. Improv is a weird calling. I've always thought of it as a tool in the performance toolkit, and that doing it by itself is a bit like calling 'stretching your hammies' an Olympic sport. But I noticed Tegan, standing there, making shit up.

Several years later, I had made my way into the entertainment industry somehow. I was hosting mid-dawns on Triple J, and was performing sketch comedy. One night I found myself at a shocking chain restaurant which had the gall to call its food Mexican. Sitting across from me in the dining area? Tegan Higginbotham. I noticed her again. She didn't look up. Fair enough; it was the late noughts, and I had straightened hair. I'd not have looked up either.

Several years later, I was at a rowdy indie dance night called Finishing School, and Melbourne institution Andy McClelland was bouncing and jiving away onstage, cranking out 'This Charming Man'. My group of friends had decided to dance, which gives me hives, so I stood back amid the heaving, thrumming mass of drunken revellers. I turned around, and there, next to the water cooler, was Tegan Higginbotham. This time, she did look up. Tegan was a bit of a big deal at this point, and to my surprise, she smiled and began talking with me, something akin to recognition in her eyes. I can't recall the specifics of the conversation, but I remember thinking . . . my god. She's gorgeous. Tegan, if you're lucky enough to know her, will quite candidly tell you she has no recollection of any of this.

Several years later, at a comedy festival, my friends and I queued up to try to see Tegan's sell-out show, *Million Dollar Tegan*, in which she was the very first female comedian to craft a festival show around a grand experiment: training to fight in an actual boxing match. Naturally we wanted to go along, but we couldn't get in. Sold out, night after night. Why were we so determined? Well, we were also performing in the festival and were sharing a dressing room backstage at Trades Hall with Watson, a comedy group made up of Tegan and Adam McKenzie. By the end of the festival, I had a crush on Tegan so vast it could've issued its own currency.

Tegan, if you're lucky enough to know her, will quite candidly tell you she has no recollection of any of this.

Several years later, Tegan and I were cast in a friend's improvised comedic web series, *Written It Down*. Tegan and I wandered up to each other, talked about how we'd rather be hiding in a corner eating the free grub, then got onto the subject of Harry Potter. I thought . . . well, as before, she'll not remember any of this. But before long, we were cast in a second series, and by the end of the shoot . . . it was game over, man. Game over. From the time the cameras rolled to when they yelled cut, we'd gone from polite to flirting so hard the lens almost shattered. It had happened. Finally. We'd fallen into each other's orbit. We've been inseparable ever since.

We got married one April morning in Paris, 2019, by the Medici Fountain in the Jardin du Luxembourg. Adam officiated the wedding, beaming at the two of us. A family of furious ducks dive-bombed his head. Mum and Dad were there, smiling broadly, next to Tegan's parents, Kevin and Carolyn, a pair of the kindest, strangest eccentrics you'll ever meet. Imagine wombles. Are you imagining wombles? Good. That's them. They're wombles. My sister Anne was there, the same sister who was in Mum when she was mule-kicked during a citizen's arrest in a department store. Our wonderful friend Rama was there, beaming at us. My best man, Josh, was there with his wife Liz. It was a small affair, and everyone applauded and cried. We drove around the Arc de Triomphe in two open tuktuks, leaning out and whooping as a storm front turned Paris dark with torrential rain. We sat in a tiny Parisian kitchen and made speeches and toasted. And Tegan and I sat across from each other, once again at a table full of our friends.

Tegan, if you're lucky enough to know her, will quite candidly tell you she will never forget any of this.

A while back, I asked my dad if he thought I'd make a decent cop. Dad wasn't shy when he told me no, I would not have made a good cop. In fact, I think he said 'Fuck no'. But when I asked if Tegan would, his response was the opposite.

'Mate,' he said. 'Mate, don't take this the wrong way, but she's very smart, and very decisive. She'd make an excellent cop.'

He's not wrong, mind you, but I may have yelled 'HOW DARE YOU' and stormed from the room upon hearing this.

'But . . . why her?' I asked, and I asked. I realised that I was a little jealous of a career path my wife never wanted to take, but that somehow Dad deemed her worthy of. Dad knows my face well. Too well. He charted the emotions flitting over it before he responded.

'Frankly,' he said, 'she's got that intensity. She's willing to do things that are unpleasant or tough, she's clearly willing to stamp things out if they escalate. You're nice. You're maybe too nice, mate.'

What I didn't say at this juncture is that this implies cops can't be too nice. And I neglected to push him on it, neglected to ask him if he thought Tegan is frightening, and if I was some kind of doughy, Kirby-esque marshmallow of a man. But I think the real reason I didn't push is because he probably paid me a compliment. Too nice. I'll take it.

I always struggled with the knowledge that Mum and Dad were so clearly in possession of skills I'd never have: heroism, decisiveness, an ability to guilt you into doing your homework from a range of thirty feet. Their knack for working together, and facing danger together, was something that transcended their time on the force.

'Dad!' I exclaim as he comes back into the apartment, holding his phone and wallet. Mum has already vacated his seat and tottered off to fuss in the kitchen, so as not to let on that she's just been inserted into the book. 'Dad, I was wondering if you had a story about the two of you on a case.' Dad looks at Mum, and Mum gives him a thoughtful look. She answers first. 'Well,' she says slowly, 'it's not on the force, that's the only problem. But John – the scuba tank?'

'The . . . oh!' Dad lights up, paces over to his chair and sits down.

And they begin telling a story. Only this time, they tell it together.

John had been out of the police force for some years, and he'd not scuba-dived in ages.

He missed diving a little, sure. But he was in the fire brigade now, which meant he was technically around water more than ever, and in an odd way, spraying it out of hoses robbed him of any desire to swim about in it. While on General Duties, he and two dear friends had suited up in scuba gear, dived into Sydney Harbour and almost been eviscerated by the house-sized propellers of an international ocean liner. The same tank that he'd sucked from deeply as he was whipped around like so much jetsam that night now sat empty. The tank sat inside a tub in the Verhoevens' garage, alongside a weight belt, a tatty scuba suit and assorted other pieces of diving gear.

'Should I sell it?' John asked Christine one morning.

She looked up from the Barbie Fold 'n Fun House she was assembling with Paul. 'Hmm?'

'The scuba stuff,' John clarified. 'Should I sell it?'

Christine said he may as well – they needed the cash, after all. Having two kids on the Northern Beaches was proving to be more expensive than they'd anticipated. So John headed down to the garage, took a pensive look at the suit he'd worn over and over to brave the inky depths, and decided the money was more important.

What he did, however, was hedge his bets a little. Perhaps he hoped that by tagging his gear with a faintly absurd price, he wouldn't actually have to sell it. He'd have created a loophole. *See?* he'd say to the universe. *I tried! Too bad. Better bundle this stuff back into the house.* So he called the *Trading Post*, a low-cost local rag designed solely for people to offload their unwanted goods, and pitched a thousand dollars for the lot.

A thousand dollars. He was, it should be noted, taking the piss. Scuba tanks were odd, arcane things back in the old days, you see. Each one comprised a steel cylinder, carefully crafted, within which was a cavity to carry a precious parcel of compressed air. But because these tanks were literally capable of both giving life and taking it away, should a malfunction occur, the user had to have them inspected and given a stamp of approval every twelve months. They had to be regularly serviced, and embossed on the top with a mark of good service. The last mark on John's was a decade old, or near enough to make little difference. And so who on earth, thought John, would be mad enough to buy this spent canister from a bygone era of submarining derring-do?

Several days later, they got the call.

Well, Christine got the call. John watched her as she picked up the phone, nodded, nodded again, then raised an eyebrow. Upon finishing the call, she turned to her husband. 'Well,' she said, 'you've got a buyer. They said they'll pay cash. They'll . . . be here in an hour.' And then Christine gave him a look. A look that said, *Is this on the up and up?* And perhaps he'd have picked up on this look, run with it, started an honest conversation, had the price not been so appealing. But it was a thousand bucks, and they needed the money. Dollar signs didn't rack up in his eyes like he was in a cartoon, but they also didn't *not* do that.

One hour later, on the dot, a jet-black Triumph motorcycle roared to a stop outside their house, and off it stepped a man who was six-and-a-half feet tall. John's jaw dropped when he saw the giant, clad in black leathers, removing his helmet and placing it under his arm. The head that had been revealed was a big bullet with eyes. Cold, black eyes.

'He's an assassin,' John muttered under his breath.

'What's that?' replied Christine, also rapt as she watched the thundering approach of the gigantic, frightening bastard up their driveway. 'He looks like a hitman,' she mumbled, not taking her eyes off the window. A knock, then a shuffling of boots met their ears.

When they reached the door, there he was.

'Paul,' Mum says, 'he was big. Very big.'

'How big?'

'I just said. Very big.'

She has me there.

'He was wearing black leather,' Dad says, 'and he offered a thousand bucks. Folding money, all fifties.'

'They looked new,' Mum says intensely. 'John? They looked fresh off the press. No marks, no creases.'

Dad looks at her and nods. 'Yeah, that's right, I forgot about that. I think I was too distracted by the way he looked to really notice. But he was just so . . .'

'. . . Big,' I finish, looking at Mum. 'She just said. Very big.'

Mum laughs.

They watched as the man, who had somehow deftly avoided providing his name, continued leafing through his cube of pristine bills. 'Okay,' he said, matter-of-factly, finishing up his count. 'One thousand. There ya go.' And he handed the bills to Christine, smiling politely. 'Listen,' he said. 'Can we go see the tank?' He clasped his hands. *Those hands,* thought John and Christine in absolute tandem, *are dangerous hands.* But they were holding a lot of money, and he smiled at them in a show of warmth, so they stuffed their misgivings down a little deeper and led him through their house, past their kids, who were skulking in the lounge room, and down to the garage.

The man walked over to the plastic tub, opened it and cleanly lifted the old oxygen tank, turning it in his hands. 'Listen,' he said, gazing at the battered cylinder. 'I live over in the city. An apartment. Haymarket – Chinatown. Why don't you run the scuba gear over to me tomorrow with the kids? It's the weekend. It'll be busy, but you can make a day of it, and I can't carry it all back on me bike, anyway.'

He smiled at them again. *Maybe,* they both thought, *he's on the level. He's a collector.*

He's certainly odd, thought Christine. *Maybe an ex-crim?*

Maybe, thought John, *he's just a scuba diver and digs the vintage gear.*

Either way, there it was again. The nudging of the bills. The hot, fresh paper in their hands. So they said yes, they could even take the kids to the Marigold, their favourite yum cha place.

'Oh!' he exclaimed, delighted. 'That's right across the road from my building. Bloody perfect.' So they all agreed to make Saturday the day of the exchange, and as the giant purred away on his beautiful British motorcycle, they squealed, clasped hands, and ferreted away their cash.

The next day, once across the bridge and heading along George Street, near Chinatown, with the kids in their dodgy Ford Falcon, Christine and John turned into the garage of the apartment building. They pulled up near the lifts, where the enormous man was waiting, bearing that same impenetrable, charming smile.

'I'll wait here with these two,' Christine said, ruffling Paul's hair. He was in a mood – he was always in a mood these days, for some reason – and so she tried ruffling little Anne's hair instead. Her daughter giggled. *Jackpot,* thought Christine.

John hopped out of the car, grabbed the tub of scuba gear, and began to walk across the half-full car park. He passed a large white flower-delivery van, nodding politely at the driver and passenger, who had stopped their conversation to eyeball him before resuming what looked to John like a hushed argument. Finally, he reached the lift and popped the tub down in front of the man.

After kneeling down and giving everything a cursory once-over, the big bastard stood up, clapped John on the back, and grinned. 'Cheers, John,' he said. 'Listen, if you still want to hit up the yum cha, it's on me. Just let me know when you want to be let back out of the car park. I'll buzz you out.' And he handed John a one-hundred-dollar bill.

So the Verhoevens left the car park, the four of them, and filed into the Marigold. It's one of those palatial Chinese restaurants swarming with people, windows crammed with tanks, which are in turn crammed with lobsters, which are in turn crammed with an awareness that they're soon to be ex-lobsters. Enormous tables, punctuated by lazy Susans, furiously encircled by a blur of angry servers doling out dumplings and rainbow jelly, buzzing about the cavernous room. John, Christine, Paul and Anne were directed to a table, and before long, they'd over-ordered and were groaning with delight.

'It's all the MSG,' interjects Dad. 'Dehydrates you.'
'Actually,' I reply, a little smugly, 'MSG is just salt.'
'What?'

'It's just salt. There was a huge movement against it, Chinese restaurant syndrome. Basically it's a weird cultural food bias — it's essentially just salt.'

Dad looks affronted, like he's about to pummel me with a grumpy counterpoint, when Mum pipes up. 'He's right, John,' she says calmly. 'Read about it in the Guardian. *Basically food racism.'*

'You two are hopeless,' he sulks.

An hour later, the four Verhoevens staggered across to the car park, were buzzed in, bade a friendly farewell to the giant motorbike man and made their way back home. It was, all in all, a brilliant twenty-four hours. A thousand dollars and free yum cha. All was well.

Until one year later.

It was a quiet morning, and John was off work for the day. He was in the kitchen, playing with a now-even-moodier Paul, when a knock almost shook the house. Christine, chopping something in the kitchen, looked up with a start. They stood as one and headed for the door, flinging it open. There, outside the screen door, stood *three* gigantic men. By John's estimates, they were as wide as they were tall. By Christine's estimates, John was prone to exaggeration. The three men, wearing suits, announced their presence.

They were spooks.

They were there on behalf of the federal police.

In an effort to create a sense of anticipation, to tease out of you a sense of excitement and intrigue, we're now going to flash back to the strong, mysterious protagonist at the heart of this uniquely odd tale. We're going to flash back one year . . . to the scuba tank.

After John, Christine, Paul and Anne bundled themselves into their practical but rather hodgepodge family sedan and left the parking garage, the giant man on the motorbike leapt into action. He threw out everything but the scuba tank – years of John's memories, his essence, jettisoned like farts in the breeze. He then picked up the tank and took it to a shady workshop nestled deep in Sydney's suburbs. Pulling up a large clacketty roller door, he greeted a man with eyes like belt holes, whereupon said man carefully took the tank and mounted it on his workbench. This rotund, pockmarked hobgoblin of a man spent several hours pains-takingly sawing through the tank until it was artfully sheared in two. At this point, an intermediary arrived, and after several grunts back and forth, which in all likelihood were intended as some form of communication, the first man went to take a slash. While he was gone, the intermediary stuffed an indescribable quantity of extremely high-quality and staggeringly expensive heroin into the now-exposed cavity.

Our hobgoblin returned, cracked his fat, gnarled knuckles, cleared his throat, and set about reversing what he'd done. With a finesse that belied his inelegant form, he magicked the cylinder back into a single piece. No marks on the surface betrayed what had been done. And our motorbike-riding leviathan, happy with how everything had gone down, nodded, grunted, and left with the tank in tow.

He then took this tank on something of a whirlwind trip.

Over several harrowing months, our protagonist and his tank full of heroin travelled all over the world, bouncing from country to country. They never stayed long, and they were always on the move, switching hotel rooms, taxis and boats with an unset-tling frequency and ease. They ricocheted across the globe, never stopping, never resting, until finally, they came to land on a small yacht moored off the north coast . . . of Australia.

Now, in an effort to create an even more heightened sense of anticipation, to tease out of you a sense of excitement, of intrigue, we're going to flash back to the two men John had noticed in the car park: the two men in the flower van.

These two men were not delivering flowers.

They were, in fact, spooks. And for the past several years they'd been tracking our motorcycle-riding man. Because – and I hate to ruin this rather handsome brute for you, but brace yourselves – John and Christine had intuited correctly. He *was* an assassin, and he had a sideline as a courier of heroin. His role, in this case, was to shuttle an enormous and vital shipment from a new supplier around the world, and he'd hit upon a novel idea: why not hide it in a scuba tank? It would have to be an old one, though. Thicker, harder to look into, and busted enough, used enough, to seem plausibly his own. So this assassin had picked up the *Trading Post* one day, at his wit's end after having tried unsuccessfully to obtain an intact workable tank. And there, in the middle of the page, was an ad. An ad from one John Verhoeven, asking a comically high price for his scuba gear. Tank included.

For someone with this man's connections and budget, the asking price was a drop in the ocean. He bought the tank. He didn't notice that he was being tailed all the way to the Northern Beaches. He didn't notice the bogus flower van parked nearby as he did his deal. But his seven-month jag, his ping-pong across the globe, was designed and planned specifically to throw off any tails. And it worked . . . at least, it bought him enough time to get his tank safely to that yacht off the north coast, whereupon the trail for the feds went cold. Turns out the asking price literally was a drop in the ocean.

The feds, however, sent scuba divers to sweep the area where the trail had gone cold, and sure enough, they found at the bottom of the ocean two halves of a scuba tank. A scuba tank registered to . . .

John Francis Verhoeven.

The men in the flower van had had their backs up about this nefarious scuba tank deal from day dot. But what disturbed them even further was the fact that after very little digging, they'd found out who this married couple were. The couple, with kids, who had given the assassin the means to transport heroin around the globe were, in fact, ex-cops. And given how corrupt cops were in the eighties, they thought they'd hit paydirt. And, unbeknownst to John and Christine, the spooks spent the next seven months tapping the Verhoevens' phone, following them, tracing every aspect of their lives back to its origin.

Of course, John and Christine didn't find this out until years later. One night, Christine was talking with her cousin. And this cousin was telling Christine about her time working with the federal government. And said cousin, after a pregnant pause, told Christine (I shit you not) that she'd been assigned to watch the assassin's apartment building from across the street the day the Verhoevens had delivered the tank. And where had she been hiding? Where had she been watching from?

From a window seat.

In the Marigold.

'You ordered too much,' Christine's cousin laughed into the phone. 'I remember thinking you all had the appetites of a Mongol horde.' Christine laughed back, nervously.

When she told John all of this, he looked at her, eyes wide. And in a quiet moment, they both agreed that the whole affair had, frankly, been the most exciting thing to happen to them both in years. And they remembered, in that moment, that their shared love of adventure – and terror – was something that would always keep them in lockstep with one another. John promised Christine, fervently, that he would never again sell a single fucking thing in the *Trading Post*.

And they agreed, both of them, that they'd never forget any of this.

17

DICKING AROUND

Right. So there might be some ways in which I'm similar to Dad. We both met women who didn't notice us for a long time, and we're both punching above our weight. Fine. That's something, and I'll cop to it.

But the fact is, we need to get back to Dad's time in Forensics, because he's just dropped a bomb on me.

'I got in trouble once,' he says, leafing through his notes.

I perk up instantly. 'What do you mean, trouble?'

'Trouble,' he mutters. 'I got into trouble. Pretty bad trouble, actually.'

I gaze at him, confused but cheered greatly. Here's a weak spot, a moment I can probe for insight. If he got in trouble, perhaps that means he has regrets? And if he has regrets, god, we're on my home turf. Because then I can maybe get him to finally admit there are things he wishes he could have done differently. It's a long shot, but it's an opening. It's fascinating. It's—

'Mate, have I ever told you about the person stealing all the dicks?' he says, now gazing at another page in his notebook.

I look up at him. He's very . . . animated. Like a bloodhound suddenly catching a scent in the air.

Looks like we're hearing the getting-in-trouble story later.

Grey liked John. It was obvious. As much as John liked having a wizened mentor – and he liked having a wizened mentor a lot – Grey liked having an eager protégé. As the weeks and months rolled on, they developed a kind of shorthand, a secret language that accrued case after case, body after body. Occasionally, John would think about his time in General Duties; about Julian, his ex-partner, who'd taken the detectives up on their offer of promotion. And he'd get a little down, miss what they'd had. But in those moments, he realised he'd more or less hit the jackpot with Grey. Even if, more often than not, their casework got a little surreal.

A couple of months into Forensics, for example, Grey and John were over at Glebe Morgue inspecting a body. They decided to take a quick, perfunctory lunch break and found themselves sitting in the sterile break room eating egg salad sandwiches. A polite knock startled them from their meal. 'Hi fellas. We are having,' said a pathologist who was now standing in the doorway, '. . . a bit of a problem.' John looked at the morgue worker, an older man with a ruddy complexion and broad shoulders. He held up his half-finished sandwich. 'Should I . . .?' he said, indicating he'd love to come and help, but would rather not abandon his meal. The pathologist gave him a look nestled somewhere between apologetic and sickened. 'Yeah,' he said, 'probably leave that here.'

A minute later, Grey and John were standing in a refrigerated side room, little puffs of steam popping and curling out of their mouths as they breathed. The stout pathologist tugged on a gleaming handle, and out came a gurney. It came to a stop with a *shunk*. The pathologist whipped off the sheet, the coarse fabric billowing off to the side. 'What do you think?' he said, gripping the fabric and eyeballing the body.

'I think someone has cut this man's dick off,' said Grey.

John couldn't have said it better himself. Someone had, in fact, clearly taken some kind of cutting implement to the penis of this very dead man. John cast his eye over the rest of the body. Nothing else was amiss, but did it really need to be? A missing penis was plenty amiss. The guy was about forty, at a guess, though dying rarely made people look their best. Tousled hair was plastered to bluish skin, and his eyes and mouth were shut, his face calm. *My face,* John thought, *would not be calm if someone took my pecker off.* 'You know,' he said, leaning in, 'if I didn't know better, I'd say this was done post-mortem.'

Grey chuckled appreciatively. 'My thoughts exactly. In fact, John, look closer at the . . . uhhh . . . *wound.*'

Loath as he was to lean in any closer to the opening, John did so. The cut had been rather precise; a circle of exposed meat and muscle and the bisected urethra peeked up at him from amid the thatch of matted pubic hair like a terrible, unblinking eye. 'This . . . wait. Very clean wound – no blood, no tearing. Did you clean this?'

The pathologist shook his head, eyeing John. Grey watched to see if John would pick up on what he'd clearly already ascertained. John finally twigged, shooting bolt upright. 'Did someone come in here and cut this guy's dick off?'

The pathologist nodded.

'Right,' John said, beginning to pace around the body. 'So . . . I'm assuming you didn't do it. But it's obviously someone who works here, right? Who else has the access?'

The pathologist went from sage-like to startled. Grey still watched on like some kind of wise owl, but he was clearly enjoying seeing John's deductive process play out with a witness for once, instead of just a broken body and a line of police tape. 'But . . . well, shit,' the diminutive pathologist said, stumped. 'I mean . . . look, that makes sense. Actually . . .' he trailed off, in deep thought, then made his way to the door. 'Come with me, fellas.' And he led them around the corner, down a corridor, through a doorway and into an office. Reaching into a filing cabinet, he pulled out a manila folder, cleared his throat awkwardly, and handed it to John and Grey. They set it down on the desk, opened it, and began riffling through the large, glossy photos inside.

Dickless bodies. Dickless body after dickless body, all the same M.O., each incision clearly performed well inside the apparent safety of the morgue.

'These are all from here?' John asked.

The pathologist gave a noise indicating that, yes, all of these bodies had been robbed of their manhood within the premises. 'It's been going on for weeks now, but we thought it was . . . Look, I don't know what we thought. But it's reached kind of a fever pitch. We thought it might be a contractor. Actually, the bodies that were getting the snip were ones on their way out of here, all our work on them done, but this latest one hadn't been autopsied yet, so of course we noticed right away.'

'You didn't think to check morgue workers?' quizzed Grey. The pathologist gave Grey an exasperated look. 'We don't do things like this. We just don't! And there are so many contractors on our books . . . Look, I appreciate the once-over, guys. I'll make some enquiries.'

And with that, he asked if they could leave. They said yes, and they left. And that was that.

Only it wasn't *that*, was it? Because if John was learning anything, it was that there were consequences to his choices. He'd spoken up, he'd stuck his nose in. And several weeks later, over at Chatswood Scientific, he and Grey got a visit from their pathologist friend. And this time, their friend had photos in tow. New photos, mind you. After some pleasantries, the red-haired pathologist sat down and, in hushed tones, relayed the following.

After John's suggestion that the incisions were performed by someone on the inside, the pathologist had begun an inquiry. Quietly at first, so as not to alert anyone. And eventually, after poking and prodding and checking timesheets, he and his supervisors had a suspect. They sent police to this suspect's apartment during an unremarkable morning, and found . . . well. They found all the penises.

'All the penises?' queried John.

'All the penises,' the pathologist assured him.

Grey nodded. 'All the penises.'

'Penises,' John added for good measure.

Inside this apartment was a kind of boutique craft display, the kind you might find at a school fete in Annandale on a summer afternoon. There was handmade jewellery everywhere, strung up mid-assembly, above a neat and tidy workspace. But instead of beads, or big gleaming hunks of colourful resin or timber orbs, the necklaces they found were made from penises. Dried, cleaned, freshly shorn penises. A makeshift clothesline bisected the room, with the tiny, sad, shrivelled phalluses hanging there on itty-bitty pegs, the breeze from the police officers' congress setting them to sway gently to and fro.

'Penis necklaces,' I say, utterly perplexed.
Dad just nods.
'But,' I stammer, 'what if they somehow all got erect when you were wearing it? It'd break your neck!'
He doesn't dignify me with a response.

The jeweller – who shall remain unnamed – was dealt with later that day. And when the authorities had returned from their grisly craft fair, John got a sincere, embarrassed thank you from the pathologist. Once the pathologist was gone, Grey gave John a very earnest thumbs up from across the office, before getting back to his cup of piping-hot black coffee.

John was finding the morgue a fascinating, albeit convoluted, place. A bustling hub of activity, its outside as complex as its inside. Years later – as you now know – he'd go on to work at a funeral home, due in part to the reverence he grew to have for the dead. Even during his time in General Duties, John had become extremely protective of the dignity of people, and who was more defenceless than the dead? Absurdity notwithstanding, the gall someone must have to defile a body, especially when that someone was entrusted with its protection, incensed him.

But people kept mistreating the dead. They seemed compelled, John reflected, to take advantage of the powerless. Less than a week after the 'case of the missing penises' – as Grey called it – yet another case of sacrilege crossed their desk. They were sent to deal with the analysis and pickup of a body found, of all places, in a white van, parked by the side of the road. As they pulled up on the grass verge by the crime scene, a patrol car was leaving, presumably with a suspect inside. John and Grey got out and were greeted by a thoroughly shaken, extremely rattled highway patrol officer, white as a sheet, standing near his monstrous Kawasaki. He gestured to the back of the van. The doors were ajar, and John could see a single leg through the gap, askew, pale.

Here is what the officer told John and Grey, as they stood by the side of the road, wincing under the blaring sun.

He'd just finished up his shift, and was heading back towards his home station, when he noticed the van parked rather awkwardly by the side of the freeway. Shaded under a copse of trees, the van was, apparently, unoccupied. The officer, thinking something was off, decided to wind back around and investigate. He parked behind the van, removed his helmet, and inspected the vehicle. He suspected immediately what the van was. You see, all funeral homes had these vans parked in a queue outside Glebe Morgue, and when a job came up, they'd grab it. They were like tow-truck drivers in that respect, only instead of towing broken vehicles, it was broken bodies they'd ferry to and from their final destinations. And this white van, thought the officer, was clearly from a funeral home. *Maybe,* thought the young man, *I should go and see if the driver is okay.*

And so he did that walk over to the van. You know the one: the walk designed to be watched through a rear-view mirror, the calm, collected, calculated build-up designed to make you sweat. And as he reached the driver's-side window, he peered in to find . . .

Nope, he wasn't crazy the first time. Nothing.

No driver, no passenger, nothing. But the engine, he noted, was still ticking away gently, popping and snapping in the heat. He touched his hand to the bonnet. Faint movement. Clearly, this engine hadn't been turned off for very long. And so, in a move the young officer would regret for some time, he had a bright idea. *What if,* he thought, *the driver is in the back of the van? What if he's back there fixing something?* So he stood up straight, put on his game face, and did his intimidating walk around to the double doors at the back of the van. He grasped the handles, flung open the doors . . .

And there, in the back of the van resting by the roadside, was a funeral-home worker having sex with a corpse.

At this point while relaying his traumatic tale, the officer had to stop to take a breath. Even Grey looked startled at what he'd said, and gently placed his enormous hand on the officer's slumped shoulder. John took another look at the leg peeking out from the van, and shivered despite the heat. He cast his mind back, trying to remember what the suspect being taken away as they'd arrived had looked like. *What kind of a person,* thought John, *would do that to another?*

But, of course, John knew already. He'd seen more barbarism in his career-to-date than most people would see in ten lifetimes.

'Dad,' I ask, 'I know I've brought this up before, many times, but . . . I know I wouldn't have been able to process any of this stuff. So with that in mind, do you think I'd have made a good cop?'

Dad knows this is a bit of a sore spot for me. I asked him this in *Loose Units*, the first book, and after it was published and he read what I'd turned his stories into, he very earnestly apologised to me: 'Sorry, mate,' he said. 'I didn't mean to make it sound like you'd make a shit cop.' And I believe him. Why would he want to be that cold about it? But I guess there must be something striking about reading how your son perceives you – after all, John in the books isn't really the *real* John. He's my version of John. And if he comes across as rude or blunt, then Dad was clearly worried that's how I see him. Which, I assured him, simply isn't true.

'Look,' he says, choosing his works a little more carefully this time, perhaps peripherally aware he's on the record, 'you'd be good at some parts of policing, not so good at others. But your strength is your speaking, your personality. So maybe the police wouldn't be great for you. Maybe a lawyer?'

I'm shocked. I'm genuinely shocked. 'Lawyer?'

'Lawyer,' he says, his expression showing signs of backpedalling already. 'But a *good* one, you know? Because they have to give speeches, convince people of things, turn crowds. I think you could do that beautifully.'

He gives me a look. A 'How'd I do?' look.

I think he did just fine.

18

TINY SHAFTS OF LIGHT

For many months now, John had been excelling in Scientific, and Grey had grown into a perpetually impressed, frequently jubilant mentor. But Grey told John one day that the next time they were called to a hairy case, a really, truly hairy one, John would have to go it alone.

'Alone?' asked John.

'Alone,' confirmed Grey.

'Hairy?' asked John.

'Hairy,' confirmed Grey. 'One of the really bad ones. After long enough in this business, you get a feeling for when they're about to happen. And by you, I mean me, naturally. I've got a feeling we're overdue for something really, truly hairy. Mark my words, John. We'll get a call.'

And sure enough, the very next day, the call came.

And it was as hairy as they come.

The phone rang so loudly it almost shook the handset off the receiver, and John, who'd almost nodded off at his desk, gave a little startled yelp. Grey was out of the office, and John had decided to peruse his fingerprint manual for the tenth time that week.

Now, however, every nerve ending in his body was firing, and he reached for the phone, snatching it up. Eyes widening at the request being relayed, he let his pen race across his notepad, fervently laying out key details.

Once he'd hung up, adrenaline was boiling in his veins. 'He was right,' John mumbled to himself. 'Hairy.' He then radioed Grey and told him about the job. Grey conceded that it was, indeed, hairy, and told John to calm down and to take a deep breath. 'You have within you,' intoned Grey down the line, 'the potential for great things. Centre yourself, and repeat after me, John. Wherever you go . . .'

'Wherever you go,' replied John obediently.

'. . . there you are,' finished Grey.

'There you are,' repeated John, confused, but definitively calmer. Grey wished him luck, and John hung up.

The Endeavour Migrant Hostel in South Coogee was a series of enormous, brown, nondescript buildings huddled together behind high fences close to the ocean. The moment John pulled up, he knew shit had gone seriously wrong. He was ambiently aware while driving over that he was flying solo this time, but he kept repeating Grey's odd mantra. *Wherever you go . . . there you are.* John's mind's eye began to drift. He pulled back, up and out of the Kingswood. He drifted further still, up and away from the road. Now he could see the whole facility humming with activity, a kind of frantic energy. And there he was, pulling into the car park out front. Just a small dot on a map. *Hi John,* he thought dreamily. *There you are.*

Well . . . shit, thought John, stepping out of the Kingswood, shoes meeting the gravel of the car park. *Grey was right. It actually worked.* He felt lighter. He'd need some lightness, if the reports were anything to go by. John popped his notepad into his bag of forensics gear, straightened his tie, readjusted his mustard suede jacket, and made his way to the main compound.

The Endeavour, named loftily after one of the longships whose arrival on Australian shores began the brutal process of colonial theft and assimilation, was set into a grassy verge. A looming, gleaming, beaming white flagpole stood to attention out front, the Australian flag lolloping in the intermittent breeze. As John rounded the corner and entered the main courtyard, he knew more or less what to expect, of course. He'd been briefed. But as he saw the emergency response team charging about the place, all he could think of were the countless war movies he'd seen. Men in bullet-proof vests, holding large, glossy, hateful guns, barrelled to and fro, and he realised that if something went wrong, he'd likely have no other defence than flinging an anal thermometer at his assailant. *It's gross,* he thought, *but it just might make them recoil. I'd have to explain what it's used for for that to work, though, by which point I'd be dead.*

'Oh!' Dad exclaims, startling me. 'Sorry, mate, sorry. I had a gun.'

'You had a gun? In Forensics?'

'Yes. Sorry. I had a gun. In one of those cool chest holsters, like detectives wear. Plain-clothes. Sorry. Does that change anything from earlier in the book?'

I look at him, and have a think. I mean . . . does it? The 'I had a gun the whole time' revelation is really an aesthetic change, as he couldn't really shoot his way out of any of the cases up to this point, right? But look. If it helps aid your reading experience, go back and re-read the whole thing, only this time, imagine he has one of those cool holsters with a gun in it the

entire time. Maybe it'll colour your perception of him. Oh,
and if you're working for the company making the inevitable
Electric Blue *action figures, please draft up a new design and*
call me to discuss. I'm thinking a 1981 Glock 17 could be a
good look.

John was approaching the entrance to the shower block, where
he'd been ordered to head. The building was long, very long, and
somewhat bleak-looking. Emergency Services, Tactical, and even
the occasional patrol officer milled by the entrance. As John neared,
he flashed his badge. A senior member of Tactical eyed it, nodded,
and gestured for John to head inside. *I've never flashed my badge*
before, John thought. *I didn't even know you* could *flash your badge*
in real life. I just sort of . . . did it. He ducked his head – needlessly,
as the doorway was rather high – and walked in. Letting his eyes
adjust to the light, he looked about the space.

The whole shower block was a single room, with very high
ceilings, and rows of shower cubicles down both sides. It smelled
like wet concrete and soap, but it wasn't the showers that seized
John's attention. It was what lay down, far down at the very far end
of the almost sepulchral space. In the distance, past the showers,
was a small door. Unremarkable. And around that door stood a
clutch of highly armed members of Tactical, guns trained on said
door. John looked about, and waved at an officer who was buzzing
past, holding a radio. 'Mate,' John said, 'Sorry. I'm with Scientific.
What's with the room?'

'Oh,' said the officer in a raspy whisper, stopping to talk and
pointing at the door. 'That, down there, is where he went. We got
him. For months, someone has been sneaking into this enormous
shower block and sexually assaulting several of the immigrants

being processed here. Always women, usually late at night. The staff have tried to figure out who it was. They always figured it was another immigrant preying on his own, y' know. Already here, easy access.

'But about an hour ago,' he explained, 'a man in a janitor's uniform cornered some poor woman about to shower and advanced on her. Then, thank god, a friend of the woman came in to have a shower too, scared the guy . . . and chased him off. Chased him right . . . there.' He pointed again at the door.

'How do you know he's still in there?' asked John, unable to take his eyes off the tiny green door, encircled as it was by automatic weapons.

'Because it's a janitor's cupboard! Well, as good as. Storage closet, basically. No other doors. Staff came running, held the door shut until we could get here. But we don't know if he's armed, and he's hurt a lot of women, so we want him stopped, quick smart. We're gonna need you to canvass the area once we have him, make this thing watertight.' He turned, looking down the other end of the room. 'Hold tight, mate. Looks like they're getting ready to go in.'

John thanked the officer and began to make his way towards the door. He already knew most of this information from his phone call, but never in his wildest dreams had he anticipated that the guy was still here, trapped like a spider under a glass. *This,* John realised, *is hairy. Grey was right, dammit.* The men with guns began to make frantic, precise gestures. *Time to slip the piece of paper under and see if the spider escapes,* John thought, bracing himself.

A well-aimed kick, and the door popped away from the wall, spinning in place and falling to the ground. Several of the armed-response units aimed their guns inside, then . . . silence. Confusion, perhaps. Several of the officers looked about, one of them yelling for a hand. The myriad of cops from different departments began to run around, make calls, all of them looking completely thrown. John had no idea what was going on, but he knew it wasn't good.

He was still wondering what the hell to do when one of the tactical-response officers sprinted over. 'Scientific?' he asked, not even a little out of breath. John nodded mutely. 'This way. Gonna need a once-over on this.' And so John followed. The two of them trotted down towards the remains of the door, and when John passed through the herd of baffled and heavily armed men, who were standing there gawping, and once he crossed the threshold into the tiny room, he saw why they were so thrown. The officer who'd explained the situation to him hadn't exaggerated, not one bit. The room was practically a closet, the walls painted the same sickly shade of green as the door, which lay off to one side, handle jutting out of it sickly like a broken tooth. John looked back; the members of Tactical were all peering in, looking . . . unnerved? Spooked? Come to think of it, there was literally no way the guy could have left the room. There were some pipes running up the wall, brooms, a bucket. But that was about it. No doors. No trap-doors, no doggy doors. No doors, period. And nobody had taken an eye off the room since he went in, meaning he'd just . . . vanished.

Could the impossible happen? John had suspected for some time that the impossible wasn't really impossible, just a little less likely than the possible. On the weird nights, the ones where he was finishing up at Chatswood Scientific and Grey had clocked out, he'd look at the jars of pickled unmentionables, at the folios full of unspeakable horrors, and think . . . maybe. Maybe we just don't get it.

And here he was, standing in a room, looking for a man who'd vanished into thin air. *No doors. Well,* he thought, looking at the

remains on the floor . . . one *door. But he didn't pass through it.*
He absently nudged it, lifting it with his foot. He turned to the
men outside. 'Well . . . he's not under here, at least.' Nobody
laughed.

Then, something marvellous happened.

The wind ruffled John's hair.

Only for a moment, mind you. The smallest of gusts, distant
and warm, lifted his fringe slightly and let it drop. Nobody was
speaking, nobody was so much as moving – everyone else's eyes
were glued to John, who'd suddenly locked up like a deer in the
headlights. He whipped his head around, then licked a finger
and held it up. A breeze. A breeze . . . and it wasn't coming from
outside. Somewhere in this room there was a draught. And this
room had no doors, John reminded himself. No doors. A draught,
and no doors. He knelt down and placed his kit bag on the floor,
stood back up, and began to stalk around the room slowly, holding
up a single licked finger, trying to figure out where exactly the
breeze had come from. A gentle stream of air hit him again, and
he held up his palm. It rushed against his skin, and he held his
hand aloft like a sail, slowly coasting across the room, cupping the
loose thread, the hint of a clue, in his hand, holding his breath so as
not to disturb it. Closer, closer, closer. 'Wherever you go . . .' John
whispered, edging his way over to a bank of plumbing on the far
wall, '. . . there you are,' he finished, closing his hand on an almost
invisible gap between the pipe and the wall.

He'd done it. This was where the air was coming from. He
pressed his face flat against the wall, eyeballing it up and down,
running his finger along the seam, until . . . he hit something. Just
out of sight between the pipe and the wall, a gentle ridge. A latch.
He gripped it, pulled, and several makeshift hinges that had been

invisible until now creaked gently. And several feet of wall came away as a single piece.

A hidden door. John swung it open all the way, and literal gasps issued forth from the Tactical units outside. Then, yells. John drew his gun. He was joined by the Tactical officer who'd briefed him outside. They peered into the muggy, misty darkness beyond the door, and without thinking, John did what he always did when a dreadful choice lay before him. He didn't think about whether he should or shouldn't. He didn't wonder what would happen if he did.

He just fucking did it.

John leapt in.

He landed in a wall cavity about a foot wide, air thick and cloying and humid. His new colleague stepped in behind him and raised a flashlight. 'The only way this guy escaped from behind here,' John said, 'would be up . . . there.' Their eyes followed the beam. A handmade ladder scaled the wall up into the ceiling, and sure enough, the crawlspace up there looked to be large enough to provide passage.

Another couple of tactical unit members approached the make-shift door. 'Dog squad is here,' said one of the officers. 'Need us to grab them, sniff something out?'

John nodded, then hauled himself up the ladder and into the crawlspace. On his hands and knees now, he looked around the cramped recess. The sight that met him was truly odd, but perhaps no odder than what he'd already encountered that day: he was looking out at the space that lay above the ceiling of the vast shower block. And as his eyes once again adjusted, he noticed hundreds of tiny shafts of light were piercing the darkness like golden threads. He crawled forward, gloved hands outstretched, while behind him, Tactical and dog squad members heaved a German shepherd up into the cramped space. And that's when John's left hand met something soft. He reached down and picked up . . .

A tissue. Scrunched up, hard and crusty. With a terrible sinking feeling, he leaned his head down, bringing his eye flush with the nearest hole. He had an unfettered bird's-eye view of a shower block. He looked back up again at the litany of holes peppering the floor of this pervert's cave, and realised there were more tissues. They were everywhere. And they'd all been . . . . Well. *Used.*

The dog, John thought, *is going to eat the tissues.* He'd seen dogs eat weird shit before, and the idea of a beautiful, well-trained police dog seizing a jizz-encrusted Kleenex in its mouth almost had him sick to his stomach. But then the dog darted past him, a bundle of fur and muscle barrelling through the darkness. 'After him!' came the yell of the dog handler, who was now cresting the end of the ladder and coming into view. 'He's got something!' So John crawled as fast as he could, flanked by several other police.

They frantically bundled themselves after the dog, banking left, then along a darkened cavity . . . and finally to a large grate. The dog had stopped, panting. John lifted the unfastened grate away from the wall, slid through, and found himself in yet another storage room. This one, however, was far cleaner. He made his way down the wall with the aid of several large crates, which had been stacked to serve as stairs, and the other police – and the dog – followed. The dog, soon on solid ground again, barked and bolted out the door. John and the police gave frantic chase. *We've got him,* John thought. *We've got the bastard.* They rounded the corner, feet crunching on gravel, and there . . .

. . . was the car park. And the police dog, looking almost as crestfallen as John, stood before a vacant parking spot. The animal looked back at them, panting, and John ran over to the dog's side. He knelt down and patted the animal, and rested a hand on the parking space.

He could smell exhaust in the air.

They'd just missed him.

They'd just fucking missed him.

I sit there for a while, watching Dad. He seems calm. Remarkably calm. Despite relaying his story about kneeling in a crawlspace, knee-deep in jizz-encrusted tissues, then chasing a German shepherd hot on the trail of a sex offender through the walls of a shower block. Calm. He seems calm.

'But what if you'd got there earlier?' I ask.

Dad looks confused. 'What do you mean?'

'Well,' I continue, 'if you'd found the hatch in the wall quicker, or if the dog had been passed up faster, or if they'd breached the room sooner and caught him halfway into his secret passage . . . What if things had happened just that little bit quicker, and you'd caught the guy? *Did* you catch the guy, eventually?'

Dad looks thoughtful. Or, rather, he puts on a thoughtful face to make a show of looking thoughtful. 'We didn't ever catch the guy, no. At least, not as far as I'm aware. Besides, my job wasn't to catch him, I just happened to play a key role in . . . you know. *Almost* catching him. But as for doing things earlier . . . that's not what happened.'

'I know that's not what happened!' I blurt, utterly exasperated. I laugh, but I plough on anyway. 'Dad, Jesus! I'm just asking you to try to see things from my perspective. The wondering what could have happened, the paralysis over which path to choose, the need to chase every stray lead . . . that's how I see the world. That's how I view stories. All I'm asking is that, when I present you with a question like this, you *try* to understand that not everyone is as rigid as you on this front.'

He's listening. Good. He doesn't look like he fully *gets* it, but he's listening, smiling kindly. I keep talking. 'Okay, Dad . . . look, let me explain a little clearer. See this?' I pick up the half-unwrapped present, the copy of the Choose Your Own Adventure book I bought him. 'In these books, you get to choose one of any number of paths, right?'

'Right.'

'Well,' I continue, 'think of this book as my brain. It wants to know what would have happened if things had played out differently. Some days I think it *needs* that. And it gets . . .'

'Frustrated?' he offers helpfully.

I clap my hands together, channelling Grey completely by accident. 'Yes! Yes, perfect. My brain, because of the ADHD, gets frustrated. It needs to know what was going to happen, what happened after, what happened before. It wants to know it all, and it wants to know it *all at once*. So I've always looked at your adventures and been awestruck, not just because of what you did, but the fact that you could do it *at all*. That you could see every one of those multiple choices, each one of those possible endings in front of you each time a big decision arose in a case . . . and just *choose one*.'

I take a breath and look at him. He's processing all of it, I know he is – it's like a tiny scrolling stock exchange readout is stamped across his head, with NOW PROCESSING drifting from left to right in bright red letters. Finally, he looks at the book, and picks it up. 'I never got these books, Paul. I never really got the appeal.

But I think I understand what you mean. I don't know if I'll ever view the world the way you do, but I appreciate you telling me all of this.'

We're both silent for a minute or two. And then, because we're father and son, we push the moment aside and carry on with our work.

19

SUNDAY ROAST

When John got back from the Endeavour Migrant Hostel, hauling his tired butt into the office and heaving his gear back onto his desk with a weary thump, Grey was back from a lengthy lunch. Wordlessly, he brought John a cup of coffee, acrid and black. John took the proffered cup and sipped, mind still entirely occupied with the sight of those tiny shafts of light. He promptly scalded his tongue, and for the following week had next to no tastebuds in working order.

But, as Grey had told him again and again, you need to stub your toe. So John asked Grey to keep him busy, distract him. And Grey looked John up and down, smiled, and wiggled his fingers. 'How do you feel about hands?' he asked. That, right there, was an interesting question.

'Hands were tricky,' Dad says, halting the story to deliver one of his horrible asides. 'One time, Grey and I were all set to do analysis on a set of hands which a visiting member of Scientific had dredged up. They were from a drowning victim, and we needed prints, so he sheared them off at the wrist—'

'EW.'

'Yes, ew. He sheared them off, carried them up to the roof, fastened them to something and let them dry off. The only problem was, of course, that by the time he got back upstairs, they were ruined.'

I raise an eyebrow. 'They weren't already ruined?'

'Not like this. Birds. They were almost entirely eaten by birds.'

My nauseated look pleases Dad a great deal. 'Another time, a lovely cop from the country got in touch and told us he'd send down something for us to get prints off; something pertaining to a horrifying, crucial case. We waited for his delivery, received it . . . and when we opened the box, we found ten fingers.' Dad pauses for effect.

'And?'

'And they'd been clipped off. Ten loose fingers, rattling round a fucking box. Do you know what you need to do to be able to take prints, Paul? You need to know which finger goes where. But we had ten fingers. In a box. Useless. Had to chuck them out. Hell, maybe I didn't flinch quite so much at throwing the bones out because I'd already had to dispose of body parts so many times. Maybe I started to see it all as just . . . meat.'

I stare at him. 'Meat.'

'Meat, yes. Oh! The story. This fits perfectly.'

Colour me shocked.

Here, then, is the case with which Grey decided to distract a slightly crestfallen John.

John and Grey, once again united as a duo, headed out to a small, pretty house in the inner suburbs of Sydney. A flight of stairs climbed up to the front door of the red-brick edifice, which John could tell was still warm from the afternoon sun. There was a smattering of emergency services vehicles and workers about the place, and the same emergency lighting they'd seen in the hoarder's house, the same house where John had mistaken Chinese food for human brains – clearly the power was out. But what grabbed John's attention was the clump of sobbing young men off to one side, sequestered away by a kindly-looking patrol officer. Grey placed a hand on John's shoulder, and with the other, gestured to the side of the house. John picked up his kit, straightened, and made his way onto the lawn.

The sides of houses are odd places. Sometimes they're thorough-fares, sometimes afterthoughts. This house's left flank was full of thick, dense trees, many of them spilling over the neighbour's fence. There was a strong earthy scent here, and the chirruping of distant birds filtered through the damp foliage. Halfway down, his arm already aching from the overloaded bundle of gear, John stopped to stretch. And that's when something caught his eye.

The fuse box.

The rusted rectangle, bolted to the side of the house, sat there calling to him. Maybe it was the mood he was in that made him want to give the hatch a poke; maybe it was the odd smell that had begun to fill his nostrils. It was like someone's home cooking, and it made him weirdly homesick. The hatch was warm to the touch, and as John put on his gloves, with Grey watching intently, he pulled it open. It stuck for a moment, then popped away with a dull *sprong* sound, and there before them was a truly awful piece of improvised electrical work.

The wiring on one of the main fuses had been replaced with what appeared to be a nail. Everything around it was blackened, and the nail itself almost coursed with residual energy. John turned to look at Grey. 'The power's clearly been turned off, but . . . holy shit. This thing has been carrying some serious current.'

Grey nodded, eyeballing the nail, which sat there like a pulsing iron tooth in a charred square mouth. 'Yes. Power was cut off. But what do you think has happened there, John?'

'Well, at a guess,' John replied, 'someone has whacked a nail in there to stop the fuse shorting out. Which would imply . . . it shorted out a lot. Maybe the owners got impatient, got sick of having to run down and fix it, thought they'd do something truly dangerous like this. Something has gone wrong inside, obviously, else we wouldn't be called. But . . . oh god. The fuse wouldn't trip, meaning that whatever happened . . .'

'Kept happening,' finished Grey. Now he, too, bore an ominous look. 'Come on,' he said, patting John in a conciliatory manner. 'Best head inside.' And so they did.

That's when the smell of food got stronger. 'Are you hungry?' John asked Grey. Grey shook his head, and stared off into the distance, like an animal that had sensed the approach of some terrible quarry. He looked over at the back entrance to the house, and trotted up the steps ahead of John. And when John headed inside and reached his mentor in the bathroom doorway, he wasn't hungry anymore, either.

Here's what John and Grey saw in the bathroom.

John was right, as it turns out. His instincts regarding the fuse box were bang on, but the inability of the fuse box to short-circuit wasn't technically the cause of what had happened. This house that they were in, this unremarkable, tidy little suburban hamlet, housed a woman. An older woman who had kids, and who'd separated from her husband before the kids had grown into young men and moved away. It happens. But this woman didn't let it get her down. She adapted.

However, this woman's electricity kept crapping out. Every few weeks, a fuse would trip and she'd be plunged into darkness. And she'd swear, and stomp around, and yell 'FUCK!', and finally realise she couldn't call any family member to help out. Then it struck her. Her neighbour, a burly man with many practical skills, had mentioned once that he used to be a sparkie. You know how you accidentally let someone know you have a useful and widely applicable skill, and then for years afterwards you find yourself called upon to perform it over and over, with no pay and no regard? That's what happened with her neighbour. Not at first, mind you. The first time our single lady headed next door, knocked on the fly-screen and asked the ex-tradie for help, he happily obliged. 'Happy to oblige,' the man obliged, happily. He whacked in a new fuse, closed the fuse box, and patted it as if it were a horse being put out to stud. Then she, glowing and grateful, said, 'Thanks for the help!' and he, foolishly, said, 'Any time.'

The next time the fuse went out, she headed next door again. 'Sorry,' she said, genuinely sheepish. 'It happened. Again. And you said any time!' And she laughed, and he laughed, and there was much good humour to be had.

But then it kept happening, didn't it? It kept fucking happening. And she kept asking for help, not in a malicious way, mind. She didn't delight in knocking and waiting and watching as the tradie put in another new fuse, then another, then another. She wasn't getting off on this dance they were doing. But she grew . . . accustomed to his help. And so she forgot to thank him. And he got a little bitter.

So one night, after the lights had gone out and she'd pleaded for his help again, he heaved himself to a standing position and made his way to the door, not with a new fuse . . . but with a toolkit. And as he knelt there before the fuse box, he assembled an absolute Frankenstein's monster of a contraption: a fuse with a nail, hammered in place, where the copper wiring should be. *This,* he thought, *will never trip. And maybe now I can get some goddamn peace.* He slid the fuse in, the power hummed on, and now it was his turn to beam at her. 'See you again next time!' she joked. And he laughed, because he knew there wouldn't be a next time. Because this thing he'd cobbled together? It wouldn't blow. A never-ending fuse. *This should hold her over until she pops it,* he thought.

And a year passed. And the lights stayed on. And the woman grew lonely, and sad, because . . . well, because people do that, don't they? They get lonely and sad. It just happens sometimes. And one night, one dreadful night up the tail end of the week, this woman headed into her spacious bathroom. She plugged in her Speedie brand radiator, the one she used to keep her house warm, and got into the bath. And she dropped the radiator in. And the water cracked like lightning. And . . .

The fuse didn't blow.

She died instantly, of course. No way a human body can carry that much electricity in one go. But because the fuse didn't blow . . . the white-hot energy roaring down the line and into the water set the water to boil. And boil. And boil.

That Sunday, in the evening, two young men walked up the small flight of stairs leading to the front door and knocked. Nothing. *Where's Mum?* they thought. *It's time for our traditional Sunday roast.* They could smell something cooking. Perhaps she was in the kitchen? So after waiting a minute or so, they trotted back down the stairs and made their way around the side of the house, then headed in though the unlocked back door. And, having

looked everywhere else – and noticing the kitchen was unoccupied – they headed into the bathroom.

The first son to enter slipped on the floor, slick with a viscous
saffron tallow. The second didn't enter – didn't need to. He saw
enough from the doorway.

He saw what John and Grey saw. A skeleton in the bathtub. The
thirty centimetres of water had cooked off, reducing and turning to
steam, but this steam had a very high fat content.

They were breathing her in.

'How the hell do you process this?' I ask, feeling sick to my stomach.
Dad's been so deep in the story he looks like a sleepwalker roused
from a walk; he looks around, taking a moment to remember where
he is. And I expect him to parrot one of his usual lines, or fall back
on Grey's much-vaunted wisdom. Or say that he just had to get on
with it. But he doesn't.

'Sometimes . . . you can't. I . . .' An uncharacteristic pause. 'I can
still see her there, in the bathtub. With her heater in what was left
of her lap. And . . . mate, if I can't stop seeing her, I can't imagine
what her sons went through. I don't think you can ever recover
from some things. Certainly not from that.'

This, dear readers, is perhaps the first time Dad has implied that
what he's seen and done has traumatised him in some way. I don't
intend to push him on it just yet, so I sit there for a bit, letting him
recover, before changing the subject.

'Dad,' I venture, 'do you remember our old heater?' He looks
at me, curious. 'You know, the crappy old one. It wasn't a Speedie,
but . . . Do you remember . . . Sorry, but I just recalled this.
Did you ever see me camping in the lounge room, and . . . this is

gonna sound weird. But do you remember me toasting bread on the heater, and pretending I was camping? I'd get a wooden skewer, stick it through, and huddle there under a blanket. It was always after school. I was really little, and I would hang out pretending I was in the wilderness, cooking something exotic I'd foraged.'

Dad looks at me with the strangest expression. Finally, he speaks. 'I don't remember that, no. But do you want to hear something weird?' I nod. 'When I was little, living in Armadale, I was very bored, and very restless. And when I was little, when my parents were out of the house . . . I'd huddle in front of our old heater in our living room. And I'd hold up a slice of white bread and toast it.'

'And you pretended you were camping?'

'I pretended I was camping.'

We both sit there for a while, suppressing smiles. This might not seem like a big moment – both of us pretending we were living wild and roasting up the haunch of some fictional beast by a roaring fire while we were kids. But god, it feels huge to me. Like I've untangled some hidden strand of shared DNA.

Like I've found a shared heritage.

20

THE HELMET

John had been in Scientific about six months when he found the helmet.

It was the end of the hellish week wherein he'd dealt with the woman boiled in a bathtub, and John was exhausted. Drained of all energy. There's something unique about the torpor that creeps over you when you know you're nearing the finish line, and right now, he knew he was right on the precipice of a weekend with Christine and the kids. *If I ever have a week left to live,* John thought, *if I ever have a terminal illness and want to make what little time I have left yawn out in front of me, then I should have another week like this. Because right now, every minute feels like a fucking eternity.*

He'd got back to the office with Grey, the smell of the woman still thick in his nostrils. He'd put down his bag and watched as Grey hummed and waltzed to his corner desk, seemingly back on the horse. How did he do it? John marvelled at the man. They'd spent little to no time getting to know each other out of work. The huge ex-hippy, with twinkling eyes and constantly moving hands, sort of just disappeared at the end of every shift. He was a ghost: a helpful ghost haunting the building. How else could Grey rise above the things they were seeing? How could he bounce back? John made a mental note to piff some rock salt at Grey if he ever got the chance. If the guy screamed, he'd know for sure.

In the days since they'd got back from the woman's house, even the most banal fingerprint duties had felt intolerable. Rote. Ever had a substitute teacher stand in front of your class? Ever had them half-heartedly insist you finish your work? That was John's home stretch before this much-needed weekend. The office felt like a hot, sleepy classroom. John was running on fumes, waiting for the final bell to ring.

So imagine his relief when he got a call that there'd been a bad motorcycle spill that needed his attention. *Relief,* John reflected. *Is that odd? Is it odd to be relieved to have something to do, even something as horrible as this?* He'd long since jettisoned any notion that such a reaction was ghoulish. It was, of course, ghoulish – the idea that someone else's misery or death might liven up your uneventful shift – but that's just how it was. He'd internalised that fact, and Grey had helped him do so. He grabbed the tail of the call and let it yank him towards wakefulness. A crash. He took down the details, gesturing to Grey once he'd hung up.

'One more before we clock off?' John asked.

Grey turned slowly, like an Ent in tweed, and blinked at John. 'Of course,' he said, stifling a yawn. *Aha!* thought John. *So he does get tired. Maybe he's human after all.*

John drove, as Grey sat next to him, riffling through a sketchpad. They sat in silence, not because they had nothing to say, but because they'd grown comfortable enough with one another to enjoy such silences. John eventually crested a hill, one which dropped down at the kind of dizzying angle that only backstreets in specific Sydney suburbs could do. It was a death drop, girt by tiny houses, that careened back upwards ten metres on. It was, John noted, like sitting atop a frightening half-pipe, the kind you'd see at a skate park. And at the bottom, through sheafs of rain, he could see the accident. Grey tapped the dash and pointed.

John headed down, found a park a little way back, and pulled to a stop. It was about five in the afternoon, and it was beginning to get a little dark. A light rain had kicked up, black clouds sitting low in the sky. The noise from the accident had drawn a few people from their houses. Several windows were now open, with heads brazenly sticking out, while other windows showed people peering through venetian blinds at the partially obscured mayhem.

John hopped from the Kingswood, wincing in the rain. There was an odd *FLOOMP*, and suddenly, there was Grey, holding a freshly deployed umbrella over them both. They stood together and walked down towards the crash site. Once they made it to the perimeter and crossed the police line, John appraised what lay before them.

A green wooden bus shelter had detonated. Slats of the chartreuse timber had popped from their framework and scattered outwards across the road and footpath, and beyond, a motorcycle lay partially crumpled. Further away was a body, curled up at a strange angle. Further still lay the helmet.

Grey and John approached the officer on the scene, and they discussed the division of the workload. The officer was in no hurry to deal with the carnage, and asked if he could question the various heads peering from their windows. John said he'd like to check the body, if Grey was amenable to that. John knew Grey was amenable. 'I'm amenable,' said Grey, needlessly.

They made their way over to a prime spot. The first thing John noticed was the blood. Not the blood on the body, mind; he was still too far off to see any of that. No, John noticed blood on the huge fragments of the bus shelter.

'There wouldn't be any on the shelter, though,' I interjected. 'Right? I mean, you hit something at that speed, surely there'd be no time for—'

Dad waved to shut me up. 'I'll get to that.'

John knelt down carefully for a closer look, Grey's comically voluminous umbrella sheltering him. 'There's far too much blood,' he said, half to Grey, half to himself.

'There is,' Grey replied, casting an eye about. 'Notice anything unusual about it?'

John looked again. Now that Grey had brought it up, he noticed a lot of it had dried, meaning it . . . meaning . . .

He stood. 'This rain started pretty recently, right?' he asked. Grey nodded. John continued. 'The call for the accident came through about twenty minutes ago, and the shower started a good ninety minutes back. So something here doesn't . . . I can't believe I'm about to say this. It sounds clichéd.'

'It's okay,' said Grey, smiling. 'Sometimes clichés are clichés because they're true.'

'Right,' replied John. 'Something here doesn't add up.'

The rain seemed to agree, doubling its efforts to drown the scene. John stood there with Grey, staring out at the crime scene. Suddenly, he felt something. A pull, something drawing him towards a conclusion. Compelled to act on a strange and sudden hunch, some kind of lizard-brain impulse, he strode out from the sanctuary of the umbrella. He began hastily arranging the largest of the bus shelter fragments on the road in front of him.

It was slow going at first. He wasn't getting soaked, as it was only really sprinkling, but the encroaching darkness made it harder to see. He picked up piece after piece of the devastated wooden shelter, turning the splintered pieces over in his hands before placing them down. It was a puzzle, that's all. A large, dreadful puzzle. After a minute or so of dashing to and fro under the watchful eye of the decidedly dry Grey, he was done. And as he gazed down at his finished puzzle, the weight of what had happened here hit him full force. It wasn't just a reassembled shelter he was staring down at anymore.

It was a target.

Someone had painted a target in blood on the shelter.

He turned to Grey, shock in his eyes. 'This wasn't an accident.'

Now it was Grey's turn to look shocked. He stared down at the bullseye, eyes wide. 'No, it wasn't, John. This . . . this was a suicide.'

John stood up a little straighter, suppressing the urge to run over to the body. He glanced towards the houses; the other officer was still busy questioning people. Another cop was cordoning off the scene. The body still lay there, prone.

'He hit his mark,' John said to Grey. 'He planned this, drew a target . . . then drove at it. And he hit it.'

Grey nodded, scribbling notes. 'John, go and check the body, would you?'

John, still reeling from what he'd discovered, approached the prone figure. Denim jacket, gloves, boots. He took in the details. About five feet ten inches. Broken leg, broken . . . well, broken everything. And . . .

No head.

John looked ruefully over at the helmet, realising he was going to have to go and get it. He walked, staring down at his shoes, rain now drenching them. And finally, he reached the helmet. He reached down.

Heavy. It was heavier than a helmet ought to be. And then, because he was curious, and too tired to be thinking clearly, he turned the helmet over. There, peeking out from inside, was a head. The rider's head, wedged there inside, eyes wide open. John blanched, almost starting and letting the helmet drop. But he held on, lowering it as calmly as he could.

He stood back up, suddenly sick to his stomach. He looked back at Grey, who'd not picked up on John's discovery yet. Only moments earlier, he'd felt like Sherlock Holmes. He'd felt high on waves of adrenaline after solving an honest-to-god mystery. An actual puzzle, one that he'd solved. A puzzle with life-and-death stakes, the last act of a disturbed mind, and he'd been buzzing, slapping himself on the back, while metres away lay this person. This actual person. He felt sick. He was furious at the residual smugness still coursing through him.

A tap on the shoulder made him jump. He turned and saw Grey, with his big, kind, wizened face. 'You doing all right? You look a little rattled, John.' John sighed. *Was* he rattled? Or was he just tired? 'Everything seems worse when you're worn out,' Grey offered helpfully. 'Good find, though, John. Excellent police work. Really, just excellent.'

John appreciated the compliment, but there was a headless young man lying in pieces around them. He shifted uneasily. Grey, sensing John's utter fatigue, gave him a pat on the back.

'Anything you need me to handle, John? Anything I can do to help, you know. Take some pressure off before the weekend?'

John thought for a moment. Eventually, he murmured a reply.

'Yeah. Take care of that helmet, would you?'

21

THE VANS

I sometimes worry about Dad. I mean: a headless body. The head, wedged inside a helmet. He goes on to tell me, seemingly non-plussed, that once they checked the driver's licence, they found out the guy was seventeen. He'd got the motorcycle as a birthday present from his family. Why would he drive it into a bus shelter, I ask? Why would he weaponise a display of love from his parents like that? Why would his first ride on a gift from them end up being his last ride ever?

Dad has, throughout this process, conceded the point that certain things are 'fucked up, mate'. He'll do so in a deep, deadpan voice, and shake his head solemnly. Rarely, very rarely, will he betray anything other than stoicism. But I'm starting to suspect it's not because he's afraid of showing his emotions. It's because he's afraid of what will happen if he does: admitting there's a problem *means there's a problem*. If you act like it's all fine, all part of the job, you can get on with life. They say to dress for the job you want. Well, Dad is dressing for the job he wants: a sane, functional man. His clothes are proof for everybody watching that he's okay. And I learned long ago that critiquing Dad's clothing choices always goes badly.

'Dad,' I say. 'Listen. This kid . . . he wanted to end his life. He planned it, and he did it. Do people always plan ahead?'

'Yes,' he replies. 'In fact, there's this bloody awful thing that people about to die of suicide will do. See, they're suddenly happy.'

'Happy?'

'Yes. Happy. Because they've finally made up their mind about what they're going to do, and it gives them . . . clarity. Finally, they've got a plan to deal with . . . whatever they're going through. So they cheer up! And they start giving things away. They start being super generous. I've seen it happen, it's very common. So that kid, on the bike . . . I'll bet he was great company. Before . . . well. You know.'

There's that face again. I'd better distract him. Better stub his toe.

'Any other cases during Forensics involving bizarre, elaborate methods of suicide?'

His eyes go wide, and I know I've succeeded in distracting him. And we dive on in.

John and Grey, near the end of their first nine months together at Scientific, found themselves dealing with more suicides than normal.

They tackled them with the same level of dispassionate detachment as always, of course. But John, who'd always run at life's problems, found suicides a little confronting. Just a little, mind you, but having to confront the finality of what these people had done – and worse, having to clean up the aftermath – was wearing. John, you see, wasn't prone to depression. Or anxiety. Or any form of mental illness, really. He was, despite his chosen profession, an optimist. Grey had noticed this in John, and commented on it one day, as they headed to yet another suicide: 'You're an optimist, John. Do you know that?'

John looked at Grey, then changed gears and took a left turn, raising an eyebrow in the process. 'An optimist? You think I'm optimistic?'

'Yes. Well, you speak in a bit of a monotone register and get lost in thought, but you also assume the best about people. It's very helpful for me, to be honest – the last lad I worked with here, about your age, actually, was a bloody downer. Wouldn't stop moaning. But you like your work, you like people, and the job hasn't made you cynical. In spite of all you've seen, you're an optimist.'

John continued driving, smiling, grateful.

'Well,' piped up Grey again. 'That, or you're profoundly stupid.'

A solid drive later, they arrived in the bush near Stanwell Tops, south of Sydney. John parked the Kingswood in a tiny car park that was full of emergency services vehicles, and ratcheted up the handbrake.

'So,' he said, wearily, 'Grey. I've noticed you never help carry the gear.'

'No,' replied Grey. 'No, I don't.'

'Is there a reason you don't help carry the gear?'

Grey thought about this for a moment. 'Yes,' he finally replied. He then nodded, muttered 'yes' once again, and hopped out of the vehicle. John stared straight ahead and considered this. If he'd ever been paired with a weirder person, he couldn't recall who.

The two men grabbed the gear – well, John did – and made their way over to the police cordon. There were a lot more cops than were normally at these kinds of crime scenes. John knew it was a suicide – after all, Grey had told him. But Grey seemed even more absent-minded than usual, which probably meant it was a bad one. Whenever it was a bad one, Grey's higher brain functions seemed to go into overtime, meaning he sort of just drifted along behind John, like a charming yet decidedly unhelpful balloon.

Grey bantered with a couple of uniformed officers, turned back to John and nodded, and they began their trek past the treeline and down the trail towards the crime scene.

It was a warm afternoon, the bush was dry, and the gumtrees around them were unfathomably tall. Twigs cracked underfoot like little firecrackers going off, and the leather strap on John's kit bag was making his shoulder ache.

'You right there, John?' Grey enquired, hopping deftly along the trail.

John looked up, wincing. 'Are you offering to help me with my bag?'

'No. Just seeing if you're all right.' Grey smiled, and gestured ahead. 'I think I see it.'

Sure enough, there it was. The crime scene, marked by police tape. It extended from an enormous chalky white gumtree all the way into the distance.

The two men ducked under the fluttering tape, and John popped his kit on the forest floor. Around the gumtree was rope. Two lengths of rope, actually: thick and tied tightly. John followed the lengths of rope with his eyes. They traced unwaveringly into the woods, and already John had a feeling. Grey clearly had it, too; the two of them eyeballed one another, gave an 'Oh well, in for a penny' look, and after nodding at the uniformed officer standing guard, began to carefully follow the ropes.

'I already suspect I know what this is,' said Grey, beginning to sweat in the heat. 'But I dearly hope I'm wrong.'

'You're not wrong very often,' said John.

'True,' replied Grey. 'But it'd be nice to get this one wrong, believe me.'

They kept walking, one on either side of the rope trail, like Hansel and Gretel following a trail of breadcrumbs. Then, in the distance, they saw it. The end of the rope. The end of the trail.

Two heads.

It was obvious, even from a great distance, what they were looking at. Each length of rope ended in a noose, and in each noose was a human head.

John halted in his tracks. 'Was . . . was this what you were expecting?' he asked Grey, panting from the hike.

Grey squinted, wiping sweat from his brow with the back of his sleeve. 'Yep.' And that's all he said. He snapped on his latex gloves and they walked over to inspect the heads, which lay there in a bed of dead leaves, staring blankly up at the canopy overhead. John realised he'd seen more detached heads over the past year than he had in his entire police career-to-date. *Should I be keeping a tally?* he thought. *No. Probably not the best idea.*

A man and a woman. That much was obvious. Necks broken, heads popped out of the bodies they belonged to with a terrible force, a shocking finality. The eyes on both heads were half open.

'If it's any consolation,' said Grey, inspecting the man, 'they would have died very, very quickly. Instantly, in fact. That's one of the only good things about losing your head, John.'

John grimaced. He then noticed that the head he was inspecting was grimacing, too, and dropped the expression, pursing his lips and standing up. Grey followed suit.

'Now, here's the interesting part, John. The part that will really get you. Look around. What do you see, hear, smell?' This was par for the course with Grey. He was still in mentor mode; every time they hit a crime scene, he'd slip into this teacher mentality, asking John to stretch out with his feelings, to intuit what was going on, to push himself. John liked this part. It helped him detach himself from the tragedy that lay on the ground in front of them.

John looked around for a full minute, eyeballing everything from the ground up. Finally, he turned to Grey.

'Two things,' he said, brain working feverishly. He pointed at the ground. 'Tyre tracks, leading from the tree to here.' Grey nodded. So far, so good. John continued. 'And . . . the smell of exhaust fumes. So I'm guessing . . .' He strolled a few feet away, then turned back to Grey, jaw set, eyes dark. 'They didn't.'

Grey nodded again. 'They did, John.'

'They fucking *didn't*.'

They fucking did.

'They did what?' I ask, desperate to know what the hell had gone down here. Dad, now looking like Grey, eyes wide and hands spread enthusiastically, begins to paint a picture for me.

'They . . . well, this couple had agreed to kill themselves. We don't know why, and figuring out the why of it all unfortunately wasn't our job at Scientific. We were there to figure out the what and the how of it all. So this couple, mid-twenties, pretty normal pair. They agree to kill themselves at the same time, and they have a panel van. So they buy two lengths of extremely long, extremely strong rope. They drive their van into the woods. But do you know what was just through the treeline past where we found their heads?'

Speaking of heads, I shake mine. Dad continues. 'A cliff, Paul. A very steep cliff. What they'd done was back up to that huge tree. Then, they opened the back window of the panel van, tied the ropes around the tree, and threaded the rope through to the front of the van. They tied the rope around their necks, probably wished each other luck . . .'

'*. . . Then fanged it over the cliff,' I finish, winded.*

'*Over the cliff. Pulled their heads clean off. Both dead instantly, at the exact same time.' He sits there, letting me stew in this dreadful revelation. It takes me a moment to process the imagery, the logistics.*

'*But . . . why was this so elaborate? Why a van? Why a cliff?'*

Dad shakes his head. 'No idea, mate. But remember how I said Grey worried he knew what this was?'

I nod. 'Well,' he says, 'that's because . . . and this is the really fucked-up part. That's because it had happened before.'

'What do you mean, this has happened before?' asked John.

'*Wait. Is he talking to you?' I ask.*

Dad looks confused. 'No, he's talking to Grey.'

I raise an eyebrow. 'Are you sure?'

'Who are you talking to?' asked Grey, confused. He placed a hand on John's shoulder as they stood at the edge of the cliff, the remains of the annihilated panel van far, far below, like a crumpled discarded paper cup.

John looked up at Grey, confused. 'Did . . . did you hear something just now?'

Grey shook his head. 'Hear what?'

'A voice,' replied John vaguely. 'You know what? Never mind. That was . . . odd.'

Dad looks a little unsettled. 'Did . . . did he just hear us?'

I laugh, waving the notion away. 'No! Of course not, Dad. Don't be stupid. Just some crossed wires.' I point at the notebook, indicating Dad should continue.

'Right,' said Grey. 'Well, it's been happening. Over and over. You've probably not heard about it because . . . well, the blokes upstairs are trying to keep it from reaching the public. People looking to do this to themselves are very . . . suggestible. Once an idea on how to do it gets out there, it's like it hits the collective bloodstream and suddenly there are copycats. Now . . . there've been no media leaks. None. But this? I've seen this twice already, and there've been a lot more up and down the coast. I don't know how the hell people are finding out about these, but we need to keep it quiet. But . . .' Grey trailed off, looking once again at the ruined van below, a gust of warm wind tousling his hair. 'But this is just such a waste. Such a waste.'

Now Dad is shaking his head. I realise that now he probably looks more like Grey did back then; he's grown into himself, become more eccentric. Clearly, working with Grey left more of a mark on him than I ever knew. I remember hearing his stories from his time in uniform, before he leapt into forensics. And I remember how . . . simple he seemed. Not intellectually, obviously, but tonally. He had a clean, precise approach to things. Now, though, he's getting a little weathered, a little more interesting. And as he tells me about Grey, I'm noticing that Dad has clearly picked up Grey's mannerisms, too; the hand gestures, the barking laugh, the raised eyebrow. And perhaps, I reflect, it's because Grey is the first person he was paired with

on the force to actually take a moment, look at a dead person,
and tell John—

'It's fucked up, mate,' Grey said quietly, patting John on the
shoulder, the two of them staring into the abyss together.

'It's fucked up, mate,' says Dad, holding his notebook up,
sighing.

22

ON THE BEAT

It's that time for the story to take a bit of a turn, folks.

'Dad,' I say hesitantly, not entirely comfortable raising the topic. Isn't that strange? All the dark things he and I have dived into, and I still haven't mustered the resolve to broach this topic. He's standing up, stretching.

'Have you mentioned yet that I soft-sand run?' he asks, distracted. He keeps bending from side to side, swinging until a vertebra or two gently pop. He sighs happily at the noise. 'Every morning. It's important to stay fit, Paul.' He's not wrong, but I resist the urge to follow his subject change, and push on.

'Bullying,' I say. He stops, looking over at me.

'Bullying?'

'Bullying. Yes.'

He approaches and sits, the soft upholstery making a lovely *FOOF* sound around him. 'Sure,' he says. 'I can talk about bullying.'

And just like that, we're talking about it.

*

Back when John was in General Duties, he'd occasionally do what was referred to as community outreach. In the eighties, the cops in Sydney had a serious image problem – they were seen as thugs, given to corruption and assaulting suspects. They were, in short, slipping out of public favour. One of the moves the New South Wales Police Force made was to enlist female officers, like Christine, but a far broader approach entailed encouraging officers to focus on the little things.

So when John received a call sending him to help a very wealthy woman in Mosman with a minor matter near the tail end of an uneventful shift, he thought . . . sure. Community outreach. Small things.

Just to be clear, he didn't know what he was in for at first. He figured he'd head along, smile, shake hands, kiss babies. But when he arrived at the palatial Mosman home and was ushered inside by the middle-aged woman dripping in jewellery, he finally found out what was going on.

'Bullied?' John asked, nursing the orange juice he'd been forced to take from the woman, her necklaces and bracelets jangling like bells. He shifted uncomfortably, casting his eye around the room. The house was incredible from the outside, but the inside was pure opulence. All the furnishings were art deco, and . . . wait. Was that a . . .

'Matisse. It's a Matisse,' purred the woman, walking over to the painting and waving a manicured hand. 'Lovely, yes? Anyway, I know this sounds silly. But Jamie is being bullied. Horribly, horribly bullied. Won't leave his room, won't stop crying. We've tried everything, talked to teachers, dropped him off every day at school, *not* dropped him off, given him time off. Nothing. It won't stop.'

John wasn't sure what he was actually meant to do. He was a

cop, sure, and cops helped people. But bullying? Bullying wasn't police business. And the family was clearly rich. *Couldn't they just . . . buy him a bodyguard?* John thought. *A suit of armour? Perhaps pay a sharpshooter to linger five miles away at all times, a little red dot appearing occasionally on the forehead of errant antagonists?* He didn't say any of this, of course. What he said instead, after exhaling deeply, was, 'Let me have a chat with the little fella.'

The mother, exceedingly grateful, practically bundled John up in a hug. She led him up a winding set of vast carpeted stairs, and into the boy's bedroom. Sure enough, there he was: Jamie. Sullen, cowering like a wounded animal in the corner. Any pretence John had of indifference, any weird class hang-ups he harboured, dissipated. And he found himself doing something he'd always been rather good at: comforting people.

He did it all. Knelt down, getting to eye level with the kid. He smiled, explained who he was. And they talked, they just talked, for a good twenty minutes. It was striking, John realised later, how much the kid opened up the second he saw John kneeling there, taking his hat off and holding it gently, turning it over and over as he talked. John had a kid, after all. *What if,* he thought, *this was Paul, or Anne? Wouldn't I want to help them, too?*

After the conversation wrapped up and the mother tearfully thanked him, John did something rather foolish, though.

He promised the kid he'd help.

The next day, during a particularly dead period in an uneventful shift, he and Julian pulled up outside the kid's school. John walked over to the fence and spotted the kid among a threatening clutch of twelve-year-olds. Jamie hadn't been lying – he was, even now, being bullied. A larger kid was jeering at him, yanking at the hem of his shirt and poking him in the stomach over and over.

Then the bully saw John. He and the other kids all turned, and Jamie's eyes practically popped out of his head. John felt like Falkor, the luck dragon from *The NeverEnding Story*, poised to swoop in and drive them into a dumpster. Instead, he beckoned the bully over. The sight of a uniformed police officer didn't appear to faze him, but as the kid sauntered over, John noticed the slight tremor in his lip. He leaned against the bars of the fence and eyeballed John. John knelt down again, glancing over at the group, all utterly rapt and terrified.

'Listen,' John whispered, just loud enough to be heard by the bully. 'See that kid over there?' He pointed, making sure the bully nodded his understanding. 'Well, he's a friend of mine. Yes? And if I find out you've done anything to him – and I do mean anything – I'll be back.' The bully stood frozen. John leaned in closer, whispering as quietly as he could. 'You got that? I'll be back,' he finished, channelling Arnie just a little. Then he stood up, waved cheerfully at the kid he'd come to rescue, and headed back to the car.

Once inside, Julian laughed. 'What did you say to him?'

John waved it off, starting the car. 'I just told him to pull his fucking head in and to stop picking on people.'

Julian shook his head. 'Better be careful, mate. This is a fancy school. He could be chief of police someday.'

John shook his head. 'Not that one. That one's gonna work at Coles, mark my words.'

I stare at Dad, speechless.

I'm not often speechless. Just to be clear, though, it's not a good speechless. See, I never knew this story. I didn't know Dad went vigilante for the sake of bullied children everywhere. And if I had known, I'd not be as conflicted, as mad, as downright confused as I am now. And let me tell you something, folks. I am fucking ropeable.

'Dad,' I say, as calmly as I can, 'let me tell *you* a story.'

And that's exactly what I do.

When Paul Verhoeven was a kid, he attended an all-boys school. It was situated, like some mean, shitful, squat thing, atop a wind-blown clifftop, a short drive from a bustling surf community. Paul's parents were incredible people, both ex-cops, and he loved them very much. But at some point, they decided to send their willowy, acne-marred son – whose favourite pastime was wilfully reading Tintin books under an umbrella in the rain – to what, by all accounts, was a prison for boys for whom necks were but a distant dream. This school, which for the sake of discretion we shall not name here, was called St Paul's Catholic College, and I can only surmise that the name is what made this simmering pubescent gulag stand out to John and Christine. When your son's name is right there on the sign out front, maybe it seems like kismet.

Paul was an odd kid. His ADHD had turned his brain into a cluster bomb of ideas, all going off at once in his head, but the friends he accrued were brilliant. They understood him. He had never really grasped the finer points of social interaction. His best friend for decades, Anthony Stenmark, had been sitting there in the playground of their primary school when Paul waltzed up to him, robotically asked, 'Would you like to be friends?' and Anthony, to his credit, said yes. People either liked Paul, not minding that he seemed incessantly distracted, restless, bored and wildly indecisive, or couldn't stand him. And that's fine. He was doing fine.

Then, one term into Year Six, John and Christine did something that changed Paul's life forever. They moved one suburb over. As part of a move Paul never really understood, they forced him to change schools. He spent the last three terms of primary school at a Catholic school in Manly Vale, ten minutes' walk from his new house, and it was at this school that he was bullied into a fine paste.

It was, for Paul, like moving from Springfield to Shelbyville. Everything was slightly out of whack; gaunt, loping bullies wandered like drunken kaiju from classroom to classroom. Many of his teachers, presumably drunk on power, treated him with abominable disdain whenever he didn't respond to their questions monosyllabically. This school simply didn't know how to cater to his popping, fizzing little brain.

Now, Paul wasn't his father. He didn't have a thick skin; he couldn't look at a problem and stare it down. He wasn't used to being treated contemptuously for being different, and he responded to it very badly.

Paul was, in short order, spat on, kicked, and covered in yoghurt. Where did they get all that yoghurt from, exactly? They seemed to have an inexhaustible supply of the stuff. In an array of flavours, too; Paul became adept at identifying brands of yoghurt by viscosity alone. Once, during assembly, Paul was out the front of the entire school, ready to give a presentation, and one of his classmates yanked his pants down around his ankles. He stood there in shock for what seemed an eternity, pale legs practically incandescent from lack of sunlight. Having four hundred of your peers laughing at you and your nether region is sort of a – if you'll forgive the choice of words – hard one to pull out of.

Eventually, the bullies found out where Paul lived, and they took to jeering his name at him outside his house at night, even going so far as to hurl food at his windows as they passed by from time to time. Once, he was lifted up in front of a group of girls by a boy named Patrick and then hurled at a rocky outcrop, where he almost shattered his coccyx. After, he had to limp home while being jeered at. And every time he arrived home, he wondered how his dad would have handled it. And he wondered why he wasn't able to exude some of his dad's air of authority.

At one point, for a class project, Paul spent a full day building a haunted house in the classroom. When the time came to set it all off and let people through, one boy jammed his hand in a door and then claimed credit for the bulk of the project. Which, to be fair, worked out well for Paul. The haunted house was contrived and derivative. In that respect, he was probably the forerunner for Jerry Bruckheimer.

Every day there was a living hell, and the only place Paul could safely retreat? Books. In particular, he kept diving back into his Choose Your Own Adventure books. Leafing through the flimsy paperbacks, pages yellowed and dog-eared, he began to wonder if he'd made a wrong choice somewhere along the line. Perhaps he could have said something differently, gone into a different room, responded in a different way the day he arrived at this hellish school.

Once he was done with his book collection at home, he'd borrow new ones from the school library where, according to their smudged borrowing slips, they'd remained untouched for years. The librarian, who hated everyone within her domain, often made it difficult for Paul to borrow more than one at a time. And so, one week before graduating from primary school, he looked into his mother's face. When an unbelievably pale, sad twelve-year-old tells you, 'I just can't cope anymore,' you tend to pay attention. So she hugged her son, assured him everything would be fine, and she and his dad said he should go and pick up anything he needed from school.

He sauntered into the library, crammed a veritable treasure trove of books into his library bag, then coasted past the librarian and out into the yard. He walked past the unattended lunchbox of the genius who had pulled his pants down and punted the shit out of it, sending sandwiches and a fruit roll-up skittering across the playground. He got home, told his parents what he'd just done – which they quietly applauded – and spent the next week tucked up on the sofa under a doona, being brought hot soup and toast so buttery it made his eyes water.

After this primary school from hell he ended up at St Paul's, the all-boys Catholic high school that we in no way name-checked earlier, where every single bully from the primary school had also ended up. Several of whom had seen the lunchbox-kicking incident, and punished him accordingly for the next six years. But thankfully, many of his friends went there, too; later in his life, Paul realised it was the littlest bit like being Harry Potter, surrounded by loyal, stalwart Gryffindor chums, but also the reprehensible, fatuous gits from Slytherin.

After a year or so of high school, Paul had managed to get back together with his old friends and make some new ones, and because this was high school, his weirdness suddenly became less weird and more appealing. His indecisiveness gained an edge of wit, and endeared him to most of his teachers. He also (somehow) managed to not reignite the ire of the bullies who'd hounded him so badly.

And then, one particularly freezing morning, the school bus deposited him and a handful of classmates off earlier than intended. It was winter, and it was a Tuesday, and the mandatory sports day uniform – naught but tiny shorts, shirt and a windcheater – did little to shield the cold. And on that freezing morning, outside that poor excuse for an educational institution, in an attempt to impress some kids who already liked him anyway, Paul's brain made a truly tragic decision.

The playground at St Paul's was essentially a vast, barren spread of asphalt, interrupted occasionally by lone gumtrees which were surrounded by timber fences about a metre off the ground. Boys would congregate around these at lunch – partly because they made good places to hang out with like-minded people, and partly because the boys were addicted to the hallucinogenic sap that the trees secreted.

Problematically, Paul had begun to like being the centre of attention, and he saw an opportunity. He listened to his brain whispering, nodded sagely, and proceeded to crawl up onto the wooden fence that surrounded one of the craggy, flaking trees the boys worshipped. He then balled himself up by slipping his legs inside the windcheater. He carefully withdrew his arms, leaving two sleeves dangling, useless, like two plaintive windsocks. Then, because sometimes young boys are absolute idiots, he sat there, perched like a supercilious bird, and began yelling, 'Hey! Hey, guys! Check it out!'

By this point, he'd failed to notice that another busload of boys had arrived. One walked quite close to Paul. Paul was startled, and began to teeter dangerously, like some drunken sunflower, swaying first back one inch, then forward two inches. Still entirely bound up inside his top, he was like a priceless vase rocking itself towards the edge of a mantelpiece. His friends were frozen, watching wide-eyed; his enemies bore sickening grins of anticipation. And then, slowly, gracefully, and with singular purpose, he toppled forward, landing face-first with a sickeningly wet crunch on the asphalt.

He somehow rolled onto his back, and his friends began laughing along with him at his apparent joke. But Paul wasn't laughing; he was coughing up what turned out to be bits of gravel, bone and gristle. And blood. There was a lot of blood; black and thick and cloying, as though someone had blended his insides. He later recalled gurgling the word 'help', at which point Anthony came forward and unzipped him. His limbs splayed outwards, deployed like four useless parachutes, and from there, things sort of went black.

Fortunately, the school was situated right next to Manly Hospital. Paul was carried there and put under the kind of anaesthetic one prays they'll accidentally be prescribed; a thick, pink fog encircled him, and he spent what seemed like days doing what he'd always done – wondering what if. What if he hadn't made such a bizarre, dickhead move? What if he'd chosen to do something else? Such as, I don't know – *not* invite disaster? And then, the worst thought of all crept in: what if he'd been inviting bullies to take pot shots at him all this time? What if he was the problem all along?

At the hospital, Paul was told that both of his cheekbones had been shattered, and his nose was not much of a nose anymore. He looked into a mirror and saw a frighteningly washed-out kid with a white plaster over his nose, and two blackened eyes.

When he went back to school three days later – the proper surgery couldn't be done for a few weeks, for some reason – the caveman holdovers still bearing grudges from primary school smelled blood in the water. Or possibly urine; Paul may have pissed himself involuntarily when he was on the ground bleeding. They gave him a handy new nickname: Panda.

Every day for the next three years, anywhere from between thirty and a hundred random boys, desperate to finally have someone else to pick on – the abused always kick downwards – would yell that nickname at Paul. It didn't matter that the panda was, and is, a delightful animal. The word 'panda' was spat out with venom and generally accompanied by another word: 'defect'. After a while, the 'defect' thing stuck, and people just went with calling him that. Then they started hitting him; shoving him down stairs, hurling his lunchbox into the road. In woodwork, he had a wire brush dragged across the backs of his legs, taking two raw, pink bands of skin away. He had fruit pelted at his head. He had dog shit left in his backpack. He was slapped, hard, regularly. And once, a bully referred to his wit as 'pedestrian'.

PEDESTRIAN.

After his final round of reconstructive surgery, Paul was a mess. His eyes were blackened, again. His acne had kicked in, his voice was breaking like that of a busted yodeller being hot-wired against their will, and his nose was covered in scabs. And again, yet again, he wondered, *Why am I not like Dad? What shitty choices could I have changed to end up somewhere better?*

'I guess what I'm asking, Dad, is . . .'

I trail off. I'm winded. Dad's expression is unreadable, but kind. 'What?'

'Why didn't you help? I know it's clumsy. I know it's obvious. But you went up, in uniform, to a school to stop a kid being bullied. Why didn't you help me?' I blurt all of this out, by the way. My eyes are burning, and I'm on the verge of tears. Dad, struggling to make eye contact, leans forward a little.

'What was I supposed to do? Walk up there, not in uniform anymore? I'd just be some guy, some dad, doing what you're not supposed to do – getting too involved. Because those fuckheads, Paul, they could smell weakness. And the second I left, they'd bully you *more* because you'd gone and sent your dad to stick up for you. It broke our hearts, and we were there at the principal's office, begging him to step in. But no matter how much we pushed them, it didn't make a difference. So we decided to do everything we could outside of school. We were there for you as much as we could be when you got home. But I couldn't have just strolled in there and thrown people against walls.'

'I wish you fucking would have!' I yell, startling both Dad and myself.

'It wouldn't have helped.' He pauses. 'I don't know. Maybe I should have. But those boys were animals, and nothing I could have done . . . shit. I don't know.'

We both sit there quietly, unsure of how to continue. Finally, I speak. 'What about primary school? Why did you make me change schools in Year Six?'

'That was a fuck-up. And I don't know if Christine and I have ever pointed this out, but we're human, and we fuck up some-times. We thought it would make things easier for you, being able to walk to school. And it was just three terms before you went to high school. We were both working multiple jobs, didn't have time to think, and before we knew it, for us, the year was over. But as you've made very clear, for you, the year was—'

'An eternity,' I finish. More silence. 'I'm not mad at you, Dad. I'm just . . . Look. Maybe I am mad. You spent your career pro-tecting people, including going to a school and stopping a bully in his tracks, and I went through hell. *Hell.* Every second day of my school life was torture. If what had been done to me happened at the workplace, those people wouldn't just be fired, they'd be charged and arrested. So how the hell is it okay for it to happen to children? And how the hell was it okay for it to happen to me? Over and over?' My voice is building in volume, and I catch myself, throwing Dad an apologetic look. 'Jesus. Maybe I should have talked this through with someone.'

'You did,' Dad says. I throw him a confused look. 'We took you to a child psychiatrist. He's the one who diagnosed you with ADHD. He also diagnosed you with anxiety, depression, a bunch of other things. So he prescribed you Ritalin, Aropax. You gotta understand, mate, you're amazing. You're just incredible. And you're unique. But having a teenager is like playing fucking whack-a-mole. There's so much going on, so many crises popping up. Spot fires everywhere. We tried as hard as we could. Of course we could have done more, of course we could. But between you, and your sister, and your younger brother, and after decades in emergency services . . . we couldn't fix everything.'

Now it's Dad's turn to look teary. And I realise that I've just yelled at my dad, my beautiful, weird dad, and upset him. The last time we both cried together was at the end of *Paddington 2*, at which point we almost passed out from dehydration. Now, though, we're two grown men, sitting across from each other, talking. Just talking. Dad wipes his eyes and perks up suddenly.

'Mate. Do you remember, after your nose was broken – you'd had your second lot of surgery, and you had two black eyes, huge white plaster? Dried blood everywhere. Real mess.'

'Yes. Thanks for reiterating that. And thanks for the colourful description.'

'No problem. Anyway, I thought . . . I thought it'd be nice, after all the bullying, and surgery, to take you out and treat you like a normal kid. Remember?'

I nod, a faint memory drifting back. He continues.

'So, I took you to see *The Cable Guy*, which was sort of terrible. Shit film. Anyway, we had a "no fast food" rule, so without Christine knowing, I took you out for a massive chicken burger and chips. And I remember you looking, just for a minute, really happy to be there. We were sitting at a shitty plastic table up the back of some Nando's down in Manly, and you looked like you'd just reached the end of a bloody war. You were so, *so* fragile. I just felt so sorry for you, mate. But I was so impressed. Not many people can go through that much and end up as . . . light, I guess, as you are. You didn't become mean. You didn't become cruel. I remember being impressed by that. And as we walked back to the car, I told you some stupid joke, and you laughed happily. But because of your busted head, you let out a kind of strangled, honking sound. And . . . remember this? You honked, and it grabbed the attention of this tiny adorable girl who was walking by with her mum, probably five years old. And then the girl looked up at your face, saw all the bandages and blood . . . and screamed! And she fucking ran away!'

Dad is now crying with laughter, doubled over. And I am, too.

Only Dad could reveal something so utterly revelatory, honest and beautiful . . . and then totally kill the moment immediately afterwards.

23

ALMOST

'Right,' says Dad, looking a little shaken. 'Paul. Can I level with you? Can I . . . What's the word for when you don't know something for sure, but you want to guess. It's an S-word.'

'Sword?'

'No,' he says, still distracted.

'Speculate. You want to speculate? That's not like you.'

And it's not. It really isn't. But hey, while we've got him here, and while he's being candid, why not let him speculate? It could be revealing.

He rolls his shoulders, sets his notebook down, and steeples his fingers.

Grey and John had spent the better part of the evening doing nothing. Absolutely nothing. Well, filing. Sorting fingerprint slides. Sipping acrid coffee. And then John did something he didn't normally do.

He headed out the door from Scientific, down the winding pathway and into the main station building to have a wander around.

It felt good to saunter among the uniformed officers, some clearly fresh out of the academy, looking him up and down with . . . if not reverence, then a moderate level of respect. He thought about his time in General Duties, his time sitting at a cramped desk, hat wedged onto his head, filling out paperwork. He gazed over at the dispatch room, catching a glimpse of the huge switchboard. He recalled one evening, early in his career, when he was working the switch and a young woman named Christine had wandered in mid-shift, taking her shoes off to stretch her calves. And he remembered a litany of fumbled meetings with her, a gradual, clumsy progression from utterly awkward to madly in love.

A uniform zipped past clutching a sheaf of papers, heading towards the switchboard, slapping him back into the present. Stray strands of conversations seized his attention.

'Another one.'

'Another one?'

'Northern Beaches. He's hit twice tonight, down the beaches.'

Curiosity piqued, John meandered down towards the dispatch room. He leaned around the corner as subtly as he could, and stood there in the alcove just outside, trying to remain discreet.

'Here's a fun fact,' Dad pipes up enthusiastically. 'You can walk into basically anywhere in the world if you act like you belong there. So I just stood there and acted like I was meant to be there, which absolutely works.'

'Wait,' I reply, unconvinced. 'I could walk in anywhere, and if I acted like I belonged there I could cruise on in?'

'Yes. The trick is giving off the air of someone who belongs there. It was easy for me, because I used to be a police officer, so I felt at home. So I just stood there and nobody noticed me *listening in. But I reckon I could walk into the UN if I was feeling confident.'*

I reckon he could, at that. Only dads have that level of confidence. The kind of confidence that says, 'I made human beings and have a home loan. Gaze upon me, for now I am become Dad, destroyer of worlds.'

And so, standing there, John imagined for a fleeting moment that he was a detective. Undercover. And he heard the phrase he'd been dreading; the one he and Grey had been rolling around. *The Northern Beaches Rapist.* And that's when he felt it. A winkle. His skin went cold, synapses crackling like popping candy in a wet mouth.

He leaned around the doorway, taking the two sergeants a little by surprise. They looked him up and down, and saw what he hoped they'd see: a plain-clothes cop, police special nestled in a shoulder holster.

'Fellas,' he said, suppressing the urgency in his voice, 'last seen where?' He was doing that thing: acting like he belonged there. *Imagine you're a detective,* he thought to himself.

'Detective Hard Seltzer?' I ask.
Dad smiles. 'Why not.'

And the two officers saw what John projected: detective. And they said, 'Ahh, Curl Curl, mate. Round there, anyway. You want an address?'

Detective Seltzer – or was it John? – shook his head. Something was buzzing around in his brain. Intuition, maybe, or paranoia. Weeks of theorycrafting and speculating in his office with Grey, whose flights of fancy could have carried the two of them skywards given the chance, had wound him up a little. Sure.

But his intuition had always served him well. So as calmly as he could, he gave a quick, curt thank you. He slipped away into the hubbub of the bullpens, cops whizzing about him like blue vapour trails. Fuzzily, he fumbled and bumbled his way out, headed down the path to Scientific, and wandered over to Grey. 'Mate. Mind if I knock off?'

Grey smiled and gave a sudden thumbs up. He then stood up, leaned forward, and booped John on his nose. He sat back down, picked up a tattered issue of *2000AD*, the grim visage of Judge Dredd leering up at John from the cover. John, beginning to feel as if this evening was going wrong on some profound level, walked out to the Kingswood.

And he drove.

The Kingswood was a blur, and felt to John like a stone skimming across the surface of a lake. John was a damn good driver, but was out of practice, having not gone above the speed limit in a year. Why would he have needed to? Forensics didn't require urgency, or at least not often. But John felt someone behind him, pushing him, urging him onwards.

Curl Curl. *Close,* he thought. *It's too close.*

What John meant, muttering to himself as he swung a corner, making a hairpin turn and rocketing away with frightening precision, was this: Curl Curl was too close to his home. The feeling he had might be nothing more than paranoia, fine. Sure. But he knew it wasn't. Somehow he felt as if he'd lifted up the piano lid of the universe and found a hammer broken. Curl Curl. It was too close.

John pressed his foot down, the needle on the speedometer wavering, straining, like the little train that could. *Almost there,* he thought, shifting gears again and running a red light, staring frantically about him to make sure he had his bearings. Satisfied, he slowed down, headed down a side street with a gentle skid, and minutes later pulled into the car park of the block of flats where he and Christine lived.

The red-brick building was a vast structure looking out over a public park, the kind that was unremarkable during the day and existentially menacing the second night fell. Across the road was a nature reserve, filled with acres of mangroves. And up, up, up on the third floor in a tiny apartment was John's family. It was late, and Christine was at home. *Asleep, probably,* John thought. *She's probably asleep, and so are the kids.*

'Paul,' Dad mutters apologetically, 'does this sound . . . stupid?'
'No,' I say. 'Doesn't sound stupid, Dad. Go on.'

John slammed the door of the Kingswood, the rubber seal sucking it shut like a fridge. *Shhhhump.* John looked around at the half-filled car park, bathed in pharmacy lighting, harsh and cold. A dog barked in the distance. And John looked at himself, at his hands, clammy, listened to his panting breath. He was panicked. Why was he panicked?

The work, said a voice coming from inside John's head. *The work is getting to you.* Maybe it was. And suddenly he felt a little silly for flipping out on a mad hunch and gunning it all the way from the station to his humble home, sitting here in the darkness across the road from a horde of oily, shifting, swampy trees.

He chuckled, slid his keys into his pocket and trotted to the glass door of the apartment block. He pulled it open, depressed the fat white button which would grant him thirty seconds of meagre light, and began to haul himself up the flights of stairs to the third floor. He walked along the landing towards his apartment door, fishing out his keys, and as he extended his hand . . .

The door creaked open.

BINK.

The light in the corridor guttered out.

John could hear his own heart beating. And there it was again: the winkle. That feeling. He felt the blood drain from his face, and for a moment insisted to himself that it was just a coincidence. *You've been thinking about this guy for a long time. You're projecting. Stop being fucking stupid, John. And if you are worried – really worried – call for fucking backup.*

He took a breath, eased the door open all the way, and peered into his apartment. Lights were out. No noise. *Good sign, John? Or bad?*

'No idea,' replied John.

He set foot into the hallway. At the very end of it lay the bedrooms: his and Christine's, and the one Paul and Anne shared. He began walking, suede shoes making no noise at all, until the corridor opened out into the lounge room. The streetlights outside cast amber shafts across the space, and John, feeling that feeling again, looked over at the sliding glass door which led to the balcony.

Open.

It was open.

With a high-pitched ringing sound suddenly filling his head, John dropped all pretence of holding it together and ran down the corridor towards his bedroom, flinging the door open. There, in the near-darkness, was Christine, asleep. John cast his eyes around the room. Nothing was amiss. And then he looked down at the bedside table. Paul had taken to playing with his police badge lately, as well as several of his mementoes from his time on patrol. And on the bedside table was his badge, his old police hat and his crisp blue shirt, kept as a memento but clearly confiscated from his son's grubby little hands.

Dad looks at me intensely.

'Now . . . here's what I think, Paul. I think he may have come in, seen the uniform and the badge, got scared, and gone out the front door. I went in, and Christine was asleep. Everything was fine. But I never . . . I never really forgot how that felt. I think I realised that night how fragile some things really are.'

Dad pauses, watching me to see how I'm handling this tale of a potentially life-altering near-miss. 'Now you know why I always made such a fucking noise about locking our doors at night. And here's the worst part. The next day, I went into my kit. I took my fingerprinting brush, and dusted the balcony window for prints.'

Dad pauses. I glare at him. 'And?'

'And,' he goes on, slowly, carefully, 'I found prints.'

'So . . . Jesus fucking Christ, Dad. Something . . . something almost happened,' I say, in utter shock.

Dad exhales, rubbing his face. 'Yeah. Almost.'

24

HYPNAGOGIC JERK

Mum comes in holding bags fit to burst full of fresh produce, bellows an enthusiastic greeting, and that's it. The bubble is broken. I look down at my third can of empty hard seltzer (Empty *Detective* Hard Seltzer to you), and check my phone. It's late. It's surprisingly late. Somehow, we've compressed years of a man's life into a single day of recording.

The man in question, sitting across from me bleary-eyed and yawning, gets up to greet his wife. My parents, everyone. There they are, decades older than they were moments previously.

One of the things about the way my brain works? When someone tells a story, I'm . . . well, I'm *in* the story. The reason I get so invested is because I'm transported there, mind and body.

This might sound weird, but the stakes of stories seem so much higher for me than they do for others. Even when I was a kid, reading those flimsy paperbacks Dad got me, I took them seriously. Every time I finished a book it felt like I was pulling myself free of the pages, as if I were swimming desperately from a sinking ship and watching it descend into the darkness below. It's the same now. Looking at Dad feels . . . wrong, somehow.

A minute ago, he was in his early thirties. Where did Grey go? Where's the Kingswood? *We have to go back!* the voice in my head bellows.

But I don't. Instead, I stick around and have a glass of wine with Mum and Dad. Dad continues combing the tassels on the rug, Mum mocks him for combing the tassels on the rug, I do an impression of him combing the tassels on the rug. We eat risotto. Make small talk. I hug them both goodbye, head outside and walk back to my Airbnb. It's a large, odd place in Kings Cross, and the rain is kicking up. As I get about halfway to the apartment, the sky breaks open, everything turns black, and suddenly it's bedlam. The air is so thick with rain that, had I the will, I could leap into the air and swim home. But I don't want to look foolish, so instead I run from cover to cover, laughing all the while.

The foyer of the building is dark – there's a long, gothic corridor, peeling wallpaper, faux-chandeliers winking in and out, and lush, red mildewy carpet so dense I almost get lost in it. I trudge up three flights of stairs and drag my sodden self into the apartment, and there's Tegan, sitting in the window seat, tapping away, working on a script. She turns to see me, laughs and runs over, and suddenly I'm out. I'm free of the miasma of the stories. That's what Tegan is to me. Oxygen.

Later that night, I have the dream.

In the dream, I'm sitting in Dad's office at Chatswood Scientific. I look around the place; it's exactly what I imagined when I heard the stories, when I took them and turned their threads into something big and weird and different. The clutter is there, the desk is crammed with files. I look down, and I'm wearing . . . chartreuse corduroy slacks, an off-white shirt, suede shoes, a skinny brown tie and a mustard-coloured suede jacket. I look down at my hands, inspecting them, delirious. I reach up and touch my face . . . Yep. My moustache is there. So I assume I'm still . . . me. Whoever 'me' is.

I look over at a glass cabinet and catch my reflection, and see myself staring back. And that's when it hits me.

I'm Detective Hard Seltzer. I'm wearing Seltzer's clothes. I'm . . . yes, I'm at his desk. A small nameplate bears my name. And then, in comes Grey.

Grey, with his grey hair, grey sideburns, blue eyes. His demeanour, however, is almost effervescently colourful. He beams and bows and claps and crows, striding over and grinning at me. 'Seltzer!' he exclaims. 'Listen, we've got a case. Just across the road! Whaddya say, John? Want to grab your gear, maybe I can show you what I do when I'm on the job?' Grey picks up a bright red plastic briefcase, waves it around above his head and gestures for the door. I stand up, shrug and follow him.

We exit the building, Grey suddenly seeming taller than before. We're jogging across a massive freeway, dancing between cars, and suddenly we reach a wire-mesh fence. Grey practically steps over it in one effortless stride, but I, Hard Seltzer, have to get help from my mentor. On the other side he brushes me off, points towards a very small clearing. 'These trees,' he says in a whisper, 'are very old.' And he's right, I can tell: this is a forest we're in. It smells boggy and cloying, and because this is a dream, I can suddenly feel the danger of it all around me.

I reach for Grey's briefcase.

'Don't worry, John,' he says kindly. 'When we get there.'

'What are we looking for?' I ask, matching his whisper and following in his huge footsteps.

'Evidence,' Grey says. 'Footprints. We need to take casts of foot-prints.' He waves the case again and we continue in silence, deeper and deeper into the bog.

Suddenly, Grey stops. He waves me over, leans down, and points. There, in a muddy puddle, is a smattering of distinct foot-prints. He grins back at me, and I stare at him, deadpan. Detective Hard Seltzer is all business.

Grey puts the case down, opens it, and hands me a small dish. He then tears open two small sachets and taps a liberal quantity of white powder into my dish. He hands me a small flask, nods, and I pour the water into the dish, mixing it with a tiny copper spoon. The mixture eventually smooths, and we're left with . . .

'Plaster of Paris,' says Grey. 'We're left with plaster of Paris.' He extends a wizened finger towards the first footprint. I pour the mixture in, watching it fill out the shape.

'And when can we take it out? Is this going to take long?' I ask, a little more surly than normal.

Grey looks over at me, disappointed but clearly trying to hide it. 'It'll take as long as it takes, Seltzer,' he says. 'Be patient.'

Suitably put in my place, I squat there, watching the thick white guck drying. After about three minutes of near-silence, a dumpy little mosquito lands on the surface, and, frustrated and impatient and overcome with petulance, I swat it. Hard. The plaster of Paris mixture goes flying, spraying Grey and myself with clotting ivory goo. Grey looks furious, but before he can say anything, I stand up and storm off. I can hear him getting up behind me, grunting with exertion as he clambers to his feet. 'Seltzer!' he calls, sounding a little sad now. 'Seltzer!'

There's a crack overhead. White light jabs into my eyes, and with a start I awake.

I'm back in the apartment. My phone reads 3 am, and I can see the storm has redoubled its efforts. Rain scrubs the windows, and a siren whizzes past. Tegan is, somehow, still asleep.

I collapse back into bed, watching the lights play across the ceiling.

I guess these stories are getting to me.

25

CLIFF

We're back at Mum and Dad's place. I'm standing in the corridor outside their apartment, waiting for them to come to the door. Don't tell Dad about the dream, okay? It'll completely derail him. I glanced at his notebook yesterday. I know which stories are lined up next. There aren't many, but they're the big ones.

And besides, today I have something to throw down at Dad's feet for once. You see, these stories have helped me make sense of him. I don't think Dad is one for self-reflection – most dads aren't, really, and that's fine. But I've been taking his true stories, the things he lived through and decided to never think about or even process again, and have turned them into narratives. I've taken matter-of-fact, sometimes threadbare anecdotes and blown them out into the kinds of stories he and I enjoyed while I was growing up.

I watched him read the first book I wrote about him, *Loose Units*. And I watched him gasp as he followed the book version of himself. 'It's like a movie!' he said, elated. 'It's like someone took the things I did and made them . . . Hollywood.' But until that moment, Dad hadn't thought of himself from the outside. He hadn't interrogated what he was actually like as a person, how he was perceived.

The stories he's told, the stories I've retold through my lens, have helped me understand him. But today, I'll be helping him understand his son a little better.

I hope.

Shh, shh. He's here.

John hadn't thought about detectives in a while.

Scientific was, as Grey had promised, scratching an itch. He wanted plain-clothes, cool cars, shoulder holsters and crime scene access. Check. He wanted big, scary problems to solve. Check. He wanted to duck under the police tape and flash his ID nonchalantly. Check, check, check. And now, after over a year in forensics, after a year cruising up to crime scenes in the Kingswood with Grey, he felt at home in his skin. He felt good. He felt shit hot, in fact.

It was summer. An unbearably hot summer. Australian summers are like pineapple on pizza: fucking awful, but some idiot will always loudly crow about liking them. And this summer was particularly awful, with humidity through the roof. In forensics, heat meant several things, chiefly that bodies would go bad much quicker, something Grey warned John about very early on. 'The smell,' he said to John as they burned down the road towards their destination. 'The smell is less than ideal.'

Here is where John and Grey were headed in such a hurry.

Early that morning, across town, a bunch of council workers were toiling by the side of the road. What they were working on doesn't matter. It mattered to them, presumably, but it has no demonstrable effect on the contours of this story. They were working away on the Old Pacific Highway, a winding, undulating stretch of road, and had decided to essentially set up camp and set up a billy.

I raise an eyebrow. 'An actual billy?'
     'Yes. An actual billy.'
     'Was this the 1980s, Dad? Or the 1880s?'
     Dad gives me his 'Don't be a smartarse' look. Fair cop from
a fair cop.

Four of these council workers, girt in high-vis, were sitting there by the side of the Old Pacific Highway, sipping scalding tea from tin cups, leaning their tired backs against bollards, hanging out, trying to stretch their tea breaks out as long as possible. We've all been there. Stretching out tea breaks, just to be clear. Not doing so on this particular bit of highway. And while they were sipping away, one of the chaps sniffed the air. What is it, the others asked. And the chap kept sniffing, and said he could smell something. Probably roadkill, right? But curiosity got the better of them, and they set down their flimsy cups, stood up, and began roaming around, looking for the source of the odour.

Eventually, the four of them headed through a thin patch of scrub, which opened out onto a vast abyss. A huge rocky slope, sitting at about a fifty-degree angle, fell away into the valley below, and as the men peered over, they saw it: a body, which had clearly fallen down the cliff, and miraculously become snagged on a small tree jutting from the precipice. They exchanged looks, pulled back, and called General Duties.

And that's where John and Grey were headed on this swelter-ing day. To the cliff, to step nonchalantly under the police tape yet again and investigate a body stuck halfway down, wedged there on the shale like something nested between two teeth.

As John pulled the gleaming Kingswood up to the cordoned-off stretch of highway and found a spot between other emergency services vehicles, he looked up and saw them. Police rescue. One of them, a bullet-headed man who John faintly recognised, traipsed over to John's door and opened it. 'Scientific,' he said. 'Good. This way.'

Grey raised an eyebrow and gave John a look, and John nodded, hopping out. He grabbed his kit, and they made their way under the police tape, passing cops from a litany of departments as they went. And there, off to one side and looking decidedly shady, were two detectives.

John could tell they were detectives. They were dressed . . . well, like him. Plain-clothes. Immaculately groomed, hair slick with pomade, tiny bellies pressing against crisp white shirts. They turned to look at John and Grey, slowly, deliberately. John tried to pay them no mind, instead focusing on the police rescue sergeant leading him towards the cliff. Once there, another member of police rescue approached, holding a harness. Now John wasn't thinking about the Ds at all. *Cliff,* he thought. *Harness. Rope. Dead body.*

I'm going over, aren't I?

'Yes,' said the officer, holding the straps and carabiners aloft, square jaw tensed, beady eyes fixed on John. 'You're going over. We're gonna need an inspection of the body where it fell, which means you're going to rappel down. Ever climbed before?'

John fumbled for a way to explain that while he had no problem with skydiving, climbing and abseiling for some reason set his teeth on edge. But the ball was already rolling, the decision made. John's jacket was removed, and a navy-blue harness pulled over his head. Buckles were tightened, ropes fastened. Beyond the dry hissing of knots being drawn closed and the tinkle of metal screwing him into his safety nappy, he heard the faint susurration of two deep, dumb, deadpan voices. The Ds, back and under a thicket of trees, watched with something akin to curiosity. Was this greenhorn going to tumble to his death? Would he piss himself? John resolved, if he could help it, to do neither.

The police rescue team gave him a few more helpful hints, but John was barely listening. Grey leaned in, and asked if John was comfortable doing this – he'd happily take over, he said. But John looked at his mentor. The guy was animated, sure. But he was getting on, and frankly, John wanted to show the detectives and everyone else assembled that the boys down at Scientific were more than just eccentrics who huddled behind microscopes or peeled fingerprints from the hands of the dead. They were capable. They were heroic. They were . . .

Walking backwards over a cliff.

John stared at his feet, at his suede shoes planted tenuously against the rock face, at his hand as it gripped the rope. With his other hand, he let out a little more slack. From above him, the faces of the assembled emergency services workers peered, faces rapt, curious or leering, growing smaller as he went further down.

'Dad,' I venture. 'You know what would make this exciting? Like, really exciting?'

He raises an eyebrow.

'Well,' I continue, 'if you, like . . . almost fell. You know, if the rope gave out and you hung there, gripping on for dear life, before making a heroic recovery.'

'Yes,' he says, 'that would be exciting. And yes, you make up loads of shit in these stories. But it didn't happen that way.'

I eyeball him cheekily. 'You sure? You sure you didn't slide down the cliff and grab on at the last moment, like in the movies?'

A *plink* sound. *Plink. Plink. Plink.* John looked around, unsure from where the gentle plinking was issuing forth, and then . . . he saw it. The rope.

The rope was giving way.

Tiny tendrils of glossy fibre were snapping and peeling away, curling gently like the fronds of a carnivorous plant. Someone from up high yelled to pull the rope up; another barked that this would only hasten the fraying. And as John looked up one last time at the line of heads, he saw Grey, horrified.

Plink.

SHUFFFFF.

The two ends of rope parted in slow motion, and with terrible certainty, John teetered backwards into the abyss. He felt the shale under his feet, and wondered if this was it. If there was room on the outcrop for one more body. And then he fell, tumbling end over end, sliding away towards the end of the incline. *WHUMP.* He bounced away, and felt something burst. *WHAM.* A rib popped like a dry branch snapping. Then he slid, down, down, down, and in a final act of desperation, threw his hands out. His body hurtled faster and faster, and then . . .

Wind. Wind, all around him. He was a bar of soap flying from a wet hand, a cork exploding from a champagne bottle. He hovered over the abyss, and then, improbably, his outstretched hands met a thick, knotted vine. He gripped on as hard as he could, and his body arced down, slamming into the rock face. Wheezing, he hung there, legs dangling into space, the forest floor spread out beneath him, the canopy of gently swaying green beckoning.

'I guess,' muttered one of the detectives to the other, 'he's dead.'

'Guess again, ballbags,' panted John, heaving himself up into view, a cigar hanging from his mouth.

'No!' yells Dad, laughing. 'No, no no no. That is not how it . . . Mate, where do you come up with this stuff?'

I'm laughing too, but honestly, what does Dad expect? He's jumped out of planes, chased bad guys at high speed. He even once got into a blue in a department store with a prison escapee. The stuff he's gone through is not that far from what I just told him. And you know what? I reckon if he read my version enough times, he'd start to get confused about which version was the real one. Or maybe not. Maybe he really does have a limited imagination.

I sigh. 'Fine,' I say. 'How did it actually happen?'

John lowered himself carefully – clumsily, if we're being candid – down the rock face. Finally, after an agonising series of badly placed footfalls and line slippages, he made it to the body. He hung there, locked off his rope, gave a thumbs up to the now-distant huddle of heads, and shimmied to the right. He peered down at the body, wincing in the sun.

The body was stuck on a large jutting branch. Female, John noted, sweating profusely. Female, and wearing a black leather jacket dotted with huge metallic buttons. Beneath that, a dark green dress, quite short. Ripped stockings covered her legs. John cast his eye to her head, and noted that her hair was done up in a bun, now covered in debris from her tumble. She was facing away from him.

John carefully, very carefully, withdrew his camera from its satchel, acutely aware of everyone watching him from fifteen metres up. He popped off the lid, drew the camera out, slid off the lens cap, and began snapping away. Somewhere in the distance, a lone kookaburra cackled wildly.

Once he'd finished photographing, he put his camera back in its case. He then double-checked to see that the dead woman's position was stable enough, then looked back up at the cops above. 'I'm turning her over now!' he yelled, his voice practically bouncing off the rock face and echoing into the valley below. Several nods of acknowledgement met him, along with a cheerful thumbs up from Grey. *Here we go,* thought John. *If this is going to go wrong, it's going to go wrong right now.*

The outcrop she'd landed on held. John reached out, carefully rolled her onto her back . . . and suddenly, he realised what had happened. She'd been partially mummified, skin leathery and desiccated from days and days in the Australian sun. She'd also, John noted, been nibbled at by rodents, small bite marks marring her arms, hands and neck. Rats, probably; they clearly didn't have the issues John did making it down this far. Her lips had withdrawn from her teeth, leaving her bearing a permanent grimace. John could tell she'd likely been in her mid to late twenties when she died.

Too young, he thought as he once again readied his camera to document her present state. *Too young.* And he hung there like a lean, perspiring tetherball, squinting down at a dead young woman who'd met her end here, baking in the midday sun, all alone.

Half an hour later, her body had been hauled up. John had been congratulated quietly by Grey, who asked him the same probing questions he always did. What did you notice when you first saw the body? How long do you think she was down there? Any signs of a struggle? And John kept answering, but all the while he couldn't take his eyes off the two detectives, looming just out of sight, smoking, muttering, weighing up him and Grey. By now, a small crowd from other departments had converged, all milling about the body, sweeping the cliff face for evidence. John, however, couldn't stop thinking about the detectives. Then, it hit him.

'Those Ds, Grey.'

Grey looked up at John quizzically. 'The ones behind me?'

'Yeah. Those ones. They look local to you?'

Grey's eyebrows billowed. 'I don't know, John. I gather they don't look local to you, though, which means they likely aren't. And what, my boy, does that tell you?'

John mulled it over, trying to look inconspicuous as he watched them, loosening his tie. 'It tells me they know something we don't, is what it tells me, Grey.'

Grey smiled and leaned in towards John's ear. 'Tell you what. Let's do a sweep of the area. Be subtle. We'll go and check by the roadside, where nobody is looking, because . . . well, I don't trust these jokers to have checked everything, frankly. There's a good lad.' He meaningfully patted John's kit, winked, and made his way to the car. John looked about the place, clocking the two detectives again. They'd wandered over to get a look at the body. John followed Grey as calmly as he could, keeping his head down.

And that's when a glint of metal caught his eye.

It was off to one side, and just for a moment, the argent midday sun turned it into a beacon. John stopped in his tracks, leaning down for a closer look. Sure enough, there was something in the tall grass, halfway between the road and the clearing leading to the cliff face. John knelt, pulled on a pair of latex gloves, and very gingerly reached in. As he parted the blades of grass, he saw it. A button. A single polished metal button, identical to that on the jacket worn by the dead young woman. John slid out his camera, snapping a photo of the gleaming circle. He returned the camera to the satchel, blew on his gloved hands, and made to pick the evidence up.

A booted foot came down on his hand, pinning it in place. John, now in agony, instinctively yelped and shot a look up at the owner of the boot. There, his dead black eyes boring downwards, was the uglier of the two detectives. The toad-like man was mostly jowls, and his face was doused in sweat. With barely a look at John, he bent down and plucked up the button. Pocketing it, he lifted a single plump finger to his drawn lips, shushed John, and receded back into the undergrowth.

John massaged his aching wrist. In all his time as a New South Wales police officer, he'd never had a hand laid on him by another cop, nor a boot for that matter. At least, not that he could recall. And as the blood began to boil in his ears, as he clenched and unclenched his hand, a hand settled on his shoulder.

'John. Let's go.'

'But . . .'

Grey looked down at him, a touch of Gandalf to his demeanour. 'John. It's not worth it. Come on. We'll go and wait for the body. We're here to do a job, with or without . . .' He gestured to where the detectives lurked. John, having long since learned to listen to Grey, accepted a hand up, picked up his bag, and followed Grey back to the Kingswood. He looked back at the trees, at the expanse that lay beyond them. 'Grey. Those buttons on that jacket.'

'Yes?' replied Grey, pulling open his door and looking at John across the hot roof.

'Sturdy. That jacket was sturdy. Nothing came off during the tumble down the cliff, which means for it to have come off back here . . . Well.' He gave Grey a look. 'A struggle.'

'Sound reasoning,' whispered Grey. 'But given the clearly out-of-area detectives who just stopped you picking up proof of that, I say we head back and wait to inspect the body close up. My guess? We'll find further proof. If, of course, you're right.' He ducked down into the car, tugging the door shut before continuing. 'Which, John, you are with increasing regularity. I'm sorry if I haven't told you that enough.'

'I don't know what to say.'

'You don't need to say anything, John. But let's get a move on to Hornsby. I talked with the lads upstairs. The body is being taken there now.' He gestured to one side, and John saw the body being trundled into a gleaming white van parked by the road. As John watched, a hand bearing scuffed nail polish slid out from beneath the white sheet, hanging there, limp and pale, jostled as the gurney disappeared into the bowels of the vehicle.

A short while later, he and Grey stood in a small, cold, clean room. The pathologist in residence had spread crinkly plastic sheeting out across the floor around the slab, on which lay the dead young woman. She was still fully clothed, and under the harsh halogen glare, John was struck by just how young she was. He cast his eye over her body, noting the spot the missing button belonged, half concealed under a thick, frayed lapel. Her feet were pointing in towards one another, crimson nail polish peeking out from behind the lattice of her frayed stockings. He stared at her face once more, wondering what her parents would think.

'It's clichéd,' he said, breaking the silence. 'I know it's a big, shitty cliché, Grey. But . . .'

'You're thinking about your daughter?' Grey finished, arms folded. He, too, was gazing at the young woman's face with a kind of abstract despondency.

John nodded. He'd long since accepted that Grey's intuition bordered on the supernatural. 'Yes,' John replied. 'But also . . . hand me those scissors.'

Grey walked over to a table bearing all manner of tools for the impending autopsy, picked up the huge scissors and placed them in John's hand. John, still fixated on the young woman, approached her. He dipped down, pointing towards a slight protrusion under the jacket sleeve. 'This,' he murmured, eyes wide. 'Did you spot this?'

Grey strode over, leaning down to get a closer look. 'No,' he said, a whiff of fascination in his voice. 'No, I did not.' He cocked his head, looking more like an owl than ever, and after a pause, har-rumphed at John. 'Well?' he said, bemused. 'Go on, then!'

John lifted the scissors, held the blade flush with the cuff, and deftly snipped clean through the leather with a dull click. He parted the leather from the lining, and, breath held, revealed a small cavity. 'A secret compartment!' He gasped despite himself. Reaching inside, he fished around and finally found it. He drew out his pinched fingers and deposited the compartment's load on the table. A small square of dollar bills, folded with almost origami-like precision so as to minimise the space they took up, stacked neatly one upon the other.

John stood up straight, placed the scissors down, and looked at Grey. 'She was a working girl,' he said finally.

Grey quirked an eyebrow. 'All right. What brings you to that conclusion?'

John pointed at the bills. 'Well, she was hiding money. Small amounts, so as not to draw attention. You only do that if you're scared of short-changing someone who frightens the shit out of you. Then, there's the clothes. Her age. I think she hid those bills from her pimp. And the button? That jacket was sturdy as hell. There was clearly a struggle by the side of the road, then she was thrown from the cliff. It wasn't a suicide, and those Ds know it. This whole fucking thing . . . I never thought I'd say this – *again* – but . . .'

Grey gave him a nod of permission.

John cleared his throat. 'It doesn't add up.'

Grey smiled. 'No, no, John. You've come to some reasonable conclusions. But we need to tread very carefully here.' He looked back at the body, rubbing his neck with his enormous callused hand. 'Let me go grab old mate, and we can get down to the autopsy. See if there's anything to this.'

Minutes later, a small bald man in white was hovering over the body, and as he made his incision, John suddenly understood what the plastic sheeting was for.

Maggots cascaded from the girl's insides, roiling and spraying out onto the plastic like a living curtain. John retched, silently thanking the Nine that Grey had seen fit to instil in him the habit of smearing Vicks under his nose before autopsies. He staggered away from the foaming miasma, maggots bursting underfoot as he cursed his luck for wearing his good shoes. Again. He came to a stop near the young woman's head, leaning on the slab for support, and looked down at her. A small voice in his head, the one that had all of the good ideas, murmured something. Gently, he placed a gloved finger on her neck. And with a small circular motion, he probed around, and—

'The hyoid bone.'

Both Grey and the pathologist stood up straight, eyes fixed on John. John, realising he'd blurted the words without thinking, looked right back at them. 'The hyoid bone,' he repeated. 'I think it's broken.'

Grey practically beamed at him.

'What do you think all of that means, Paul?' Dad looks at me from across the room. He's never asked me this before. He's never quizzed me, never tested my working theory on a case, even one that he already knows the answer to. And, almost unbidden, an answer bubbles up from within me.

'Well,' I begin, 'the hyoid bone is a small bone in the throat. It's not foolproof, but in over a third of strangulation victims, it's broken. Meaning she was probably strangled. There was a struggle, the button came off, and whoever did it thought they'd hide her body by throwing it off the cliff. But they didn't count on the body becoming stuck there. And the detectives – I'm guessing they were bent, maybe with ties to organised sex work? So maybe they were there to make sure nobody figured out what happened, hence the button.'

It's the first time I've summed up a theory about a case to Dad, and frankly, I'm a little breathless. So is Dad. Is that . . . pride on his face? It could be pride, but I'm not sure. He's hard to read. And while I don't get anything like a Grey-level reaction, I get an exhale. It's as if he's winded by my answer. And then, a small smile tugs at the corner of his mouth.

'Spot on, mate.'

For a moment, just for a whisper of a moment, I feel like Detective Hard Seltzer.

'Years later,' continues Dad, 'I ran into an old colleague of mine. Undercover cop. We got to talking, and I told him this story. And you know what he said?'

I shake my head.

'He said,' Dad whispers, 'that the cops were involved, and that she was murdered. And I realised that that day, when that D stood on my hand to stop me digging into the evidence . . .

that was the day I decided, somewhere deep down inside, to leave the police force. It took a little while for that decision to filter up to my conscious mind, but I knew. I knew soon, very soon . . . that I'd be done.'

26

CRASH

'You know what's weird?' I ask Dad, standing up to grab a glass of water.

Dad's eyes follow me across the room. 'About this? Apart from everything?' he says.

I fill the glass, take a belt, and sit back down. 'No, about that last case. Hornsby. I didn't ask . . . but did they have their own scientific division? Was it in a full-blown morgue?'

Dad shakes his head. 'No, no. This was in Hornsby Hospital. It was an impossibly small room, actually. Not sure if it still exists, really, but there was only one other case I actually dealt with that called me there. Want to hear it?'

'Does the pope shit in the woods?'

'Probably not.'

'. . . Are there woods in Vatican City?'

Dad stares at me blankly.

'Probably are,' I continue. 'And they're probably full of those Swiss Guards, bloody perverts.'

*

There were two young brothers, both from a phenomenally rich family. They were in their late teens, and came from a stunningly affluent Sydney suburb. One of the brothers had, on impulse, purchased a Lamborghini. In the 1980s, cars like Lamborghinis were like unicorns – in that you never saw them around, not that they were prized for their horns. The brothers knew their car was exceptionally rare. That's why they drove around in it: to get attention. Which, it's safe to say, they most assuredly did.

Now we drift across to the streets of Ryde, a rather well-off Sydney suburb. It was nine in the morning, and a young mother had just dropped her two children off at school. She sat in traffic, seated comfortably in her Subaru station wagon, her car idling. On the other side of the road, however, were the two brothers. Their Lamborghini was purring away, and all eyes in the cars around were on the brothers. Peak-hour traffic had created more congestion than this high-octane car seemed able to tolerate. And so the brother who was driving made a fateful, final decision.

He fanged it.

In an attempt to swerve around traffic at blinding speed, he revved the engine and buzzed in a clean arc all the way past the nearby cars. Then, the mistake. He clipped the median strip. Median strips, it's worth noting, have edging that slopes up at a forty-five-degree angle on all sides. And because the Lamborghini was a piece of precision engineering made to go as fast as possible, because it was already going staggeringly fast, and because it was made to be incredibly light . . . it flew. It flew in a straight line at a clean forty-five-degree angle, tyres spinning away, desperate to find purchase on road that was now several metres out of reach.

The car flew through the air, whooshing as it went, coasting in a canary-yellow blur above the several lanes of traffic, until it met with a telegraph pole on the opposite side of the intersection. It hit the pole halfway up and compressed like a stomped Coke can, and the pole, not designed for this kind of trauma, snapped in two. The pole teetered. And then, the car fell. It fell hard, and it fell fast.

And it crushed the Subaru.

John, as it turned out, was asked by Grey to inspect the bodies of the two brothers.

Grey explained the injuries suffered by the woman, who, he assured John, had died instantaneously. Her head had been driven down into her abdomen by the weight of the Lamborghini landing on her, and the task of extricating her from the car was going to be laborious. But John was tasked with heading to Hornsby Hospital, for the second and final time in his career.

Once he arrived there, as he made his way down the corridor to the place where he'd be getting to work, he was stopped by a General Duties officer. This young officer explained that he was fresh out of the academy, and that the brothers' grandfather was nearby, insisting that he was a doctor and could identify them. He said that one of them had a birthmark.

John looked at the young cop, who looked decidedly pale and a little panicked, and noted the trembling of the young officer's hands. *That was me,* he thought. *Back in 1980, that was me. I wonder if my hands shook.*

He patted the young officer on the shoulder, pushed through the double doors, and found himself staring down at the remains of the joy-riding brothers heaped onto the rather compact slab. Both of them lay there, huge black plastic garbage bags covering their bodies from the waist up. Which, the nearby attendant reminded John, wasn't in any way normal procedure. John could feel his heartbeat in his ears. The room was unbelievably, improbably small, and suddenly he wanted to leave. To run. To ask Grey to take over. But he reminded himself of his job, then got out his gear and got to work.

He made sure to delay taking the bags off the boys for as long as possible. First, he spent what felt like an age removing pieces of glass from their hands, then set about carefully fingerprinting them finger by finger. It became a countdown, each finger marking a crawl closer and closer towards the final, terrible reveal. To the dual unveiling.

Finally, he realised he had to take the bags off. He couldn't buy any more time, and the attendant was eyeballing him impatiently. He looked down at the table; a femur had speared through one of the boy's jeans. Whatever was under the plastic shrouds was, he realised, going to fuck him up. It was going to ruin him a little. But he had to pull these huge bandaids off sometime.

John turned to the attendant. 'Listen,' he said. 'I'm going to need to take a look at the bodies. Is that . . .' The attendant nodded. It was necessary. *Damn,* thought John. *You could've said no, you prick.* He grimaced.

Years later, he still wished he'd never looked.

The attendant approached and withdrew the plastic bags. The heads were gone. All that was left were two neck-holes, ragged and pulped, with a tongue hanging limp from each one. Two tongues. Heads obliterated.

John looked down at his hands.

They were shaking now, too.

I have to level with you all. I don't think Dad is okay. His hand has been shaking a little, just a little, as he tells the story.

'Dad,' I say gently, pointing at his hand, 'I know we talk

about this all the time, but do these stories affect you?'

He laughs gregariously, waving me off. 'Mate! No. How many times do I have to tell you? It's fine. Seriously.'

Now it's my turn to wave *him* off. 'Dad, I actually have a pretty thrilling story of yours. Mum told it to me. Do you . . . do you want to hear it? It's got a car chase, it's got thrills, it's bloody, it's exciting . . . I don't know, maybe you'll remember it better than Mum did, but I wouldn't want to leave it out of the book. What do you say?'

Profoundly grateful for the subject change, Dad shrugs. 'Sure, mate. Sure.'

Well. He asked for it.

It was eleven in the morning when John got the call.

He was in the car in a flash. Almost flinging the door off its hinges, he threw himself in, slammed it shut and belted up. He drove the key into the ignition like a spear into the eye of the cyclops, sweating, and swearing, and cursing. The engine belched to life, the tyres span, and with a monstrous shudder the car exploded from the driveway.

A block later, he pulled up in another driveway. And there was his mate, holding his face. It was sliced open, lip hanging loose. Two panicked eyes met John's, and he ran out to grab the man, who was staggering and tottering from side to side. His eyes began to roll back into his head, and John ushered him over to the back seat of the car, opening the door with one hand and carrying his near-unconscious friend with the other. *My radio,* John thought angrily. *Where the fuck is my radio?*

Hospital, he thought. *We need to get him to a hospital. Drive, idiot. Drive, now.*

The car burned out of the tiny street, and before long they were travelling at breakneck speed towards their destination.

John's hands gripped the wheel. Blood soaked his shirt. The man writhing next to him screamed and groaned through his ruined face.

This, thought John, *is shaping up to be a really shit day.*

He checked the dash. Not because he needed to glean anything from the speedometer or the fuel gauge, but to distract himself. His friend, he was certain, was going to die. He wasn't ready to admit that just yet – best not to admit defeat, even when it's nuzzling up your leg – but things weren't looking good. The car was dancing below the speed limit, skirting the very edge of it, a warm hum pulsing as the engine threatened to overheat and gutter out entirely.

Another noise, this one more of a bloody burble, yanked John from his trance. *Focus,* he thought. *Focus. You're not far from the hospital. You can fix this. You can make this work. You can get the shit back into the horse, John.* A confused, wet, garbled scream drew John's eye. He looked over at his friend, doubled up, utterly wet through with his own blood, clenched hands holding his face in place.

John flashed back, somewhat inappropriately, to himself as a child, holding stolen apples in his shirt and sneaking into his house round the back. Just as he was about to make it to his bedroom, the buttons popped and the shirt burst open, unable to bear the burden of his stolen goods. The apples tumbled forth. His dad yelled at him for an hour. *Why am I remembering this?* John thought in a daze, foot stamped down on the accelerator. *Oh. He looks like he's about to let go, too. He can't carry any more.*

They were, John realised, snapping back to the present, still a long way from the hospital. They were in the backstreets now, burning up and down long roads, coursing along winding avenues, and into the kind of dips and troughs you only really saw on the Northern Beaches of Sydney. *We aren't going to make it,* John thought. *He's collapsing. I'm going into shock. I'm—*

And with a rather pleasant *FLOOMP*, the car mounted the gutter at high speed.

And everything went dark.

Dad has the strangest look on his face. Even when he sees that I'm done talking, he can't quite bring himself to say anything in response, so I get up and sit right next to him.

'Dad, Mum told me that story.'

No reply.

'And it wasn't a police story. That happened to you fifteen years after you left the force. Your best mate at the time cut his lip open while assembling some furniture, and was bleeding. It was a bad cut, sure, but far from fatal. We lived around the corner from him, remember? You drove over, and took him to hospital.'

Dad nods. 'I remember.'

'Only you didn't crash. You got fifty metres down the road, then you sort of just hit the gutter and pulled over. And then do you know what happened?'

Dad looks old all of a sudden. I don't like seeing him old. Somehow it scares the shit out of me. I'm scared most of the time, true, but he looks more vulnerable than ever. Finally, he responds, clearing his throat. 'I lay down on the grass and had a panic attack.'

'Yeah,' I reply. 'But you called another mate of yours first. He rocked up a few minutes later and found the two of you there, took you both to the hospital. They patched your friend up no worries, but Dad . . . I think it's pretty clear you had PTSD.'

Dad has the gall to throw me a defensive look. 'No, I—'

'Yes, Dad. And it wasn't because of the blood – it didn't start there. I think years and years and years of car chases and car crashes, dead bodies . . . Fucking hell, Dad, for the first book you told me about how a girl died in your arms underneath a train. How the hell are you supposed to keep all of that out? Where do you put all of that stuff? Of course it got to you.'

'Maybe.'

'Definitely. Those things that happened to you affected you, Dad. I think they affected us all. So please . . . please stop pretending they just breezed past you. They live inside you now. You're going to have to come to terms with this stuff.'

And that's when Dad says something that takes me by surprise. 'Mate, I'm thinking that maybe you telling my stories is helping. Maybe . . . I don't know. Maybe the books . . . maybe the stories live in them now, instead of me.'

There's a lengthy silence. I brighten suddenly. 'Dad. Are you saying this book is a fucking ghost trap?'

'Sure,' he says. 'Just don't cross the streams.'

'So, Dad,' I say as kindly as I can. 'All of these things affected you. I think it's okay to say that. And that feels like . . . well. It feels like progress. But do you now feel comfortable admitting that it would have been interesting to go back, do things differently? If your choices led to you being traumatised, is it not kind of fair to say that you could have done certain things better?' Before he can protest, I plough on. 'Okay, okay. How about this – I have an idea. Give me a forensics case, one of your big ones. But make it . . . well, make it one that ended badly. Very badly.'

'Why?'

I grin. 'I have an idea.'

27

INTO THE WOODS

John was sitting in his office one evening. He had his feet up and was daydreaming when the phone rang. Sometimes phones trill sweetly, but this one practically vomited. Startled, John hurtled forward and picked it up.

The call was fairly straightforward, at least to begin with: he was needed for a job, quick smart. There was something that needed digging up, needed his eye. Something deep inside Ku-ring-gai Chase National Park. 'Bring a shovel,' one of John's higher-ups told him rather tersely. At least, John assumed he was a higher-up. He certainly spoke like one. 'Make sure you bring a shovel, and be outside in five minutes. Someone will swing by to pick you up.'

John said fine, he'd be there, and hung up the phone. He headed to his gear cabinet to find something to dig with. He saw a small trowel, insultingly small, and his hand hovered over it. Nearby was a full-sized garden spade, or something close enough to make little difference. John considered grabbing it, but he was in Forensics. He wasn't a bloody gardener. And besides, there was no way he'd need something *that* big.

'Paul,' Dad says, looking a little uncomfortable, 'I should probably tell you what the shovel is for. I was going to dig up a body.'

I pause. 'A body.'

'Yes. He actually may have mentioned it during the call.'

'May. Have mentioned.'

'Yes, he may have.'

I'm kind of lost here, but Dad should hear what I'm thinking, so I carry on. 'Dad, if you knew you'd be digging up a body, why didn't you take the proper shovel?'

Dad looks at me, and has the gall to act like he's thinking it over. 'Well,' he sagely replies, 'I didn't want to look stupid.'

'Why would you look stupid? They told you to bring a shovel. Pick up the shovel, and bring the fucking shovel.'

'Paul,' Dad admonishes me, 'these detectives were burly blokes. Important guys. I didn't want to look like I was trying too hard, rocking up with this huge shovel. I wanted to play it down a bit.'

This is the saddest yet most relatable thing Dad has said to me in quite some time. I motion for him to continue.

John popped the insultingly small trowel into his kit, cracked his back, and headed out. He sauntered down the drive, and moments later was met by a large Kingswood (not his Kingswood) that rolled up with a gentle skid of the tyres. Inside, a weary-looking driver gave John a nod. 'Hop in,' he said. As John did so, he noticed the man eyeballing his digging implement, and suddenly, he felt very sheepish. He slid into the back seat, curled up into himself, and tried to disappear into the seat leather. A minute later, he was fast asleep.

A jostle woke him, and, wiping a trail of drool from his chin, he looked about and realised it had got dark during the drive. Ku-ring-gai, you see, is big. Really big. It is – like much of Sydney – uncommonly beautiful, but it is also unbearably big. The idea of anything being hidden there and being somehow located again was a stretch. With this in mind, John and his companion finally arrived in a small car park encircled by towering trees. It was completely dark by this point. John hopped out, got his gear – and his tiny shovel – and was directed to an unmarked vehicle over by the entrance to the woods. Standing there were three men. Two were clearly detectives, and one was a man whose face John couldn't quite make out. This man, he realised, was wearing prison greens.

In short, he was in the middle of a forest, at night, with two detectives, and an inmate from a prison, and somewhere in all of that bush was a body.

'You see, Paul,' Dad interrupts, 'we'd been given these bizarre instructions on how to get to this specific spot. Because once you get to the actual national park, there's no directions . . . you're in a bit of an eerie no-man's-land. So these two detectives had relayed their cryptic instructions through a third party, and had us meet them at a certain point in the national park. Once we met them, they'd give us more information, but not before. Then we see their cars, and I realise they're not local.'

'What do you mean? You mean, not from that area? This isn't their bailiwick?'

When I say bailiwick, Dad looks like he's been slapped in the face. 'Bali-what?'

'No, it's pronounced "bail-i-wick", Dad. Bailiwick. It means the area in which a bailiff, or a sheriff, or whatever, is allowed to actually do their policing.'

Dad looks impressed. I don't tell him that I specifically looked up a bunch of big law-enforcement terms before these sessions specifically to impress him.

'Anyway, it's a bit weird. Normally the local Ds like to be kept abreast of everything on their turf, but these ones were from Homicide. And these homicide squad detectives, in New South Wales, were regarded as minor deities.'

I nod thoughtfully. 'Well,' I muse, 'you can't spell detective without deity. Provided you . . . misspell . . . detective?'

Dad looks mad. I let him get back to the story.

Fetid branches fractured underfoot. Mud was everywhere. John noted, with some dismay, that he'd once again worn suede shoes to the scene of a murder.

'Nice shoes,' drawled one of the detectives, right on cue. John looked at him askance, shifting his bag of forensics gear from one numb shoulder to the other. He nodded at the man, struggling to see more than a metre or so ahead of him.

'Suede?' asked the other detective, positioned just off to his right, wearing a blue suit. John nodded in reply. A pause. The group continued their trek in silence, picking their way through the busted, fusty undergrowth.

'You waterproof 'em?'

This time John replied. 'Did I what?'

'Did you waterproof them.'

He side-eyed the detective on his left. The man was dressed immaculately, all clean lines and pressed linen, an ostentatious tie pin fastened to his chest like a gleaming insect. The detective looked genuinely concerned about John's shoes.

The other piped up. 'He's right. You really oughta waterproof suede. It'll stop fading and stiffening.'

'What are those, pigskin suede?' asked the detective with the tie pin.

'Cowhide,' replied the detective in the blue suit, helpfully. 'Look at the finish.' He swung his flashlight towards John's feet.

'Cowhide,' agreed Tie Pin.

The group resumed their hike in silence once again. *I'm surrounded,* thought John, *by staff writers from fucking* Vogue *magazine.*

After a time, just when John thought the trees wouldn't allow any more progress, the man in the prison greens cleared his throat and spoke. 'We're here. It's over there, in the clearing. To the left.'

In unison, the group turned the beams of their torches to the left, where, sure enough, through the bracken was a tiny clearing. They forced their way through the treeline, John now even more self-conscious about his shoes than before.

'It was here,' said the prisoner, gesturing his cuffed hands at a spot on the ground. John cast an eye over it. In this light, he couldn't tell if the earth had been disturbed or not, but the detectives seemed sold on it. 'Right,' said Tie Pin. 'Guess we'd better dig.'

All of the assembled men slowly turned to look at John. And John, who was fast realising the score here, wearily reached into his kit and withdrew the small trowel. Very small. Comically small. 'Time to build a sandcastle' small, he realised. Feeling like he ought to defend his loyal trowel's honour, he rather churlishly deployed the telescopic handle, adding a meagre five inches to the handle's length. Tie Pin chuckled. They weren't buying it. They weren't digging it. So John got to digging.

Digging, John already knew, is a shit job. The act of displacing soil and putting it in another place was, John reflected, not his bailiwick. His tiny trowel was strong, but the body willing it into action started to flag a little. The detectives loomed above him, watching, or gazing out into the darkness. The prisoner shifted uncomfortably, even giving John a look indicating that he wanted to help but couldn't. He raised his cuffed hands as if to illustrate the point, proffered a barely perceptible apologetic shrug, and stamped his feet to keep warm.

After a solid half-hour of digging, something dreadful happened. The dry, relenting *shhhhhhhufffff* of a trowel meeting little to no resistance was cut off by a declarative *shunk.* He'd made contact with something. Trowel, meet body.

Like bloodhounds, the previously inert detectives looked down, suddenly ready and willing to do their jobs. 'Here we go,' slavered Tie Pin, rubbing his hands together and getting down onto his haunches. The other cast about, an excited pep in his step.

'See?' declared the prisoner. 'See? Right here. I said it was here.'

'Shhhhh,' shhhhhed Tie Pin. 'Shhhhhh.'

Shhhhhhh, went the trowel in response, sliding through a tract of coarse earth, sounding like a wet hard broom breezing across hot asphalt.

Another *shunk.* John snapped on his gloves, the sound of the latex whapping against his hand echoing around the clearing, sharp and fricative in the murk. Without taking his eyes off the spot where his trowel had found its mark, he reached back and cleanly withdrew a brush from its tiny holster, unclipping it with a diminutive *pop. They're watching me now,* thought John. *They're not talking shit now.*

Like Indiana Jones gingerly clearing stray grains of sand from a deliciously valuable artefact, John swept the brush left, then right. Left, then right. Left, then . . .

Bones.

Human bones. A rib. And ribs tended, John thought dryly, to come as part of a set. So he moved the brush south a little, and repeated his prior motion. Left, then right. Left, then right. Left, then . . .

Bones.

After a few minutes, during which all assembled were craning forward in rapt silence, John revealed a series of ribs. Then, as he continued, he found hip bones. Then thigh bones. Then knee bones.

'Now hear the word of the lord,' John sang to himself.

Shins. Ankles. The clothing that had kept the bones hidden from the world was largely rotted away, but what soon lay revealed before them all was the bulk of a body, crammed in a hole about a foot deep. There was, John soon found, a twist, though. A kink in the tale. Not a tail, no. Something John expected to find wasn't there. Several somethings, in fact. As John returned ribwards and began to unearth the rest of the body, he suddenly realised what was going on here. With a sinking feeling deep in his gut, he hovered above the remains of a man who no longer had a gut to get a sinking feeling in. And he realised that the detectives had been expecting to find this.

They were expecting to find a body with no hands.

And with no head.

John paused after brushing up the neck and finding nothing there, nothing where a head *ought* to be. The traditional, conventional space a head typically resides. But what he realised, almost instantly, was that from a murderer's perspective, removing the head of someone you'd killed caused all kinds of logjams for the authorities, not to mention one very big problem for the owner of said head.

First of all, identification became an absolute bastard. Ballistics couldn't assess entry and exit wounds, which would allow them to deduce what kind of weapon – if any – was used, not to mention the range said weapon was used at. They couldn't obtain dental records, because the teeth and the head came as something of a package deal. They couldn't measure lividity in the eyes, provided the eyes hadn't long since turned to vitreous jelly and been eaten away by carrion. And they couldn't get a positive ID based on, you know, the face that resided on the head in question.

The hands were similarly crucial for the authorities. Say there'd been a struggle, and DNA from the assailant was trapped beneath the nails. Maybe there was a gauche tattoo, some kind of unique identifying brand on the hands. A friend who knew the victim could claim the victim bit their nails. And then, John's area of expertise: fingerprints.

You can't fingerprint a man with no fucking fingers.

There was a man who used this specific M.O. And John twigged, right away, that he was staring head-on at the headless body of a victim of—

'Mr Asia,' says Dad, with bombast. He lets the words hang in the air.

'Dad, I don't know who Mr Asia is.'

Dad does what he always does when I say I don't know precisely what he's talking about: feigns shock. Eyes wide. Blinks disbelievingly. 'What do you mean, you don't know who Mr Asia is?'

'I don't think there's any way I could put this any clearer.'

'You don't know who Mr Asia is? Really?'

'Oh, no. Wait. You're right. I do.'

'You do?'

'No! Of course I fucking don't! There is a blisteringly quick fix to this, however – tell me who he is!'

'Mr Asia,' says Dad with affected gravitas, 'was a terrifying . . . charismatic . . . problematic—'

'Hyyyyydromatic,' I offer, helpfully.

'—heroin bigwig,' finishes Dad, either refusing to acknowledge the reference, or simply evincing a low-key disdain for the musical Grease. *'From New Zealand. And his signature means of killing people involved—'*

'—Running them off the road in a drag race using blades that come out of his wheels?'

'Shooting them in the head, then removing the head and the hands. Any idea why?'

'No identification,' I reply.

'No identification,' he says, as if I hadn't just said this very thing. 'No fingerprints, no dental, no bullet.'

John paused, putting down his tools and looking up at the two detectives. His clothes clung to his body after an hour of feverish digging, and a deathly silence pressed down on the small clearing.

'Did you boys know this body was here?' John asked.

Tie Pin and Blue gave each other a furtive though guiltless look. 'Well . . . old mate here—' Tie Pin said, gesturing towards the prisoner '—had info on the location of a murder victim, offed in a . . . contentious case.'

'Contentious,' agreed Blue. 'Claims someone on the inside told him exactly where the body was, so we got dispensation to bring him out here and find the body. Said he was killed by—'

'Mr Asia,' John finished, pinching the bridge of his nose.

John, as you may have gathered, was rather on the ball. And hunched there, filthy and sweaty, shoes ruined, he realised that there was no way this prisoner was 'told' where the body was. The path he'd led them all down was incredibly specific. 'You were here,' John told the prisoner.

The man looked uncomfortable. 'Nah, mate,' he mumbled, unconvincingly.

'I think you were,' John retorted. 'You knew exactly where this bloke was. Which means . . . you were here when it happened. And if this is Mr Asia . . . fellas, there's a royal commission going on! The entire Australian legal system is currently zeroed in on Mr Asia, on all of this shit. It's all over the bloody news. This is . . . *we can't be here!* If anyone knows we're here, we'll . . .'

And just as the detectives were about to cut John off, it happened.

From deep within the murky depths of the forest, there was a flood of unnatural light. The whole clearing was lit up, and bizarre noises filtered towards them. As John looked up and squinted into the light, the sound of footsteps – many footsteps – reached him. The detectives puffed up, sucking their guts in. Tie Pin checked his hair, and Blue, inexplicably, smelled his breath in his hand. Satisfied, he stood as tall as he could manage.

And suddenly, John saw it. Bursting through the treeline came a cumbersome Channel Ten news camera, held by a small man wheezing with exertion. Behind him, a sound guy holding a boom mike, and then . . . there he was. Harry Potter.

'The boy who lived?' I exclaim with wonderment.

'No,' Dad replies. 'There was a news reporter called Harry Potter.'

'Did Channel Ten make him sleep under the stairs?'

Dad does not dignify this with an answer.

Potter's dense, aggressive eyebrows sat atop two vigilant eyes, and he strode over to the detectives. The camera swept across the scene, coming to rest on . . . John. John, holding his idiotic trowel in one limp hand, kneeling over a headless, handless body in a crude grave, sweaty and exhausted, hunched in a tiny clearing in the middle of nowhere.

Harry started a bombastic introduction to the camera, then began firing off questions. And as John watched the scene unfold, he realised that the detectives' calm demeanour and their unusual level of grooming, coupled with the fact that the news crew knew exactly where to find them, indicated one thing very clearly.

Glory boys. They'd tipped off the press. Good exposure, hell of a get – the two detectives who unearthed an undiscovered victim of Mr Asia. And they'd known that if John knew their plan, he'd have never gone along with it.

And that, for John, was that. The closest he ever came to getting into deep shit with the men upstairs, the police as an organisation, was as a result of this fuckery. He was never able to confirm that the Ds told the press, but it didn't take a rocket scientist to put two and two together. Ironically, it was basic detective principles that had led him to deduce their involvement: who stood to benefit? The detectives, clearly. And John was sent there to help them get ready for their big moment on camera.

As a result, he spent weeks being cross-examined, grilled and dissected by Internal Affairs. The case, you see, was part of a frighteningly high-stakes and complex royal commission. The goal? To bring down Mr Asia. And John had unwittingly wandered in and risked it all. *Should I have been more vigilant?* he thought. *Could I have done things differently, avoided nearly ruining my career? Should I have stopped and thought, rather than just run off after another case, something else fantastical and bizarre to cram into my ledger of oddities?*

It's too bad, John thought at the time, when he was at this crossroads in his career. *Too bad you can never do things over.*

But this is my book. This is my version of his story.

So I'm going to try something out.

THE BODY IN THE WOODS

BY PAUL F. VERHOEVEN

ILLUSTRATED BY PAUL F. VERHOEVEN

DISCLAIMER

Warning: do NOT read this story one page after another. *The Body in the Woods* is full of many different stories, with many different endings! As you read, you'll be asked to make choices. When you're presented with a choice, simply turn to the page indicated, and WHAM! You're off on another branching path of the adventure.

Your choices matter. Everything you do in this adventure will have consequences, sometimes fatal ones. If you fail – or die – follow the instructions to try again!

In real life, we're confronted with terrible, unchangeable decisions. But what if you could do it all again? Do things over differently?

Consider your options and have fun. And if you perish, or things end badly . . . go back to the beginning. Perhaps you'll find a way out that you never dreamt possible.

Remember: you always have a choice.

Start

You are John Verhoeven, a police officer in the New South Wales Police Force.

You've had many adventures over the years, but at this point in your career, you work in forensics. Right now, you're sitting in your office. Above you, a small halogen globe pings on and off occasionally. The room is full of the instruments of your trade, such as it is, and smells of disinfectant. You catch your reflection in a glass cabinet. *Not bad*, you think.

That's a well-made cabinet.

You're wearing a mustard-coloured suede jacket, an off-white shirt, a skinny brown tie, chartreuse corduroy slacks and suede shoes. You're in your late twenties, but after the week you've had you feel like you're in your early forties.

Suddenly, the scuffed bakelite phone squatting on your desk begins to bleat loudly, making your eyes water.

If you decide to pick up the phone, turn to page 3.

If you don't pick up the phone, turn to page 2.

2

You sit back in your chair, folding your hands behind your head.

What are you doing, John? Are you trying to make them sweat a little? What if this call is important? Hell, you work in forensics. It almost certainly *is* important.

If you decide you've had your fun, pick up the phone and answer 'Hello, John Verhoeven speaking,' turn to page 4.

If you let it keep ringing, turn to page 18.

You lean forward and snatch up the phone from its cradle. Clearing your throat, you . . .

Wait. How do you want to introduce yourself? Let's think this through. This is a huge deal, John. Not to put too fine a point on it, but the decisions you make even at this early stage could *drastically* change your sense of self-worth for the foreseeable future.

If you answer with 'Hello, John Verhoeven speaking,' turn to page 4.

If you answer with 'Ola, John Verhoeven here,' turn to page 5.

4

'Hello,' you say into the phone. 'John Verhoeven speaking.'

'John,' comes the reply. 'Pack your shit up, you're heading over to Ku-ring-gai Chase National Park. We've got a body. Someone will pick you up and take you there in five. Make sure when you hit the road heading into the park, you take a left, then a right. Cheers. Oh, and bring a shovel.'

The man on the other end hangs up without saying goodbye. *Just like in the movies*, you think. *Nobody ever says goodbye, they just issue commands and dump the phone back into the hook.*

You replace the receiver, stand up and get ready to leave. You smile at your reflection in the cabinet. 'Hey, handsome,' you mutter. There's no reply. You sigh. You're talking to yourself, John.

Remembering what the man on the phone said, you head over to the equipment cabinet. *A body*, you think. *We're digging up a body.* You've dealt with bodies before, too many times to count, but you've never actually dug one up. After a minute or two rifling through the cabinet, you come to the shovels. There's two to choose from.

If you grab the trowel – its diminished stature might, if the lighting is just right, make you look like a giant holding a regular shovel – turn to page 9.

If you grab the garden shovel – it's a big one – turn to page 7.

'Ola, John Verhoeven here,' you say, inexplicably.

There is a genuinely concerning pause. Then, the gruff voice on the other end of the line finally answers. *'Hola. Por favor, ¿puedo hablar con el jefe?'*

You pause. You furrow your brow.

. . . Who is El Jefe?

If you decide to bail – which is probably advisable – by just saying, 'Hello, John Verhoeven speaking' (you can still turn back from this madness), turn to page 4.

Who is El Jefe? YOU are El Jefe. Turn to page 10.

6

Here's what's clearly happened, John. You've felt a sudden, commendable compulsion to spontaneously liven up a dull night by providing the caller with a fun, breezy nom de plume. But you neglected to plan ahead – if you did, it would scarcely be spontaneous now, would it?

So you cast about, and on a colleague's currently vacant desk is a can of Hard Seltzer, a fizzy alcoholic beverage that you're convinced was bought because said colleague lost a dare. *Good enough,* you thought.

'This is Senior Detective Hard Seltzer. Can this wait? I'm in the middle of a case. There's a dame outside, and she smells like trouble.'

Nice work, John. Now for the droll laughter on the other end of the line.

But there is no droll laughter. Instead, there's an odd click, a clearing of the throat, and then a response you weren't expecting. 'Seltzer. Where the hell have you been all night? This is the commissioner. Tell that dizzy dame she'll have to come back tomorrow. We need you downtown, pronto – you got that?' And the man on the other end of the line hangs up. *The commissioner? That's fucking weird*, you think.

Then you look around the office, and everything becomes immediately, inexorably weirder.

This is not your office.

Whose office is this? Turn to page 74 to keep inspecting.

Look, you think, *if I'm going to dig up a body – and I'm fairly certain that's what the rest of my night is going to entail – then I'm not going to dick around. And besides*, you continue, *if they didn't want me to use the big shovel, why did they put it here at all?* You wrap your hand around the handle, pick it up, and lean it against the desk.

You stand up straight, crack your back, and put on a pair of white protective overalls. You then head back to the cabinet and look at yourself. The overalls look stupid. But they're regulation, dammit, and you're not going to have a repeat of the Chinese food case. Nothing ruins corduroy like decaying viscera.

You head outside, clutching your enormous shovel. 'Am I a coward?' you think aloud, walking towards the driveway. 'Am I a coward for carrying this unwieldy garden tool to a potentially delicate crime scene?' The answer, you realise, is likely a resounding yes, but you don't care. It's going to be a long night, and hacking away with a shovel worthy only of building diminutive sandcastles would be the greater evil.

You head down to the car park. In the distance, a train whistles by. You shiver uncomfortably at the sound. Finally, after another lonely minute or so, a gleaming Kingswood pulls up next to you.

'John. Let's go,' says the man inside. He eyeballs your shovel. He keeps eyeballing your shovel. He sniffs and looks up at you with an utterly unreadable expression. Then, finally, he speaks.

Turn to page 8.

8

'That's a nice fucking shovel, John.'

Incandescent with smugness, you slide into the passenger seat, do your seatbelt up, and give him a thumbs up.

Your colleague raises his hand, and you give him a high five.

A nice fucking shovel, you think. *Goddamn right.*

The car pulls away.

You drive to the crime scene. Turn to page 12.

You grasp the trowel and weigh it appraisingly in your hand. Sure, it might be comically small. But you're sure, right down to your bones, that this will in no way cause you any problems later on.

You stand up straight, crack your back, and put on a pair of protective overalls. You head back to the cabinet and look at yourself. The overalls look stupid. But they're regulation, dammit, and you're not going to have a repeat of the Chinese food case. Nothing ruins corduroy like decaying viscera.

You head outside, locking the door behind you, then head to the car park. In the distance, a train whistles by. You shiver uncomfortably at the sound. Finally, after another lonely minute or so, a gleaming Kingswood pulls up next to you.

'John. Let's go,' says the man inside. He eyeballs your trowel, and, ashamed, you slip it into a crate of forensics gear in the back. You get in the car, fasten your seatbelt, then give a thumbs up.

Your colleague nods vaguely, and the car pulls away.

You decide to take a nap. Turn to page 11.

10

Damn right you're El Jefe. You swell up, imagining yourself standing on a sunburnt mesa, your luchador mask clinging to your face. Your breath is stifled by the pleather hood, but your spirit is free. You survey the outskirts of your town.

A shot rings out. Your people need you.

You coil your muscles and narrow your gaze, and prepare to leap down and sprint towards danger. It is time, yet again, for the people of Peñíscola to witness the hot, blazing justice of . . . El Jefe.

'El Jefe means "boss" in Spanish,' the voice on the other end of the line pipes up, interrupting your imaginings. Pulled back into your body, you reflect upon what life would have been like had you been a Spanish vigilante. But you're John Verhoeven. *You're John Verhoeven. El Jefe means 'boss' in Spanish.* You're the only one here, so you're the senior man. You're the boss.

Which means, technically, you *are* El Jefe.

. . . But you're not *that* El Jefe.

You decide to backtrack. Turn to page 4.

The *shunk-shunk* of the car gliding over seams in the road begins to gently hammer your brain, and gradually your eyes begin to shut. You drift off into a well-earned rest.

You dream. In the dream, you're driving the Kingswood. The speedometer reads 95 km/h, and the car is practically floating along, the trees outside an absolute blur. You almost reach out to touch the number on the speedometer, the tiny digits dancing before your eyes. The whistle of a train echoes around you, and with a start you realise the Kingswood is a train. You're driving, and you're pulling into a police station. There's a screech of brakes, and you awake with a start.

You've arrived at the road heading into Ku-ring-gai Chase National Park. It's dark, and you're confused.

'Shit,' remarks the driver, looking a little lost. 'They tell you which way we need to go?'

You rack your brains. What do you tell him?

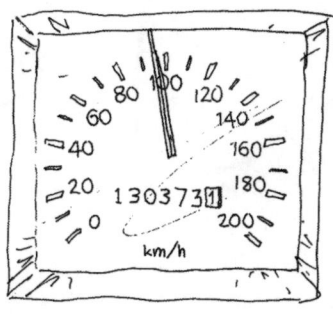

'Yeah. Take a left, then a right.' Turn to page 32.

'Go right, then left.' Turn to page 33.

You turn to face the driver. And in a clear, declarative, brazenly sudden British accent, you say, 'Second star to the right, and straight on till morning.' Turn to page 31.

12

The drive to the national park is largely uneventful, though as the Kingswood breezes down freeways and through backwoods, things become decidedly creepy. There's an energy in the woods at night, and as the headlight illuminates the ghostly branches, you can't help but grip your shovel a little tighter.

There's a silence. It's not uncomfortable yet, but it could get that way. You should probably do something to break the tension.

If you decide to ask the driver what music he has, turn to page 22.

If you take a closer look at the driver, turn to page 23.

If you play idly with some random buttons on the dashboard, turn to page 24.

The first thing Dad does – and I acknowledge this is a little extreme – is make a few more harried calls, and arrange for the detective department to try to kill John. I point out to Dad that this is something a therapist would have a field day with. 'You don't think that, perhaps, wanting to kill yourself . . . or a version of yourself . . . seems a little . . . unhealthy?'

Dad waves me off.

As we watch, another odd thing happens. After answering the phone as this Hard Seltzer character . . . John *becomes* Hard Seltzer. And Hard Seltzer . . . looks like me. Is me. Maybe that's how books work; authors are unable to stop writing themselves in. Or maybe it's a defence mechanism. Maybe it's so Dad can't kill him by breaking the fourth wall, I don't know. Maybe it's a very literal way of Dad finally seeing his world through my eyes. This whole thing is getting a bit too *Truman Show* for me to understand completely. But I see from Dad's expression that he's very cleverly figured out he's going to need to make the whole thing 'work', now that John is Seltzer. So he runs to a whiteboard and, like a mad scientist, begins frantically mapping out ways in which this could all still lead the reader – that's you! – to his desired logical endpoint. To prove a point.

And that's when he turns to me and, eyes wide, throws his hands skywards and floats the most batshit idea yet.

'Paul! I have it. Seltzer . . . IS . . . the prisoner!'

And with that, I realise I now have a chance to create an opening. A very small, very subtle one, but an opening nonetheless. So. What should *I* do?

Tell Dad you need to go to the bathroom. Turn to page 96.

Tell Dad to stop this madness. Turn to page 97.

14

You clamber out of the vehicle, clutching your tiny trowel. As you take a deep breath of the clear forest air, you look around to get your bearings.

The car is parked in a small clearing alongside a black sedan. Trees explode upwards into the sky, and a faint wind can be heard drifting through their upper branches. It is a soft, strange, soothing sound.

Your driver comes around from his side of the car and points. You follow his finger.

Standing by the entrance to the woods are two detectives. You can tell right away that they're detectives from the way they're dressed. Glory boys. Next to them is an odd man whose face you can't quite make out. He's wearing prison greens. They've got a prisoner here, at this hour? You can't quite see from this distance, but you're pretty sure he's been cuffed. He gives you a cryptic look. Fear? Whatever it is, you're sure it means something.

This whole scene is giving you the creeps.

If you approach the group of men, turn to page 25.

If you run screaming into the woods, turn to page 83.

You wake up six months later in your prison cell. Today is the day, Seltzer. You've endured six months of deep cover in Pentridge Prison, six months of pretending to be a low-level enforcer in a fictional crime family. Six months of scrapping, fighting to stay alive, greasing palms, collecting intel. Six months pretending to be someone else. And now, finally, is the day your debts are paid.

You yell for a guard, and when one comes, you tell him you need to talk to your lawyer.

An hour later, you're clutching a filthy receiver to your ear, cupping your hand around it to be heard over the din around you. 'McGruder,' you say. 'I need you to get in touch with the Ds up at the Northern Beaches. Ask for Detectives Jack Holsworth and Flynn Beveridge.'

You take a deep breath. This is it.

'. . . I need you to tell them that I've made friends with someone on the inside. I managed to get something out of them. The location of a murder victim, mate.'

'Right,' McGruder replies dryly. 'So who killed the bloke, and where is the body?'

'I'm not gonna tell them exactly where. I'll need to be let out to show them. Just make it happen, all right? I don't care what you have to do. And as to your questions . . . Mr Asia. And the body is at Ku-ring-gai Chase National Park.'

Turn to page 84.

16

You clamber out of the vehicle, clutching your huge shovel. You look around to get your bearings.

The car is parked in a small clearing alongside a black sedan. Trees explode upwards into the sky, and a faint wind can be heard drifting through their upper branches. It is a soft, strange, soothing sound.

Your driver comes around from his side of the car and points. You follow his finger.

Standing by the entrance to the woods are two detectives. You can tell right away that they're detectives from the way they're dressed. Glory boys. Next to them, however, is an odd man whose face you can't quite make out. He's wearing prison greens. They've got a prisoner here, at this hour? *This is odd*, you think.

'This is odd,' you remark to your driver.

'Yeah. I got a bad feeling about this whole scene.'

You hold your shovel aloft, wave at the detectives and make your way over to them.

Turn to page 17.

The car the men arrived in is unmarked. This would, perhaps, imply that these two *are*, in fact, detectives. They've also parked outside the lines indicated on the asphalt. This would, perhaps, imply that these two are loose cannons, not deigning to 'play by the rules'.

As you approach, the two detectives nod. The man in the prison greens doesn't nod so much as squint at you.

'Shit, mate,' says one of the detectives. 'Glad you came prepared. This could get hairy.' He gestures towards your shovel.

Suddenly, they're all looking pretty impressed with you. You're glad you went with the real shovel. *Somewhere*, you think, *in some alternate universe, I took the trowel. And there I am, probably crying into my overalls, as I get rinsed by the glory boys in a car park.*

'I'm Jack,' says the detective on the left. He reaches out his hand to shake yours, and you do. You shake it. The shaking motion makes his tie pin jiggle, catching the moonlight brilliantly. He's a gregarious-looking man sporting neat hair and a red suit.

The other detective approaches and you shake his hand, too. He introduces himself as Flynn. Flynn is wearing a blue suit which has a delightful pocket square peeking out. While you're shaking his hand, you look down and notice his shoes. He, in turn, notices yours.

'Ha! Suede. Tell you what . . .' He then darts back to his car and grabs two grocery bags from his boot. In what can only be described as a tender yet manly fashion, he kneels down and lashes one around each of your feet. Your shoes, it seems, shan't be getting wet and scuffed tonight. 'There ya go,' Flynn says matter-of-factly. 'Sorted.'

That was adorable. What's your next move?

You look over at the prisoner. Turn to page 57.

You start to get moving into the forest. Turn to page 58.

18

You lean back a little further, feeling a gentle stretch in your shoulderblades. The room, you realise, is humid.

Little do you know, but soon, roomfuls of people will pay good money to stretch in the heat. Had you more business acumen, you could get in on this trend early. Sadly, however, the phone keeps ringing, distracting you. You feel a twinge of guilt. The poor thing is just sitting there, trilling away to itself. This has gone on long enough.

You pick up and decide to answer with a crisp 'Hello, John Verhoeven speaking.' Turn to page 4.

You pick up and resolve to introduce yourself as a fictional detective. Just for the hell of it. If only you could think of a cool, fake detective name . . . Turn to page 6.

Stay the course, my friend, and turn to page 19.

And just like that . . .

The ringing stops. And you're left hanging there, leaning back on your chair, alone in your office. Truth be told, you're not entirely sure what to do next. The way you see it, you've got two options.

You decide to get up and explore the office. Turn to page 20.

Keep on leaning, baby. This chair ain't gonna tilt itself.
Turn to page 21.

20

The office is a dank little space, crammed with several poky little desks. Yours is bustling with forensics ephemera – kit bag, files and a framed photo of your wife, Christine. All pretty clichéd, truth be told, but it's your desk. Nobody else can use it. In General Duties you were used to hot desks: impersonal, cold spaces. So this is special. You earned it, John. You can be as clichéd as you want. For example: did you know that your chair is one week from retirement? Better go easy on it.

Your boss's empty desk has what looks like a small pickled foetus in a jar on it. You're almost certain it's illegal to possess, whatever it is, but there's no way you're getting close enough to actually check it out. On the wall is – and this is in no way a joke – that famous, awful poster with the cat hanging on a washing line. The cat looks like it's about to hurtle to its death, panic in its eyes, and beneath said cat in cheerful writing is the tagline HANG IN THERE.

You dealt with two hangings in the last month. You wonder if your boss, Grey, put the poster here as an attempt at gallows humour. Then you realise that even the phrase 'gallows humour' is on the nose given all the hangings, and are frankly relieved when your phone starts up yet again.

Turn to page 3.

You lean back just a little further. The timber on the chair creaks, gives a groan of protestation . . . and gives out. You fall.

Normally, a fall from a couple of feet wouldn't do any lasting damage. You are, after all, a relatively young man. Someone even called you spry once. You've also had years of experience sky-diving, which means you're kind of a natural when it comes to hurtling downwards.

Unfortunately, someone left a rather savage-looking paper-weight on the floor in the centre of the room. The back of your skull connects with it, hard, and with a dreadful snap your neck breaks.

But hey! At least they won't have to move the body far to do the autopsy.

The End

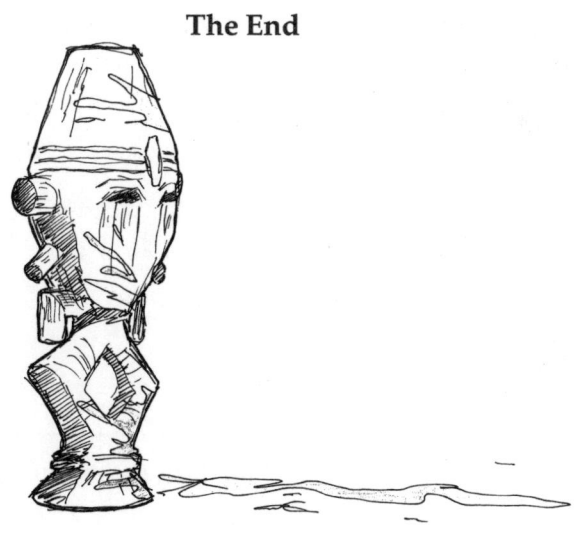

Your adventure is over. You failed. If you wish to try again, turn back to the beginning at page 1.

Or, if you're done, wrap things up and go to page 369.

'Hey, mate. Got any tunes?'

The driver nods and slides a tape out of its case, then blows on the ribbon and slips it into its little home with a satisfying click. He depresses the button. A whir issues forth, then, on its tail, the telltale track 'Drive/Driven' by Swiss duo Yello. Surprisingly, the song helps.

'Did you put this on because we're driving, and it's about driving?' you ask, utterly fumbling any cool you accrued with your awesome shovel.

'Yes,' he says. Then he gives you a look as if to imply you've made an astute observation. *Maybe he's a bit thick*, you think. You decide to shut up and let the drive continue.

Eventually, you arrive at the road heading into Ku-ring-gai Chase National Park. It's dark, and you're disoriented.

'Shit,' remarks the driver, looking a little lost. 'They tell you which way we needed to go?'

You rack your brains.

'Yeah. Left, then right.' Turn to page 29.

'Right, then left.' Turn to page 30.

You turn to face the driver. And in a clear, declarative, brazenly sudden British accent, you say, 'Second star to the right, and straight on till morning.' Turn to page 31.

You peer at the driver. He has blond hair, eyes like the opening of an overstuffed wallet, and a broad, expressive mouth. He's just the right size to be sitting all the way back in his seat and still have his arms fully extended as he steers. You can make out how fit he is; his muscles keep clenching and unclenching every time he needs to make a turn.

'What's your name?' you ask.

He thinks this over, as if having a name, or giving one out, has never occurred to him. 'Tell you what,' he says eventually. 'If you guess my name right, I'll tell you a little secret.'

You nod. Challenge accepted. So, John – what do you think the driver's name is?

If you think his name is Kevin Tyrell, turn to page 72.

If you think his name is Steve McQueen, turn to page 71.

If you think his name is Beberly Bellbo, turn to page 70.

24

You gently lean your huge, manly shovel against the car door and begin fiddling with buttons. This Kingswood is . . . well, it's a hell of a lot nicer than yours. More advanced. Honestly, compared to your car, it's like being on the deck of the Starship *Enterprise*.

'This is like being on the deck of the Starship *Enterp*—'

You are, sadly, cut off mid-observation. Your elbow catches the shovel, and the shovel knocks the handle of the door, which, as it turns out, was in a state of mild disrepair. You turn, startled by the sudden noise of wind rushing past, and you realise that, because you were distracted by the kudos you received for your shovel, you neglected to properly fasten your seatbelt. There was, you faintly recall, no *click*. You overbalance, and tumble from the car.

Your neck breaks.

If it's any consolation, however, your high-quality shovel does not.

The End

Your adventure is over. You failed. If you wish to try again, turn back to the beginning at page 1.

Or, if you're done, wrap things up and go to page 369.

The car the men arrived in is unmarked. This would, perhaps, imply that these two *are*, in fact, detectives. They've also parked outside the lines indicated on the asphalt. This would, perhaps, imply that these two are loose cannons, not deigning to 'play by the rules'.

As you approach, the two detectives nod. The man in the prison greens doesn't nod so much as squint at you.

You come to a stop, trying your best to hide your shameful digging implement.

What's your next move?

You look at the detectives. Turn to page 26.

You look at the prisoner. Turn to page 60.

You introduce yourself. Turn to page 28.

26

You assess the men. One thing that always struck you about detectives is their impeccable dress sense. Often called 'glory boys' by those among the constabulary, they have a reputation for wearing the finest clothes, essentially trying to look as cool as all get-out around the clock. These two, however, look better dressed than normal.

The first detective is dressed immaculately, all clean lines and linen, an ostentatious tie pin fastened to his chest like a gleaming insect. His fine brown hair has been, you realise, sprayed down to prevent any flyaways. This is a man who knows his mirror.

The second detective is leaner and wears a navy-blue three-piece suit. He doesn't have a tie pin, but he doesn't have a tie, instead opting for a stylishly splayed collar and several buttons undone, revealing a hairless chest. Oh! But he has a pocket square. *Damn*, you think. *These two look good.*

. . . A little too good for a jaunt in the woods, in fact. You file this trivia away for later.

How do you proceed?

You take a look at the prisoner. Turn to page 60.

You introduce yourself. Turn to page 28.

'What's going on, boys?' you ask as gently as you can. The balance of the dynamic between you and the detectives seems very delicate, tenuous. The last thing you want to do is upset the apple cart, so to speak. The group trudges on silently for a little while, then finally Jack approaches, walking alongside you while Flynn takes point with the prisoner up front, shining his torch and following the occasional direction change from the man in green.

'Right,' Jack says. 'The shovel is for digging up a body.'

'That much I got,' you reply. 'Which body?'

'Well,' replies Jack as carefully as he can, 'the victim is a bloke this lad here—' he gestures at the prisoner '—reckons he heard about on the inside. From someone in the yard, won't say who. But he's trying to get a reduced sentence in exchange for helping us out with the case.'

And now, the six-million-dollar man's worth of a question: 'What case,' you venture, 'is this body a part of?'

For a second, you see the gears turning in Jack's noggin. He wants to tell you, you think, based on the micro-expressions dancing across his pink face. Or, at least, he *wants* to want to. It feels like under different circumstances he might be inclined to tell you. But the fact remains, you're not Homicide, and you've only just met the guy.

Jack doesn't say a word.

Maybe if you'd asked Flynn instead you'd have had more luck?

But it's too late now. You can't go back and change things, John. That's not how life works.

Turn to page 61.

28

Time for some niceties, John. 'Evening,' you venture. 'John Verhoeven – I'm here with Forensics. What's the deal?'

The detectives nod and introduce themselves. You sort of tune out at this point, as you're frankly driven to distraction by the prisoner, who keeps looking at you with an odd expression. But one detective has a tie pin, and one is wearing a blue suit, so let's call them 'Tie Pin' and 'Blue'.

(Just to clarify, don't call them that to their faces. These names are what you can call the detectives in your mind palace so you don't get them confused. And you could ask for their names again, sure, but you already got given their names and forgot, so if you do have to address them, go with 'mate'. Nice and safe.)

Tie Pin pulls out a large torch, has a word with the prisoner, then turns back to you.

'Old mate here knows where a body is buried. So provided he's on the level, we could be heading for something very, very big. And important.' He glances at the prisoner. 'How far off do you think it is?'

The prisoner looks back at Tie Pin. 'Bit of a walk. Bit of a walk.' He has a nice voice, you think.

Tie Pin nods and walks over to where you and Blue are standing. You lean in and mutter to him, 'This prisoner got a name?'

'Yes,' replies Tie Pin. He blinks, whacks Blue on the arm, and Blue, in turn, nudges the prisoner. And so begins a trudge into the thick, pitch-black depths of Ku-ring-gai Chase National Park.

Turn to page 35.

The driver nods. He pulls into an impossibly dark road and follows your directions.

After twenty seconds or so of rally-driving along a bumpy stretch of road, courtesy of your laconic driver, your vehicle emerges into a small car park. Your headlights illuminate some people standing near a car. Your companion exhales with relief. You think back on the obscurity of the turn-off to the right, which, frankly, you'd have missed had you not been looking for it.

'Thank god you knew the directions, mate. That right turn was a turn which, frankly, I'd have missed had you not been looking for it.'

That's odd, you think.

The car comes to a stop, and the engine ticks away to itself.

Turn to page 16.

30

The lumbering vehicle banks to the right, and begins down an unremarkable stretch of road. After about a minute, as the driver stares at the left side of the road for a turn-off, he makes a soft *hmmph* sound.

'You think we're lost, don't you?' you say to him.

'Do *you* think we're lost?' he retorts, still gazing out for any sign of a turn-off.

You consider your options here. You're driving around a very, very large national park at night, and there aren't any road signs. Firstly, from a planning and infrastructure perspective, that makes no sense. Why *aren't* there any signs? There should be signs! If you ever make it out of here alive, you're going to call whatever council manages the park and tell them: signs. Top priority. Make it happen.

Secondly, you now have a choice: do you admit you might have got it wrong and tell him to head back and take a left, then a right? Maybe you got it twisted. Or you can double down. It's your call, John. You're in control here.

'Fine. Left, then right.' Turn to page 16.

'Just keep driving. I'm not wrong.' Turn to page 34.

He smiles, nodding at the glove box. You open it and reach inside. There, nestled among the rego papers, is a small velvet bag. You weigh it in your hand. There's something inside. Powder?

You hold up the bag and look at him, warily. 'Fairy dust?' you venture. He grins broadly and nods in the affirmative. This is it, John. Fairy dust. Like in *Peter Pan*. All your childhood suspicions have just been confirmed in an instant. It's real. All of it. You pull the drawstring and down the lot. Off you go!

. . . To hospital, that is! The driver explains that he was having a laugh, and that the bag was very strong, very real heroin. Naturally, he doesn't explain that he was going to plant it on someone (doesn't matter who). He was crooked, you see. Crooked as they come. He kept that heroin there in his glove box for emergencies, and not in a million years would he have guessed someone would mistake it for a fictional substance from the works of J. M. Barrie.

But as they pull the sheet over your very, truly dead body, the driver rests easy in the knowledge that even if his evening was horrifying and surreal – which it was – at least it wasn't dull.

The End

Your adventure is over. You failed. If you wish to try again, turn back to the beginning at page 1.

Or, if you're done, wrap things up and go to page 369.

32

The driver nods. He negotiates his way onto an impossibly dark road, takes a left, and then a right, which, frankly, you'd have missed had you not been looking for it.

'Thank god you knew the directions, mate. That right turn was a turn which, frankly, I'd have missed had you not been looking for it.'

That's odd, you think.

After twenty seconds or so of rally-driving along a bumpy stretch of road by your laconic driver, your vehicle emerges into a small car park. Your headlights illuminate some people standing near a car. Your companion exhales with relief.

The car comes to a stop, and the engine ticks away to itself.

Turn to page 14.

The lumbering vehicle banks to the right, and begins down an unremarkable stretch of road. After about a minute, as the driver stares at the left side of the road for a turn-off, he makes a soft *hmmph* sound.

'You think we're lost, don't you?' you say to him.

'Do *you* think we're lost?' he retorts, still gazing out for any sign of a turn-off.

You consider your options here. You're driving around a very, very large national park at night, and there aren't any road signs. Firstly, from a planning and infrastructure perspective, that makes no sense. Why *aren't* there any signs? There should be signs! If you ever make it out of here alive, you're going to call whatever council manages the park and tell them: signs. Top priority. Make it happen.

Secondly, you now have a choice: do you admit you might have got it wrong and tell him to head back and take a left, then a right? Maybe you got it twisted. Or you can double down. It's your call, John. You're in control here.

'Fine. Left, then right.' Turn to page 32.

'Just keep driving. I'm not wrong.' Turn to page 34.

34

Look, John, maybe you're not wrong. If there's one thing you've become certain of over your years in the New South Wales Police Force, it's that you are – more often than not – right on the money. And you have a feeling that something important is just around the next bend. It's called police intuition. Either that, or it's run-of-the-mill paranoia and you're putting too much stock in it. Guess we'll find out soon, John!

The driver looks confused. The headlights are sputtering out, as are the cabin lights. The two of you can barely see a foot in front of the car. 'Shit,' the driver mutters. 'Can't see a fucking thing, John. Can you see where we're headed?'

'No, but . . . there's something out here, I'm sure of it.'

You squint ahead, trying to discern the next turn-off as the car continues to hurtle down the bumpy road into the abyss. And then, just as you think you see something . . .

WHUMP.

A body collides with the hood of the Kingswood. It hits the windscreen, punching through the glass and partially entering the cabin. You and the driver scream in unison, and the car veers drunkenly to the left. It hits a tree with terrifying force, sending your neck forward with a sickening snap.

And this is why you should always listen when you're given directions, John.

The End

Your adventure is over. You failed. If you wish to try again, turn back to the beginning at page 1.

Or, if you're done, wrap things up and go to page 369.

Fetid branches fracture underfoot. Mud is absolutely everywhere. You seem to recall it rained recently, but this is a big place, so who knows what you're walking on. Something in the back of your mind clicks, and you look down at your feet. You note, with some dismay, that you've once again worn suede shoes to a crime scene. A crime scene in a forest, no less.

'Nice shoes,' drawls Tie Pin, right on cue. You look at him askance, shifting your bag of forensics gear from one numb shoulder to the other. You nod at the detective, who is currently treading carefully over the bracken while struggling to see more than a metre or so ahead of him.

'Suede?' asks the detective.

Well?

You decide to answer in the affirmative. Turn to page 36.

You decide to stay quiet. Turn to page 37.

36

You mumble and nod in reply. A pause. The group continues their trek in silence, picking their way through the busted, fusty undergrowth.

'You waterproof 'em?' asks Tie Pin.

This time, you *do* say something. 'Did I what?'

'Did you waterproof them,' he repeats.

You cast an eye over at the detective. In these surrounds, his gleaming, gauche insect tie pin looks almost real. Tie Pin, to his credit, looks genuinely concerned about the welfare of your shoes. Here he is, clearly a fashionista of sorts, fretting about the structural integrity of your shoes.

'He's right,' pipes up Blue in the same helpful tone. 'You really oughta waterproof suede. It'll stop fading and stiffness.'

'What are those, pigskin suede?' queries Tie Pin, an inquisitive eyebrow raised.

'Nah, mate. Cowhide,' replies Blue, helpfully. 'Look at the finish.' He swings his torch towards John's feet.

'Cowhide,' agrees Tie Pin.

'OW,' says the prisoner in the lead, who, deprived momentarily of torchlight, has walked into a shin-high tree root. The beam turns back towards him with an apologetic mumble from Blue. The group resumes their progress in silence.

I'm surrounded, you think, *by staff writers from fucking* Vogue *magazine.*

After a time, just when you think the trees won't allow any more progress, the man in the prison greens says, 'We're here. Over there, in the clearing. To the left.'

You enter the clearing. Turn to page 38.

You keep trudging through the dark forest, clutching your kit bag to your side, trying to ignore the utter destruction being wrought upon your shoes. Tie Pin doesn't seem to know how to deal with your silence.

'Cow suede?'

'No,' you answer with a dryness your shoes would envy. 'Bison suede.'

A pause.

'Are you . . . are you being serious? Bison?'

Blue speaks up. 'Of course he's not being fuckin' serious, mate. It's suede. Ergo, it's cowhide,' he says to Tie Pin, helpfully, though a touch snarkily. 'Look at the finish.' He swings his torch towards your feet.

'Cowhide,' agrees Tie Pin. And while you're still worried about your shoes, you're sure you see a glimmer of respect from Blue for your pithy rejoinder towards his colleague's dumbass question. Which won't fix your shoes, true. But what will?

The group resumes its progress in silence.

After a time, just when you think the trees won't allow any more progress, the man in the prison greens pipes up. 'We're here. Over there, in the clearing. To the left.'

You enter the clearing. Turn to page 38.

38

You and your group reach an almost obstinately dense wall of trees. Just beyond it, the torchlight bleeds through enough to illuminate a very distinct, very small clearing. It looks like it'll be damn near impossible to get through, though.

'Shit,' curses the prisoner. 'It's just through there. Does anyone have anything we can use to cut through?'

If you wait for someone to figure something out, turn to page 39.

If you use your thermal lance to cut through, turn to page 40.

After a moment, Blue steps forward and, with strength you wouldn't have suspected he possessed based on his slender frame, he starts tearing trees away, flinging plant matter aside with ease. After a minute or so of work, there's a gap big enough for each of you to work your way through.

'You know what would have been useful?' remarks Tie Pin, almost to himself. 'A thermal lance.'

The group squeezes, one by one, into the clearing, and eventually the detectives, the driver and you turn to the prisoner. He's currently busy inspecting the ground, kicking at random spots and squinting. After a moment, he nods, satisfied, and addresses the detectives.

'It was here,' he says assuredly, gesturing his cuffed hands at a spot on the ground. You cast an eye over it. In this light, you can't really tell if the earth has been disturbed or not, but the detectives seem sold on it.

'Right,' says Tie Pin. 'Guess we'd better dig.'

All assembled slowly turn to look at you.

You draw forth your shovel for all to see. Turn to page 41.

40

Don't be a liar, you fucking liar. You don't have a thermal lance.

Do you even know what a thermal lance is? Get the fuck out of here. Thermal lance. Fuck, man.

You wait for someone to figure something out. Turn to page 39.

Look, we all knew this would happen, John. You picked the small trowel spade thing, whatever you want to call it, even though you *knew* it would be too small. Why? Well, only you know the answer to that. But enough prevaricating! Everyone is waiting to see what you'll pull out of your huge, useful-looking kit bag!

You wearily reach into the kit and withdraw the trowel. Part of you hopes it'll have somehow grown larger, as if, nestled among the other tools, it had time to blossom and grow.

But no. It's small.

Very small.

Comically small.

'Time to build a sandcastle, my tiny baby child son' small.

But . . . wait! Improbably, as you draw the tool out and hold it aloft, trying not to look like you're feeling like a bit of a tit, you notice a slight ridge along the underside of the handle. Come to think of it, the handle feels heavier than it ought to. What's that on the handle? A strange bump? Everyone is watching you very closely now, barely suppressing laughter. Your next step should be taken *very* carefully.

There's no point putting it off – you shrug and get to digging.
Turn to page 42.

You depress what is clearly a small button on the handle.
Turn to page 43.

42

John, look. As you may have gathered, or guessed, or divined, digging is a shit job. And the act of displacing soil and putting it in another place is, you reflect, not exactly your bailiwick. Your tiny trowel is strong, nobody is disputing that. But the body willing it into action – yours – is going to have to use the damned thing to unearth what the prisoner has dragged you all here for.

You begin by clearing aside some of the knotted vines, leaves, twigs and assorted fragments of sodden undergrowth. The soil awaiting you beneath this blanket of decaying matter is dark earth, and it looks a great deal denser and harder to dig into than you'd anticipated. You find a good spot, cross your fingers . . . And start digging.

Turn to page 98.

Look at these judgemental schmucks, you think. Guess what, John? This button is your saviour. It's the answer to the question all of these people are thinking: why didn't he bring a bigger shovel? Because, you idiots, this shovel can *get* bigger.

Ready to defend your loyal trowel's honour, you emphatically depress the button. Sure enough, you feel something loosen inside the handle. You hold the shovel out and watch, rapt, as . . .

Five inches of handle slide impotently forth from their hiding place. Guess what, big man? Now you're holding a stupidly small shovel with a slightly longer handle, *and* you've put on a big show to everyone in the process of revealing it. You know what? Probably should have just got straight to the digging, John. You made it worse.

No point putting it off any longer. You shrug and get to work.

Turn to page 42.

44

I edge open the bathroom door and look down the corridor towards the control room, where Dad is freaking out and/or plotting. His angry call with someone is reaching fever pitch. I close the door as quietly as I can and tiptoe to another door, marked MUNITIONS. I open it and sneak inside.

There's a lot of cool stuff here, but I've gotta plant something that makes sense within the context of the story, so Dad won't suspect I did this. And whatever I plant, it can't be seen as anachronistic.

I scan the wall of firearms, grab a 1981 Glock 17, and check the magazine. Shit. Four bullets. If he misses, he's dead. Let's hope there aren't more than four people for him to deal with. And how the hell will he know it's for him? I need to make it stand out. I pull out my penknife, and carve his initials into the handle. 'H.S.'

I dart out of the room, checking the coast is clear, then run down more corridors, past banks of server rooms, and into the generator room. I can smell hot ink, and the fumes make my eyes burn. But I head to the portal, spin a few dials, and heave open the steel sliding door with a grunt. There, through the doorway, is an eighties-era lift, floor covered with orange shag carpet. I spot a loose panel of the carpet, prise it up and slip the gun under, with the initialled end of the handle visible. As I shut the portal and spin the dials back to neutral, I hear a *ding* and the shuffle of footsteps.

Close. That was too close. One more thing to do: go back, write in the single stupidest item I can think of into the story, then pray to god Seltzer figures out how to use it without blowing himself up. That he pays close attention to the readout number. Then . . . then we might have a real fighting chance here.

Time will tell if I've somehow pulled any of this off.

Your adventure is over. If you wish to try again, turn back to the beginning at page 1.

Or, if you're done, wrap things up and go to page 369.

Like bloodhounds, the previously inert detectives look down at you, suddenly ready and willing to do their jobs, almost as if they've sniffed a treat on the wind.

'Here we go,' slavers Tie Pin, rubbing his hands together and getting down onto his haunches. His knees give little muffled pops as he reaches ground level. Blue looks about the place, off into the woods, an excited pep in his step.

'See?' declares the prisoner. 'See? Right here. I said it was here.'

'Shhhhh,' says Tie Pin.

Shhhhhhh, says the trowel in response, as it slides through a tract of coarse earth, sounding like a wet hard broom breezing across hot asphalt.

Another *SHUNK*.

Great work, John. You found the body. But what do you do now? Think carefully.

You put on your gloves. Turn to page 46.

You keep digging a little further. Turn to page 47.

46

Safety first, John. Very good.

You snap on your rubber gloves, the sound of the latex whapping against your hand echoing around the clearing, sharp and fricative in the murk. Without taking your eyes off the spot where your trowel just found its mark, you reach back into your kit bag and cleanly withdraw a brush from its tiny holster, unclipping it with a diminutive *fffffut*.

They're watching me now, you think. *They're not talking shit now.*

Like Indiana Jones gingerly clearing stray grains of sand from a deliciously valuable artefact, you sweep the brush left, then right. Left, then right. Left, then . . .

Bones. Human bones.

A rib. And ribs tend, you muse dryly, to come as part of a set. So you move the brush south a little and repeat the motion. Left, then right. Left, then right. After a few minutes, during which all assembled crane forward in ecstatic silence, your progress reveals a series of ribs. Then, as you continue, you find hip bones. Then, thigh bones. Then, knee bones.

'Now hear the word of the lord,' you sing to yourself.

Shins. Ankles. The jacket, shirt and pants that had kept the bones hidden from the world are largely rotted away, but what soon lies revealed before you all is the bulk of a body, crammed in a hole about a foot deep.

What's next, John?

You decide to inspect the hands. Turn to page 48.

You inspect the face. Turn to page 49.

You search the clothing. Turn to page 50.

You check the shoes. Turn to page 51.

You leave your gloves where they are, snug in a tiny cardboard sleeve in your kit bag. Who needs protection? You're John Verhoeven. You've had to deal with a siege on the job. You've driven at breakneck speed pursuing evil men. You've encountered a witch. You're a seasoned police officer with a skill set second to none. *Who cares,* you think, *how small my trowel is. I don't need a trowel. I don't need gloves! I'm a maverick!*

Unfortunately, you're so carried away with this newfound surge of (frankly justifiable) confidence in your abilities that your next dig comes in far too hard, too fast, and your trowel bursts through the bones lying inches beneath the surface. You've just destroyed evidence needed for a massive court case, with two senior homicide detectives watching, both of whom have been growing more and more impatient over the past hour as you dug and dug and dug.

Tie Pin seizes your shoulder.

The next day, you're fired.

The End

Your adventure is over. You failed. If you wish to try again, turn back to the beginning at page 1.

Or, if you're done, wrap things up and go to page 369.

48

John, John, John. You are in for a dreadful surprise.

You carefully, oh-so-carefully, trace a line down the sleeve of the corpse lying in front of you, the body curled up like some dead beetle found desiccated underneath a bed somewhere. You reach the cuff, and you begin brushing to unearth the hand. Maybe there's something grasped in it, some grisly artefact, some clue as to who did this. And in a way, you're right on that front.

You brush.

And brush.

And brush.

And . . . brush.

There's no hand. It's been sheared off at the wrist. You look up at Tie Pin and Blue to gauge their reaction to this frankly startling revelation. They look back at you with expressions that imply . . . something odd. A decided lack of surprise, for one. Did they know this person was going hands-free?

For the sake of thoroughness, you head across to the other wrist. The forest seems even more silent than it did before. You brush, brush, brush . . . nothing. *Nothing up your sleeves,* you think, looking down at the deceased. *Quite the trick someone pulled on you.*

Where do you look next?

You decide to inspect the face. Turn to page 49.

You search the clothing. Turn to page 50.

You check the shoes. Turn to page 51.

You conclude your preliminary investigation. Turn to page 52.

Being shot in the head is a remarkably common way to die at the hands of a firearm, at least in circumstances like this one, where it looks like the murder was probably planned. You figure out where the chest is, delicately chart a course up to the collar, and begin clearing away the sodden earth. Bit by bit.

And . . .

Wait.

There's no head.

This is a headless body.

'This is a headless body,' you exclaim, shooting a look up at the detectives. They don't look entirely shocked, nor do they have the common decency to feign shock. Perhaps they knew this body would be here? But if that's the case, why didn't they tell you before you started digging? Questions. Questions.

And not a lot of answers.

What's your next move?

You decide to inspect the hands. Turn to page 48.

You search the clothing. Turn to page 50.

You check the shoes. Turn to page 51.

You conclude your preliminary investigation. Turn to page 52.

50

The body is wearing a ruined, decayed jacket of some sort. It's dark in colour, and bits of it are already peeking up from the soil, so it doesn't take much digging to reveal the garment for all and sundry.

You check the pockets. Nothing. Nothing at all.

You know you shouldn't, but you can't help wondering what it felt like to be buried in this place. You have no way of knowing for certain at this stage whether this poor sod was killed here, or killed off-site and brought here later, but instinct tells you it's the latter. You look up at the trees gripping the tiny clearing, as if they're threatening to close ranks and engulf it completely.

There are worse places to die, you suppose, but offhand you can't think of any.

You decide to inspect the hands. Turn to page 48.

You inspect the face. Turn to page 49.

You check the shoes. Turn to page 51.

You conclude your preliminary investigation. Turn to page 52.

You trace your way down the trousers, towards the feet. Retrieving a different brush, you begin clearing loose soil from around the shoes of the deceased. And after a minute or so of clearing, you squint at them. That can't be right, John. Can it?

An odd noise from Tie Pin, some kind of surprised harrumph, tickles your brain. But you barely hear it.

Suede shoes. Remarkably similar to yours, in fact. Maybe even the same make. The feet are large, like yours, meaning the body is likely that of a man. No intel is bad intel, but you feel a little sick. Those are your shoes.

'Oh my god,' mutters Blue, leaning down for a closer look.

You swallow nervously, beads of sweat breaking out over your face.

'. . . See? He's waterproofed his. They're in fantastic nick.'

You lean in closer still. The bastard is right. They look less ruined than yours do, and they've literally been buried in a forest on a decaying body.

What's next?

You decide to inspect the hands. Turn to page 48.

You inspect the face. Turn to page 49.

You search the clothing. Turn to page 50.

You conclude your preliminary investigation. Turn to page 52.

You put down your tools and look up at the two detectives. Your clothes cling to your body after an hour of feverish digging, and it's so quiet you could hear a pin drop.

'Did you boys know this body was here?'

Tie Pin and Blue give each other a furtive though guiltless look.

'Old mate here—' Tie Pin says, gesturing towards the prisoner '—had info on the location of a murder victim, who was offed in a . . . contentious case.'

'Contentious,' agrees Blue. 'The prisoner claims someone on the inside told him exactly where the body was, so we got dispensation to bring him out here and find the body. Said he was killed by—'

'Mr Asia,' you finish.

The lack of head, the lack of hands. It all makes sense. It's the M.O. of Terry Clark. Other aliases include Terry Sinclair, Alexander James Sinclair, Tony Bennetti, the Australian Jackal and Mr Big. You strongly suspect those last two were penned by Clark himself to make himself sound cool, but you can't back that up. Just a hunch, really. Clark is head of the Mr Asia drug syndicate, which flooded heroin into New Zealand, Australia and the UK in the seventies. He would, rather smartly, make the task of identifying his victims sublimely difficult by ensuring the removal of their hands and faces. How, after all, are you supposed to fingerprint this fellow, John, if he doesn't have any fingers?

You also realise there's no way this prisoner was 'told' where the body was. This path he led you all down was incredibly specific.

'You were here,' you tell him.

He looks uncomfortable. 'Nah, mate.'

'I think you were,' you retort. 'You knew exactly where this bloke was. You were here when it happened. And if this is

Mr Asia . . . fellas, there's a royal commission going on right now, a massive court case! This is . . . we can't be here! If anyone knows we're here, we'll . . .'

And just as the detectives are about to cut you off, it happens.

From deep within the murky depths of the forest, there's a flood of unnatural light. The whole clearing is lit up, and bizarre noises filter towards you.

You look closer into the light.

Turn to page 67.

54

You give the two detectives curt handshakes, ask them not to involve you any further, and make a break for it back the way you came. The driver follows you, holding your kit bag and whipping out a penlight of his own to light the way. That was a close one, John. You have the strangest feeling you just dodged a bullet there.

After a torturous twenty minutes trudging through the undergrowth, you slow to a stop. This, you realise, isn't the way you came. It's almost impossible to see, but you're fairly sure there's the rough outline of a track before you, forking off in two directions. You nudge the driver's shoulder, and he swings his feeble beam forward. Yep. Two paths. Not good ones, but paths nonetheless.

'Shit,' remarks the driver, looking a little lost. 'Do you remember which way we needed to go?'

There's that deja vu again, John.

There's that deja vu again, John.

Go left, then take a right. Turn to page 68.

Go right, then take a left. Turn to page 69.

Over the coming week, you're hauled into Internal Affairs and raked over the coals. Who told the press? You don't know, you tell them. You approved the prisoner's release? Not you, and you don't know who did, you insist. Hours of relentless grilling, accusations of potentially jeopardising a vital case being built against one of the world's most notorious drug kingpins. You should have asked more questions, Internal Affairs tells you. You should have pushed back against the detectives. It's your job to call bullshit. You're complicit. Or, at the very least, you're lazy. Maybe even negligent.

You don't know how much of what they say is real, and how much is being hurled at you just to make you sweat, but you're sweating all right. You're dripping.

You reflect on what happened, and consider how things might have played out had you made different choices.

It's your call, John. Care to find out?

You decide to start all over again. Turn back to page 1.

You decide to finish this. Turn to page 100.

56

I look closer at the man on the tiny cathode-ray monitor. The picture is grainy but adequate, and you see him checking out his reflection, seeming to look straight at us. Dad stares right back. He seems less unnerved by all of this than I am, which given what he's lived through – which is to say, this – isn't all that surprising.

Hiding a camera in the cabinet was, I realise, a canny move.

Then, something occurs that is a little . . . odd. The John in the monitor stands up, leans towards the cabinet, and pauses. Then, he says just two words.

'Hey, handsome.'

And Dad, who is transfixed, says back, 'Hey.'

I can't tell whether John has seen Dad, or whether Dad even knows he's responding. But the moment passes, and John leaves the office. I realise I've been holding my breath, so I exhale and cross the room to check some readouts. Maybe I should check on Dad.

Turn to page 94.

You look at the prisoner. He's wearing prison greens, the kind worn by those in prison, hence 'prison greens'. The actual colour you're looking at is fondly known outside of prison as 'British racing green', a name that conjures up images of freedom: breezing down a country road, past a village, on a warm spring day; cottages; glens; babbling brooks. *Probably best not to tease the inmate by mentioning this,* you think. *Probably best just to refer to his clothes as 'prison greens'.*

You notice that his shoes are green, too, and bound with two velcro straps apiece. His hands are, mercifully, cuffed. He looks like he's clutching something in them, but on closer inspection you realise he's probably just cramped from the cuffs.

You look up at him. He's momentarily distracted by the crunchy little protectors your shoes have been fitted with. While you can't get a clear read on what's going through his head, an unsettling thought flits through yours: you've seen this man before.

Before you can ascertain where, it's time.

Time to get moving into the forest.

Turn to page 58.

58

Fetid branches fracture underfoot. Mud is absolutely everywhere. You seem to recall it rained recently, but this is technically a rainforest, so who knows what you're walking on. Something twigs, and you look down at your feet.

Bone dry, baby. Bone dry.

Noticing you noticing his handiwork, Flynn pipes up from next to you. 'Little trick my wife taught me,' he says. 'Last family holiday. We were up at Byron, doing an impromptu bushwalk after we had lunch at some restaurant. I had a few too many tinnies in me, and before I could plough into the bush wearing my best boat shoes she grabs a waiter, tells me to hang on a tick, and then *whaps* two bags on me shoes. Neatest trick I ever saw. You married, John?'

You answer in the affirmative, telling him about Christine and about your two young children, Paul and Anne.

Jack speaks. 'Can't be arsed having kids, but good for you. No time for it, honestly.'

There's something nestled in the notably awkward pause that follows. You look over at the detectives. They look like they're about to say something, without knowing quite how to say it.

You decide not to push your luck, and keep walking. Turn to page 59.

You decide to ask them what's wrong. Turn to page 27.

You've somehow managed to gain some cred with two seasoned homicide detectives. Best not to push it. This elevation in status does, however, give you a few precious minutes during the ensuing silence to reflect on your evening thus far.

You're currently tracking in what feels like large, aberrant loops in what you're worried may be an abstract, unquantifiable space within a lightless national park. And while it's a beautiful place for families to visit, it's also the wilderness. Who knows what's out here. You have an overactive imagination this evening, John, and that imagination begins to wander. Is that a dingo scampering just out of sight? You're fairly certain you heard something out there, in the morass of trees. It's a living thing, this thing you're in. You're out of your depth now.

And just as the tongue of panic begins lapping at your door . . .

You realise you've reached the spot.

Turn to page 61.

60

He's wearing prison greens, as you suspected. His snug tracksuit is a pleasing shade of what you will later come to learn is called 'British racing green'. His shoes are both fastened with two velcro straps. The feet in said shoes are shifting uneasily on the spot.

His hands are, mercifully, cuffed. The hands in said cuffs are fidgeting uneasily on the spot.

You look up at him. He has a fairly nondescript face, the kind you'd likely not be able to describe after tonight. It's a nice face, you think, but you can't be sure. What is 'nice'? He is, after all, fresh out of prison. You wonder how long it has been since he stepped outside the confines of his cell, how long it has been since he smelled freedom. Is he happy to be here? Perhaps that's why his face struck you as nice. Upon closer inspection, you realise he's looking right at you.

You realise you're staring. Stop staring, John.

You look at the detectives. Turn to page 26.

You introduce yourself. Turn to page 28.

You and your group reach a seemingly impenetrable wall of trees. Just beyond it, the torchlight bleeds through to illuminate a very distinct, very small clearing. Jack and Flynn direct their torches at the wall of trees, trying to figure out how to get around it.

'Shit,' curses the prisoner. 'Shit. It's just through there. Does anyone have anything we can use to cut through?'

After a moment, Flynn steps forward and, with strength you'd never have suspected he possessed based on his slender frame, he starts tearing trees away, forcing them aside. After a minute or so of hard work, there's a gap big enough for each of you to work your way through.

The group squeezes, one by one, into the clearing, and eventually the detectives, the driver and you turn to the prisoner. He's currently busy eyeballing the ground, kicking at random spots and squinting. After a moment, he nods, satisfied, and addresses the detectives.

'It was here,' he says assuredly, gesturing his cuffed hands at a spot on the ground. You cast an eye over it. In this light, you can't really tell if the earth has been disturbed or not, but the detectives seemed sold on it.

'Right,' says Jack. 'Guess we'd better dig.'

All assembled slowly turn to look at you.

Turn to page 62.

62

You smile grimly, pop down your kit bag on one side of the spot, and start carefully digging.

'How deep?' you ask the prisoner, before really sinking the boot in.

'About a foot,' he says, noncommittally.

You nod, and begin. The soil has a bit of fight to it. It's a good thing, you think as you begin shovelling, that you packed a real shovel.

Fifteen minutes later, you've not only cleared the entire grave, you've also got the body lying in front of you, largely cleared of the dark, damp soil that lay atop it. You're sweaty as hell and out of breath, but everyone seems very pleased with your work. Well done, John.

Good call on that shovel.

You drive it into the ground to one side of the grave, wipe your brow, and kneel down to assess the body in front of you.

You reach into your kit bag and snap on your rubber gloves. The sound of the latex whapping against your hand echoes around the clearing, sharp and fricative in the murk. Without looking away from the grave, you reach back and cleanly withdraw a brush from its tiny holster, unclipping it with a diminutive *pop*.

Then, without further ado, you start your inspection. It's time to very carefully wipe off any dirt or muck from the bones. It's time to get to work.

Where do you look first?

You have a closer look at the hands. Turn to page 63.

You have a look at the face. Turn to page 64.

You brush.

And brush.

And brush.

And . . .

Well, shit. There's no hand. It's been sheared off at the wrist. You look up at Jack and Flynn to gauge their reactions to this frankly startling revelation. The look you get back is one of guilt, combined with a clear urge to explain, to clarify.

'Look, mate, we kind of expected a lack of hands. He may have mentioned it to us.' Flynn jerks his thumb at the prisoner, who gives you an oddly informal wave.

You head across to the other wrist. You brush, brush, brush . . . nothing. *Nothing up your sleeves*, you think, looking down at the deceased. *Quite the trick someone pulled on you.*

You have a closer look at the face. Turn to page 64.

You decide to wrap this up. Turn to page 65.

64

You delicately chart a course up to the collar, and begin clearing away the sodden earth. Bit by bit.

And . . .

Wait.

There's no head.

This is a headless body.

'This is a headless body,' you exclaim, shooting a look up at the detectives. They don't look entirely shocked. Perhaps they knew this would be what you'd find? But if that's the case, why didn't they tell you before you started digging? Maybe they would have told you, if you'd handled your conversations with them differently. But it's too late now.

Damn it.

Over to you, John. What do you do now?

You have a closer look at the hands. Turn to page 63.

You decide to wrap this up. Turn to page 65.

You stand up and look right at the two detectives and the man in his fetching prison greens. The driver lingers quietly off to one side. *Now*, you think, *is the time to get some answers.*

'So,' you say, 'based on the size, this is likely a dead male, age indeterminate at this stage. Cause of death . . . given the destruction of the head and hands, probably an execution.' The detectives are nodding along with your preliminary assessment, watching keenly to see what you'll say next.

'Old mate here—' Jack says, gesturing towards the prisoner '—had info on the location of a murder victim, who was offed in a . . . contentious case.'

'Contentious,' agrees Flynn, carrying on Jack's point. 'The prisoner claims someone on the inside told him exactly where the body was, so we got dispensation to bring him out here and find the body. Said he was killed by—'

'Mr Asia,' you finish grimly.

The lack of a head, the lack of hands. It all makes sense. This is the M.O. of Terry Clark. Heroin bigwig. Real piece of shit, you reflect, conjuring up details from cases involving a few of his associates. Mr Asia's signature move? Making it bewilderingly difficult for anyone to identify his victims by removing their hands and heads.

But you're on a roll now, John. You turn to face the prisoner. 'There's no way you were "told" where this body was, mate. This is all too specific. You were here, weren't you?'

The man looks uncomfortable, floundering a little.

You keep pushing. 'You knew exactly where this bloke was. And if this is Mr Asia . . .' You turn to the detectives. 'There's a royal commission going on! This is . . . we can't be here! If anyone knows we're here, we'll . . .'

You pause. Your eye hurts, a sudden throbbing seizing you

66

like a vice. The driver steps forward, looking concerned, but you wave him off. The pain passes. 'If anyone knows we're here, we're fucked. And . . . hang on, where are you two stationed?'

That gets them, John. And that's probably what you almost got out of them before you all reached the clearing – they *knew* this body was here, and they're *not* from this precinct. Meaning, not only are they trying to claim credit for a find that will complicate an ongoing case making its way through Australia's highest court, but on top of that, they're not even legally allowed to work this area.

Something tells you you'd better make tracks, John. You say your goodbyes and leave.

Turn to page 54.

The sound of footsteps – many footsteps – reaches you. The detectives puff up. Tie Pin gently pats his hair back into place, and Blue inexplicably smells his breath in his hand. Satisfied, he stands up tall, clenching his jaw heroically.

And *WHAM*. Bursting through the treeline comes a Channel Ten news camera, a small floodlight affixed to the front. A sound guy clambers into the clearing, along with the camera operator, and . . . there he is. Harry Potter, criminal reporter for Channel Ten. His thick black eyebrows sit in an almost horizontal line across his face, like two blackboard erasers. The camera sweeps past the two detectives, both posing like two marble-hewn juggernauts, and onto you.

You, holding your idiotic trowel in one limp hand, kneeling over a headless, handless body in a crude grave, sweaty and exhausted, hunched in a tiny clearing in the middle of nowhere.

Harry monologues to camera, then fires off a barrage of questions. And as you watch the scene unfold, with the blood draining from your face, you realise that the detectives' calm demeanour and their unusual level of grooming, coupled with the fact that the news crew must have known *exactly* where to find you, indicates one thing very clearly.

Glory boys. They tipped off the press. Good exposure, hell of a get – the two detectives who unearthed a victim of Mr Asia. And if they'd told you their plan before you'd come all the way out here, you'd have never gone along with it.

And now you're in deep shit.

Turn to page 55.

68

You begin down the path and take a left, then take the next right. You figure that if that route was good enough for the Kingswood, it'll be good enough for the two of you on foot. And sure enough . . . you're somehow spat out into the car park. Sure, you're across the other side from where you initially took the path to the clearing, but you've made it. The night is still pitch black, but thanks to the moonlight you can see the detectives' car is still here. You're once again buoyed by the feeling that you've pulled off something quite miraculous here, but you're not entirely sure what it is.

You trot over to the Kingswood, open the boot, and throw in the shovel. You gesture for the forensics kit, which the driver hands to you, and rifle through it quickly to make sure you didn't do anything stupid like leave behind one of your brushes, marked as they are with your name in tiny, immaculate handwritten letters.

As you're finishing up your inspection, you hear a noise. From behind you, the purring of a motor. Your shadow is cast across the car as a pair of headlights get closer.

For some reason unbeknown to you, a thought echoes through your head: *I was too slow. They're here.* You turn to face the head-lights. You hear the slam of a door, and a small floodlight is cast upon you. And there he is: Harry Potter, criminal reporter for Channel Ten. His thick black eyebrows sit like two blackboard erasers across his face. The camera is aimed at you, and Harry is hurling questions your way. Two questions in particular: Where is the body? And what are you wearing on your feet? You swallow and begin to attempt an explanation.

You're in deep shit.

Turn to page 55.

One of the least enjoyable elements of any adventure is when you're dumped in an unwinnable scenario: a Kobayashi Maru, as it were. As you and your driver scramble through the undergrowth of the forest, you think to yourself . . .

Running through the forest, on a frightening adventure. Wouldn't it be just the worst if I fell prey to some kind of stupid, pointless death, this close to a meaningful conclusion?

And because the universe can be a merciless bastard, that's exactly what happens, in a manner of speaking. Your shovel – your wonderful, enormous shovel – tumbles from your grasp. You trip on a vine, and in a freakish yet completely preventable tragedy, fall neck-first towards the head of said shovel.

SHLUMP.

Your head falls to the forest floor. And as the driver panics, screams and runs off into the darkness, gripped by an existential dread and soon to be hit by a vehicle driving hard down a dirt road into the darkness, you pass on. And you realise that it is, in fact . . .

The End

Your adventure is over. You failed. If you wish to try again, turn back to the beginning at page 1.

Or, if you're done, wrap things up and go to page 369.

70

'Beberly Bellbo,' you venture.

The driver turns to you slowly and gives you the look someone might if you'd walked into a christening, shat in your hands, and clapped. 'Beberly Bellbo? Did you have a fucking stroke?'

Look, you don't *think* you had a stroke. But saying Beberly Bellbo out loud was an odd thing to say, even for you. Were you trying to say Beverly? Maybe if you explain what you meant, that you were trying to say Beverly, he'll calm down. Maybe.

But after reading the room – which is, in fact, a car – you decide to just shut up and ask the red-faced driver what music he has.

Turn to page 22.

You stare at the driver, taking in every aspect of his appearance, his posture, his demeanour. It strikes you like a backhand to the face that this man looks exactly like the actor Steve McQueen. And not just a little bit like Steve McQueen, either: *exactly* like Steve McQueen. He can't be that Steve McQueen, obviously; the actor died back in late 1980. You remember being properly devastated by the news.

But you've had a long shift, John. You've had a long year. You're tired, it's dark, and you have a strange feeling in the back of your skull, flickering like a wasp trapped between blinds and a window. Maybe, your brain posits in its current state, he *is* Steve McQueen. In which case . . . may as well bite the Bullitt.

'Steve McQueen,' you guess aloud.

He looks thrown. Then he laughs, throwing his head back. 'Steve McQueen! Steve . . . no, John. Not Steve McQueen. But that's quite a compliment. Tell you what . . . I'm so tickled by that, I'll give you your prize anyway. I'll let you pick some music to listen to.'

You wonder if this was what you'd have won if you'd guessed his name correctly.

You ask the driver what music he has.

Turn to page 22.

72

'Yeah,' Kevin states matter-of-factly. 'That's . . . incredible, actually. Hole in one. How'd you . . . You know what? Never mind. You're all right, John.' Between this and the shovel, you seem to be on a roll.

You give Kevin a look as subtle as you can manage. Eventually, a look of realisation crosses his face. 'Right! Your reward. Of course. I don't often do this, but . . . I'll let you put on some tunes.' He smiles pleasantly, as if he's just handed you the keys to the kingdom.

'Level with me, Kevin,' you reply. 'If I'd asked you to let me put on some tunes without having guessed your name right, would you have still let me put on some tunes?'

'You'll never know, John. You'll never know.'

It occurs to you, somewhere in the deepest recesses of your mind, that you will know. At some point, you will know. 'At some point, Kevin, I will know,' you say. The words come out unbidden.

Kevin looks confused.

You ask him what music he has.

Turn to page 22.

You pull up outside the detectives' office, climb out of the Kingswood, lovingly shut her door, and head into the foyer through the huge double doors. The lighting is uncharacteristically low. There's some bad energy in here, Seltzer. But they want you upstairs, so upstairs you must go.

Two burly detectives enter the foyer behind you, walking around you and making a beeline for the lift. You watch as they depress the UP button and wait, arms folded, conspicuously avoiding eye contact with you. Their loss. You have eyes like sapphires, Seltzer.

You reach into your jacket pocket and withdraw a battered pack of cigarettes and a matchbook. You make a show of busying yourself lighting the damn thing, but really, you're keeping one eye on the two cavemen. Never can be too careful.

Finally, the lift arrives with a lurch and a woozy ding.

What do you want to do, Seltzer?

You run to make the lift. Turn to page 75.

Forget the lift – you're taking the stairs. Turn to page 80.

There's a glass pane on the door. The writing on it is reversed, so as to be readable for anyone standing outside. Go ahead, hold this up to a mirror if you like, John.

-HARD SELTZER-
DETECTIVE AGENCY
o o o
EST. 1983

You cast your eye over the rest of the office. Formica floors, venetian blinds. A half-smoked cigarette idling in a glittering crystal skull that serves as an ashtray. But you don't smoke, do you?

Icehouse's 'Electric Blue' is playing on the stereo. Your clothes, you notice, are different now: a dusty pink linen suit jacket, sleeves rolled up. White henley. Powder-blue slacks. White boat shoes. As you fumble about, panicked, you touch the moustache on your face. You . . . have a moustache now, John. Which is odd. You can't grow a moustache.

Or maybe you can, Seltzer, maybe you can. Also, you just referred to yourself as Seltzer. That's odd, too. Probably just a typo. To calm yourself, you reach a shaking hand down to seize the tiny, ashy cigarette from the jaws of the crystal skull and take a drag. The filthy smoke roils in your lungs, sending a wave of energy crashing into the back of your cerebellum.

'If the commish wants me downtown, well, shit. Downtown is where I'm going,' you mutter to yourself. You mash out the cigarette, stand up, crack your back, and grab your car keys. You head to the door and open it, step outside, lock it, and saunter downstairs to your car. The Kingswood sits waiting, like a polished steed, eyes dark, engine ready to purr. You slip inside, and push a Tatsuro Yamashita cassette into the player. Time to roll out, Senior Detective Hard Seltzer.

Turn to page 73.

'Hold up, fellas!' you bellow, running over and sliding a hand between the two doors as they close. Sensing your extremities, the doors belatedly creak back open, and the two detectives inside exchange a look. You cross the threshold, and stand facing the doors as they close. You press for the fourth floor, and wait.

The lift is slow. Very slow. You can hear the two men behind you, but only just. They're being very quiet. Very, very quiet. Almost . . . *too* quiet.

There's another ding, and the lift stops on the second floor. The doors yawn open, and in step another two detectives. These fellers are as big as the first two, and they stand between you and the door.

SHUNK. The door closes. You're literally surrounded by large, quiet men. Should you be worried? Well, Seltzer, here's your answer.

'Seltzer,' mumbles one of the blokes behind you. 'Come with us. Someone wants a word with you.' And to illustrate his point, the muzzle of a gun nestles into the small of your back.

Sloppy, Seltzer. Very sloppy. Should have known this was a set-up. The commissioner wouldn't have had someone call on his behalf; he always calls in person. You two go way back, back to The Murder in Montmartre. This whole thing stank from the beginning, Seltzer. And you just blocked your nose, didn't you?

One of the goons in front hits the emergency stop button, then presses the one for the below-ground car park. You're never gonna make it to your destination. You have about thirty seconds to try to fix this.

You leap into action, Seltzer-style. Turn to page 77.

You go along with them . . . for now. Turn to page 76.

76

Suddenly, the lights in the lift gutter out. The tiny capsule shakes, and a deafening roar fills your eyes. You can't see a thing, Seltzer; you're in agony. You wonder if the commissioner is okay, if he's even still alive. You get a flash of something, something odd . . . a man, in his fifties, sitting over a bank of cathode-ray screens, depressing a red button with reluctance. You see a flicker of trees, whooshing to and fro in the wind. You see . . . a body? Is that a body, in a grave somewhere? Then you see the door to your office, your name reflected back at you in reverse. The glass pane bearing the letters shatters. You're back in the dark lift. It's utter chaos. You feel the cable snap, and it plummets into the abyss.

And you die, obviously.

But you're Hard Seltzer. You've survived worse. And something tells you you'll do better next time.

The End

Your adventure is over. You failed. If you wish to try again, turn back to the beginning at page 1.

Or, if you're done, wrap things up and go to page 369.

One of the goons begins humming to himself. 'Electric Blue'. And with a flood of terror, you realise what's going on. They've been bugging your office. You see an earpiece in the brute's ear. He's probably still listening to your office right now.

You look down. Beneath a fold in the orange shag carpet, up against the lift wall, is a small, dark nub. And you know what it is. You don't know how it got there, but you know what it is.

A still-lit cigarette hangs lackadaisically from your mouth. You take a puff, let the smoke swirl in your lungs, then hold the cigarette between your thumb and forefinger, lifting it in front of your face. 'Anyone want a smoke?' you ask casually. And then, as the lift continues to totter down the shaft towards your final destination, you drop the lit cigarette. You catch it with your free hand, then swiftly swing the lit end into the eye of the man behind you.

There's a startled scream. You throw yourself to the floor, reach for the concealed object beneath the carpet, then grasp it and draw it out. A 1981 Glock 17. Your initials, 'H.S.', are carved improbably into the handle. *Someone meant for you to find this.* With a blur of movement, you whip out your handkerchief, wrap it around the muzzle of the gun, and look up at the three men, who are startled but starting to converge.

SHUFF. SHUFF.

SHUFF. SHUFF.

A series of thumps. A ding. The lift door groans open, light spilling out into the subterranean car park.

A moment later, you peek out. Behind you, four bodies lie sprawled in the lift, a tiny third eye punctuating each of their enormous foreheads. If men's lives are sentences, you just laid down a quartet of fatal full stops.

Turn to page 78.

78

You drop the now-flaming handkerchief, your makeshift silencer, to the ground. A pity. Lottie got you that handkerchief.

But who the hell hid the gun? You inspect it now. Empty. Good thing you never miss.

You can't see far into the car park, but if the men were bringing you here to kill you, there's no saying how much more muscle they have waiting.

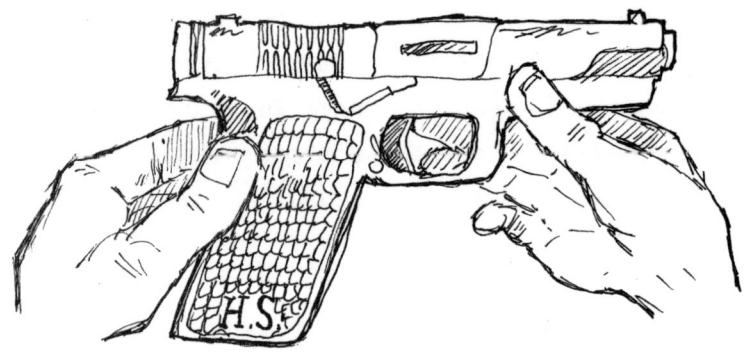

You head back up to the ground floor. Turn to page 76.

You venture into the darkness. Turn to page 81.

80

You make a beeline for the stairwell. You open the door and step inside, shoes sending echoes into the concrete ziggurat winding its way to the top of the building. You, Hard Seltzer, are going straight to the top. And god help this 'commissioner' when you find him. And you will find him, Seltzer. You always find your mark.

As you trot up the stairs, you begin to realise there aren't any numbers signifying which floor to exit on. After a while, you realise you're getting sweaty. Confused. The light in here isn't quite right, and there's a sound somewhere in the distance. It's either a busted air-conditioning unit, or an orchestra warming up in hell. Probably, you concede, the former.

But as you continue up, up, up for what feels like hours, it becomes readily apparent that something has gone very wrong in the building. And that maybe, just maybe, it wasn't an air-conditioning unit you heard. And as you reach the top floor, impossibly, ruinously tired, you see it.

The seventieth floor.

You reach for the doorhandle, but there's a stabbing pain. Your heart, taxed from the climb, seizes like a fist. You collapse, and die. But you're Hard Seltzer.

You can always try something else next time.

The End

Your adventure is over. You failed. If you wish to try again, turn back to the beginning at page 1.

Or, if you're done, wrap things up and go to page 369.

You hold the gun aloft, step out of the lift, and watch it close. The bodies sprawled inside are utterly motionless, and you give them a doleful nod as they disappear from view. Your instructor at the academy always said you were a hell of a shot, Seltzer, but you doubt this was the kind of marksmanship she'd approve of. But she's dead now, you think, a moody jazz lick drifting in from nowhere. She died in your arms. Maybe if she hadn't taken that bullet for you, you wouldn't be here now, on the run, alone, out-numbered. But that's love, kid. That's love.

The problem here, Seltzer, is that you've spent so long mono-loguing in the darkness that you didn't notice a fifth man, creeping up behind you with his revolver raised. Just as you're about to head into the garage to try to hotwire one of the nearby vehicles, the revolver handle connects with your skull. *I never should have gone out tonight*, you think as the lights do exactly that: go out.

Turn to page 82.

82

'Wake up, Seltzer.'

You don't want to wake up. Because you're almost certain that when you do wake up, something very unpleasant will happen. And you've had just about your fill of unpleasant tonight. Your whole life has been a litany of unpleasant events. But you have a splitting headache, and blood is likely pooling in your brain. They hit you hard, perhaps a great deal harder than they intended to. And if you're going to make any sense of this, you need to wake up, Seltzer.

Your eyes open like busted blinds being drawn up at a dizzying angle. Light pours in. So much light, in fact, that you can't see anything *but* the light. You go to move, but you've been tied to a chair. The voice speaks up again from somewhere past the wall of light.

'Ahh, good. You're awake. I was wondering if they'd hit you too hard, Seltzer.' They absolutely did hit you too hard, for the record. You know it, and you suspect he knows it. Something is going wrong in the old noggin, Seltzer, and you're having trouble keeping your eyes open. 'Stay with me, Seltzer. Listen. You've pissed off a lot of people.'

'Who and how?' you mumble dizzily.

'Well,' continues the voice, 'the "who" doesn't matter. As for the how . . . you've been a busy little bee, haven't you? Going off the beaten path. Poking your nose where you don't belong. Lying about who you are, what you are. Always scurrying behind the drywall, Seltzer. Breaking things. We don't like people who break things, Seltzer. But it just so happens you can help us fix something. Maybe then we'll strike your debts from our ledger.'

And then the voice tells you what it will need you to do, step by step. And it tells you that if you do not follow its instructions to the letter, you will die. A very slow, very painful death. And for the first time in your life, you realise you're going to have to do as you're told.

Turn to page 15.

Throwing caution to the wind, and gripped as you are by a sudden existential terror, you drop your kit. 'Something is coming!' you yell inexplicably. 'I'm not supposed to be here!'

Your driver looks scared, but there's something more to his expression. Like he expected this to happen somehow. Regardless, he seems unsure of how to react. You, however, have made your decision. Your legs are surging with adrenaline, and you pelt headlong across the car park and into the treeline. The group of men watch you go, uncertain about how to respond. Or perhaps they don't care.

You care, though. You can't *not* care. Your every organ, every muscle, every bone *strains* with an acute caring. There's something wrong with where you were all headed, something irrevocable, and you know it in every fibre of your being. You're deep in the woods now, John. The branches whip and lash at your face. You neglected to bring a torch, so all you have to guide you is the faint – very faint – light of the moon.

Finally, you reach . . . good lord, it's a miracle. A road. You've reached a road! How is this even possible? There's something out here, you're sure of it. You can't see much, but as you gaze out, you *think* you can see something coming towards you.

There's an odd, dreadful crunch, and everything goes dark. Well, darker than it was already.

Too bad, John. You might have been onto something there.

The End

Your adventure is over. You failed. If you wish to try again, turn back to the beginning at page 1.

Or, if you're done, wrap things up and go to page 369.

84

Later that night, you're standing next to your two detective buddies. You're cuffed and wearing your prison greens. The two are making small talk. You wager that if they knew what you did to four of their colleagues six months back you'd be the one buried in the woods. But mainly, you're wondering just how long it's been since you stepped outside the confines of your cell, how long it has been since you smelled freedom. Are you happy to be here? When was the last time you were happy, Seltzer? This is why you shouldn't break the rules. Things are meant to play out a certain way. There's a natural order to these things. A theme. You messed with that.

Speaking of 'meant to play out a certain way', here they come. The Kingswood – didn't you own a Kingswood once, Seltzer? – peels around the corner, and out steps the driver. Then, out steps a young man in white overalls. Suede shoes peek out from underneath. He makes eye contact with you.

'He's the one,' you mutter to yourself. Gripped by the urge to help the man, to help him escape this grim tableau, you glare at him. Your expression is implacable, you hope, but inside you're screaming. RUN, your brain bellows silently. RUN AS FAST AS YOU CAN.

He doesn't hear you. Time to lead them to the body. Turn to page 85.

He hears you. He runs. Turn to page 86.

The two detectives continue to make pleasant small talk, and you lead the group through the woods to the spot you were made to memorise in your concussion-riddled briefing six months back. At one point, as you're trudging through the pitch-black forest, you make eye contact with the driver. He subtly raises his finger to his lips, miming a silent shush your way. Then he winks. It's unsettling, Seltzer. It's extremely unsettling. You push onwards.

Finally, you reach the clearing. Once inside, you point at the agreed-upon spot, and the young man begins digging. You stand there patiently as he toils. At one point he looks up at you, exhausted, and you give him an apologetic shrug, gesturing to your cuffs. He gives you an understanding look, then keeps digging. This whole thing is weird. But you're almost there. You've almost got it all back on track. Good boy.

But you're Hard Seltzer. You're not *meant* to cooperate, you realise. You're not *meant* to help these people. You don't want to help them. You like breaking rules. You're disruptive. Disruptive is good.

With a start, you realise that if you're going to properly fuck this whole thing up, you don't have much time. You look down at the man digging and realise his digging implement could, in a pinch, get you and him out of this debacle. But your vision swims before you, and you can't quite make out what he's digging with. You also realise that it's sort of up to you, which is . . . odd. Roll with it, Seltzer. Make it happen.

He's digging with a hand trowel. Turn to page 87.

He's digging with a shovel. Turn to page 88.

He's digging with a FUCKING THERMAL LANCE, BABY.
Turn to page 89.

86

You did it! He looks genuinely panicked, so he drops his kit and bolts. The detectives look confused, perturbed and unsure how to proceed now.

'Do we . . . go after him?' one asks.

The other detective thinks for a moment. 'I don't know, honestly. I really don't—'

SHUFF.

SHUFF.

Both detectives drop to the floor. Shit. You look up and around, and see the driver striding towards you. 'Right,' he yells up at something you can't make out. 'He fucked it.' The man stops in place, adjusting the silenced pistol, which is still smoking in his gloved hands. He nods as if he's listening to some unseen figure talk his ear off. '. . . Right. So restart? Sorry, guys. Honestly no idea how he broke this one, I could have *sworn* we had it.' He taps his ear, clears his throat, and finally acknowledges your presence. He tuts at you condescendingly.

'You almost had it, didn't you? You were so close this time. Oh well. Don't fuck it up next time, okay? Every redo costs us, so stop taking the piss. Bye-bye now.'

He raises the pistol and you realise that, for the first time in your life, you are more like your namesake – seltzer – than ever before.

You are well and truly shaken.

The End

Your adventure is over. You failed. If you wish to try again, turn back to the beginning at page 1.

Or, if you're done, wrap things up and go to page 369.

You glare at the man. Again. He doesn't see you, exhausted as he seems to be, slogging away with his emasculating implement. He's going to be here for an eternity, and frankly, you simply don't have the time to dick around. You decide to go with the old 'I'm sick, help me, cough cough', WHAM routine.

You begin coughing. Subtly at first, but after a few minutes you're hacking your guts up, veins popping and eyes bulging.

'He's choking. Shit – he's choking!' yells the nearest detective.

'He's not choking, you dickhead. He's doing the old "I'm sick, help me, cough cough" WHAM routine!' replies the other tersely.

The driver wanders over, kneels down in front of you, and calmly looks you dead in the eye. 'Seltzer,' he murmurs, completely breaking your cover in the process. 'Is this nice man right? *Are* you doing the "I'm sick, help me, cough cough" WHAM routine?'

You nod.

SHUFF.

You collapse. The driver stands up straight and looks around. He yells skywards. 'Okay! Close it up, close it up, close it up. Let's take it from the top, people!'

The End

Your adventure is over. You failed. If you wish to try again, turn back to the beginning at page 1.

Or, if you're done, wrap things up and go to page 369.

88

A shovel is a useful thing, Seltzer. They're used for a myriad of tasks. Penetrating loose, tilled soil. Extracting columns of dirt for the sinking of fence posts, bulbs, or patio supports. Patting down flowerbeds. Shovelling manure. Or, in this case, staging a thrilling, improbable escape.

You glare at John.

John. *His name is John*, you repeat to yourself. He looks right at you. He has blue eyes, like yours. And just like that, he's inside your head, and you're inside his. He stands up, swings the shovel down, and your cuffs burst apart from one another.

You grab the revolver from the detective nearest you, aim it at the driver, and pull the trigger. The man's brains billow out the back of his skull with a pop, decorating the trees behind him. His body shudders, and as he falls, an earpiece drops to one side.

John draws his gun, aiming it at the two detectives. He's clearly in shock. 'We're off-script now,' you say to him. He nods, eyes wide, sweat coating his brow.

You lean down over the driver, and delicately pick up his earpiece. The squeaking of a tinny voice echoes from within.

You put the earpiece in and listen. Turn to page 90.

Don't put the earpiece in, you absolute spanner. Turn to page 91.

Hang on, you think to yourself. *He's not holding a shovel. I mean, he could have been, but fuck it, he isn't.*

He's holding a thermal lance, baby.

And that's impossible. Isn't it? And if he's holding a thermal lance . . . if he's participating in an impossible thing that you made happen . . . maybe you're not properly cuffed. Maybe they didn't press the wristband all the way in. As subtly as you can, you test the cuffs, not quite ready to believe your own burgeoning convictions. But sure enough . . .

They slide loose. It's happening, Seltzer. You're doing it.

What sounds like the drone of bees fills the air, and you realise it's static. Something very big and important is about to break, and somehow John senses what you're about to do.

You seize the lance. It's unwieldy, like a cyberpunk jousting pole. A huge steam vent on the side barks at you. John looks at you expectantly. You stare down at the readout on the power dial: 92 rpms. Next to it is a blinking green button. You crank the throttle, grin demonically, and turn to face the driver. The look that crosses his hateful little face is delicious.

'A thermal lance?' he exclaims pathetically. Your answer is the roar of an engine. The lance glows white hot, and shears clean through the driver. You did it. The detectives bolt into the woods, and you let them run. John whoops ecstatically. You . . .

Wait. The lance is overheating. Shit. Shit shit shit. It begins to oscillate crazily in your hand. And then . . . it detonates. Damn.

Your adventure is over. You failed. If you wish to try again, turn back to the beginning at page 1.

Or, if you're done, wrap things up and go to page 369.

You lift the earpiece, wipe off the viscera, and pop it into your left ear. Now you can clearly hear the voice on the other end.

'You shot him!' it exclaims. It's the same voice you heard that day in the room with the bright light, you realise.

'Yeah, I shot him,' you reply.

There's a pause, then a sigh. 'Look, I get it. I get why you'd want him dead. He keeps killing you, you want to get even.' This strikes you as true, though you can't seem to figure out precisely why. 'But look, there's a lot at stake here. There's beats we have to hit. You can't just come in and pull your Hard Seltzer schtick. There's a system, all right? There's—'

There's a cacophony of noise behind you. The tie-pin-wearing detective has drawn his gun and is aiming it at you. John, panicked, fires, hitting the man in the shoulder. The detective, in turn, reflexively pulls the trigger . . . hitting you. Square in the noggin.

You were close, Seltzer. *You were so close.*

The End

Your adventure is over. You failed. If you wish to try again, turn back to the beginning at page 1.

Or, if you're done, wrap things up and go to page 100.

You decide to leave the earpiece in place.

John raises an eyebrow. 'You're not curious?'

'Sure I am,' you say to him. 'But it's got brains on it.'

John gives you a look. He reaches into a pocket, pulls out a handkerchief and plucks the earpiece from the dead man's ear. Wiping it off in the same way that a deadpan mother wipes muck from her child's face, he hands you the tiny earpiece. 'There you go,' he says in a monotone voice. 'Clean as a whistle.'

'Sure,' you say, raising the earbud to your ear hesitantly. 'But you should see some of the places a whistle can fit.'

You put the earpiece in and listen. Turn to page 90.

92

You crank the throttle, grin demonically, and turn to face the driver. The look that crosses his hateful little face is delicious.

'A thermal lance?' he exclaims pathetically. Your answer is the roar of an engine. The lance glows white hot, and shears clean through the driver.

You did it. The detectives bolt into the woods, and you let them run. John whoops ecstatically. And then, just as the thermal lance begins to vibrate and build towards some manner of lethal miscalibration, you're struck by an idea: hit the blinking green button next to the readout for 92 rpms. You depress it. And just like that, the terrible whirring stops. The lance stills in your hand, and you're left in the clearing with John. The two halves of the driver lie wetly, gurgling gently. The light from the torch Flynn dropped casts strange shadows on the two of you.

John turns to you slowly and speaks.

'What now?'

You're not meant to be here.

No, seriously. You're not meant to be here.

Hello?

'Hello?' answers Seltzer.

Good, you can hear me.

Seltzer looks thrown. It's like there's a voice in his head, speaking right into his cerebral cortex.

I clear my throat. John, can you hear me too? John nods. He's nodding. Good, you can both hear me. Listen, guys. I'm breaking the rules here. I'm not meant to be doing this. Things are meant to pan out in a very specific way. See, John, the guy you're based on wants this story to end in a very set way. He's trying to . . . illustrate a point. I, however, don't agree entirely. I know how things went in real life—

'In real life?' John and Seltzer ask in unison.

Yes, guys, in real life. But this is a story, my story. I'm telling it. So I'm going to reach in and break the rules. But just this once. And do you know why?

They're both shaking their heads.

Because I believe it's important to shape your own reality. And if you want to make a happy ending for yourself, go right ahead.

'But . . . is this real?' asks Seltzer.

Yes, Seltzer. It is. So run. Run back to the Kingswood, throw the lance in the trunk, and drive. Consider yourself free of the confines of this story. The rest . . . well, the rest is up to you, really.

They leave in a hurry.

Now . . . listen. If you're reading this, we're about to jump back to the regularly scheduled programming. I had to trick Dad into leaving, so whatever you do, do NOT let on that this happened. We're just gonna skip to the end, and I'm gonna pretend none of this ever happened. But you and I know they secretly got away, okay? So don't worry. They're probably off in a spin-off book of their own somewhere, having adventures. Or maybe – and this seems more likely – they're in-between the pages of some grimy paperback. If you see something blinking up at you from the page, some subtext between the words, some unseen force . . . that could be them.

Okay. Here we go. Put on your game face.

You decide to finish this.

Turn to page 100.

94

Dad waits a moment, then calls again. A click signifies the call has gone through, and Dad sighs with relief. This time, though, the most marvellous thing happens.

John goes off-script.

It's not meant to happen, and Dad isn't expecting it, either. I can tell by the way his breath catches. He looks at me with a 'What the fuck do I do?' expression, and I shrug, feigning panic. Really, though, I'm riveted. This story keeps going the way it's meant to, with Dad's point being proven again and again . . . but now, there's this dickhead iteration of John pretending to be . . . hang on. I'll let you listen in.

'This is Senior Detective Hard Seltzer. Can this wait? I'm in the middle of a case. There's a dame outside and she smells like trouble.'

Dad is riffling through papers like a madman. He clears his throat and winches on a bizarre New Jersey accent. 'Seltzer. Where the hell have you been all night? This is the commissioner. Tell that dizzy dame she'll have to come back tomorrow. We need you downtown, pronto – you got that?'

I give him a thumbs up. Gotta roll with it, I guess. The call ends.

'Paul, what the fuck is going on?' Dad asks, exasperated.

I answer him honestly. 'I don't know, Dad. But I guess we gotta adapt.'

Time to adapt. Turn to page 13.

'Wow,' I say to Dad. 'They touched the speedometer.'

Dad looks at me, confused. 'Were they not meant to touch the speedometer?'

I pause. 'Look, I didn't put it there to have them touch it, but these stories are a fucking nightmare of interlocking beats and crisscrossing time shifts and whatnot. I think this might be a glitch of some sort?' Dad looks somewhat thrown. He's currently holding a microphone and sitting in front of a bank of CCTV monitors, watching the various story threads play out.

'Don't tell them what I'm doing!' he yells, spinning in his chair. 'They're not meant to see any of this – don't give them an edge. The whole point of this is to prove that you can't change anything in real life. Every story thread needs to draw them irrevocably towards the conclusion that wanting to go back and change things is futile and unhealthy!'

Dad grabs a sheaf of paper, leafs through it, and looks startled. Like he's missed something. He sits up straight, eyes alert, grim and focused. He picks up the receiver of a red bakelite phone, punches in a number, waits, then speaks into it with a gravelly voice.

'Hello,' says the distant voice on the other end. 'John Verhoeven speaking.'

'John,' Dad says, doing his best gruff-bastard impersonation as he reads off a page full of scribbled notes. 'Pack your shit up, you're heading over to Kuring-gai Chase National Park. We've got a body. Someone will pick you up and take you there in five. Make sure when you hit the road heading into the park, you take a left, then a right. Cheers. Oh, and bring a shovel.' Then he hangs up without saying goodbye. *Just like in the movies,* I think. On the monitor, a young John puts down the receiver and looks pensive.

If you decide to keep watching Dad, turn to page 94.

If you instead watch young John on the monitor, turn to page 56.

'Dad,' I say calmly. 'I need to go take a slash.'

'Mmhmm,' he replies distractedly. I smile, nod, and head to the bathroom.

I need to figure out a way to help, and I need to do it as quickly as I can, because Dad is not going to buy that I'm in the bathroom for very long. We're at a pivotal point here, and I need to make this count for something. Let me think.

Dad is going to get Seltzer into the prison. Which means an ambush, probably at the detectives' headquarters. It'll be in the lift. Derivative. And Seltzer can't escape that – he'll be out-numbered. Which means Seltzer will likely end up at prison, do some time, and then *he'll* be the prisoner showing the group where the body is buried. Clever! Which means . . . Ha! The idiot. He'll put Seltzer and John in the same spot eventually. Doesn't he get it? *John's not alone anymore.* But what can I do to help Seltzer survive the ambush, in order to tip the scales in your favour?

Hide a gun in the lift. Turn to page 44.

Hide a sword in the stairwell. Turn to page 99.

I stand up, crack my neck, and approach Dad in as chill a manner as I possibly can. He's in full creative mode now, and is checking the monitors regularly. He's also apparently on the phone to the prison, posing as some kind of district judge with an order to set up Seltzer with a fake cover. It looks to be going pretty well, all things considered.

'Listen,' I interrupt as politely as I can, 'Dad. Don't mean to bother you, but I think this might have gone on a tad too far.'

Dad looks crestfallen *and* annoyed. He holds a hand over the receiver. 'What do you mean, too far?'

'Well,' I venture as delicately as I can, 'maybe if the character in the story – based on you, I might add – is trying to bust out of it by any means necessary, then that could perhaps imply that he's . . . I don't know . . . *meant* to?'

And it's now that I know I've made a mistake. Because Dad might not be writing this book, or be in control of it, but he's figured out a way to do what he used to when I lived at home as a teenager: kick me out if I'm being unruly. He coolly walks over to a newly appeared button on the wall and, before I can scream a response, presses it.

The lights sputter out.

The End

Your adventure is over. You failed. If you wish to try again,
turn back to the beginning at page 1.

Or, if you're done, wrap things up and go to page 369.

98

You dig. You dig for quite a long time. Probably an hour, if we're being honest, John. Thankfully the overalls you're wearing protect your rather snappy outfit, but your shoes are shot before long. This makes you sad, primarily because your wife, Christine, bought them for you. You make a mental note to apologise when you get home. If you get home.

Around the hour mark, your digging hand is raw, and the other men assembled here look well and truly bored. You're flagging somewhat, and both of the detectives hover near you, alternating between watching you and gazing out into the darkness. Neither of them offers to help, nor does the driver, nor the prisoner . . . though in his defence, he's cuffed. He glances at you uncomfortably once in a while, at one point even giving you a look indicating that he wants to help, but can't. He raises his cuffed hands as if to illustrate the point, proffers a barely perceptible apologetic shrug, and stamps his feet to keep warm. It isn't, you realise, cold.

Then, finally, something dreadful happens. The dry, relenting *shhhhhhhufffff* of your trowel meeting little to no resistance is cut off by a declarative *SHUNK*. Well done, John. You've made contact with something.

Trowel, meet body.

Turn to page 45.

I nudge open the bathroom door and I look down the corridor towards the control room, where Dad is freaking out and/or plotting. His angry call with the warden is reaching fever pitch. I close the door as quietly as I can and tiptoe to another door, marked MUNITIONS. I open it and sneak inside.

Look, I gotta be honest with you . . . there's some insane stuff in here. And if I'm being candid, the ol' ADHD is having a real hard time sticking to the task at hand. So I reach for a sword. A huge, literal samurai sword. I turn it in my hand and observe the blade, trying to figure out a way I could hide this in the stairwell for Seltzer to find without it breaking the flow and logic of the story.

And then I see the tsuba. That's the round metal thing that guards the handle and ensures that during a fight the opponent's blade won't slide down and take the hero's fingers off. And this tsuba is the same one Dad got me when I turned thirty-one. See, when I was in my teens, Dad knew how badly I wanted a proper samurai sword, so he tracked down a replica. Then, a year later, he got into some financial strife and asked me, tearfully, whether he could sell it. And when I was thirty-one, he handed me this tsuba – this actual tsuba – and wrote me a letter apologising for not being able to afford a real sword, and that he hoped this would do.

So now, I'm racked with guilt. Crippling guilt. I love Dad. And maybe he has a point here. Maybe this story does need to always end a certain way to prove a point.

I trudge back to the control room, sigh, and hit the large button on the wall. Let's try this again, shall we?

And no swords this time.

Your adventure is over. You failed. If you wish to try again, turn back to the beginning at page 1.

Or, if you're done, wrap things up and go to page 100.

100

'Paul,' Dad cuts in. 'You can't change how things panned out.'

'Dad,' I reply, exasperated, 'I know that. Of course I know that. But now you know what it's like for me listening to your stories. While you were still in emergency services . . . I was reading Choose Your Own Adventure books. The damn things were everywhere in my bedroom.'

'I remember. We had to buy them,' he replies.

'Point is,' I say softly, 'the ADHD made focusing *impossible* for me. And it made hearing your police stories impossible too, because I'd be screaming internally at some of the choices you made. I was young, and I didn't realise that the misadventures, the mishaps, the fuck-ups, were what made your stories great. So when you tell the story of how you packed the wrong shovel, which in turn gave the news crew time to get there and get you into deep shit, I think . . . what could you have done differently? And as a kid, the only stories my idiot brain could parse were ones that let you choose. So I guess I want to ask . . . how did it feel, reliving this case? Getting the chance to choose again?'

Dad, to his credit, has been absorbing everything I've said. Finally, he speaks. 'I wish I could go back, Paul. And I . . . look. Sometimes I wish my brain worked the way yours does. Because if it did, if it couldn't ever rest on a single choice, maybe I'd have made some bolder ones back when I was on the force. But – and I don't want to labour the point here too much – you have to live with your choices, good and bad. Going back and playing with them isn't healthy. Wondering about what-if is fun . . . but I think if I did that too much, with all the shit I've seen, I'd go nuts.'

'Okay.' I sit for a moment before leaning forward, smiling. 'But do you want to dive back in again? Just one more time. I think there are a few . . . well, really weird choices worth revisiting.'

Dad smiles back. 'Sure. Just one more.'

Well, you heard the man. To do it all over again, go back to page 1 – or continue to the next page for the epilogue.

EPILOGUE

Dad sits there, holding the Choose Your Own Adventure book in his hands. He has a slightly euphoric look to him, like he's crossed through some giddy threshold. He pops it down and turns to me.

'I think I get it now,' he says, sounding brighter than he has in years.

I give him a quizzical look. 'Get it?'

'Yeah. I think I get it. I think . . . Hmm. I think maybe I get what it's like to be in your head.' He picks the book up again. 'You . . . struggled when you were little, Paul.'

'I know,' I say.

'No, I don't think you do. You were . . . different. Not from me – from everyone. And it's hard being the father of someone who sees the world so differently. When I bought you this book, I didn't do it because I knew it would cater to how your brain worked. I did it . . .' And he taps the cover, pointing at the kid detective standing proudly below the title.

And then it hits me.

I think back on all those years I spent worrying Dad didn't think I was enough like him to become a cop, or be as heroic as he was.

Now, I see the first book he bought me was practically a how-to guide on solving crimes. The kid on the cover even looks a little like me. A confused, slightly pained expression flits across my face, and Dad notices.

'The way you saw . . . see . . . the world is different from how I do, but I don't know if that's a weakness. Not really. It's fucking exhausting . . .'

I laugh.

'But,' he continues, 'it's what makes you special. Look. Sorry if I sound like Happy Healthy fucking Harold from the Life Education van, but it's true, mate. The people around you who gave you a hard time – they didn't get you. I mightn't have always understood, but I always, *always* wanted to. And if I didn't help enough when they were hard on you . . . honestly? I thought you were amazing enough to deal with it. And I didn't want you to think I didn't think you could, if that makes *any* fucking sense.'

I'm so floored by this emotional unravelling that I stop the tape, stand up and give Dad a hug. A big, tearful hug. Mum comes in and sees two men ugly-crying, the kind of crying that men who don't cry enough do. You know the kind. Like two walruses barking at each other. It's a disgrace, frankly. A right mess. And Mum comes over and hugs us, we have dinner, and I head back home.

Months later, I call Mum and Dad up, and on a whim, I tell them all about the dream. Remember, the one where I was Hard Seltzer, and I was in the swamp with Grey, looking for footprints? And they go quiet, Dad sounding a little choked up. And he tells me one more story. And I realise, with a start, why that dream seemed so damned real.

*

John opened Paul's door and looked down at his son. Fishing elbow-deep in a bucket of loose LEGO bricks, Paul turned and looked up at John with a kind of distracted indifference. John, determined to make this happen, beamed and bowed and clapped and crowed as he strode over to Paul, grinning.

'Paul!' he exclaimed, sounding as animated as he possibly could. 'Listen, I've got this case for you. Just across the road! Whaddya say, mate? Want to chuck your shoes on, maybe I can show you what I do when I'm on the job?' John waved a bright red plastic briefcase, held it out to Paul, and gestured for the door.

Paul stood up, confused. He shrugged and followed John out the door.

They exited the block of flats, John feeling suddenly taller than before. He'd told Grey, now retired from the job, what he intended to do. Grey chuckled down the phone, telling John he thought it was a brilliant idea, but telling him to temper his expectations. 'Sometimes,' Grey said, 'those we're trying to teach take a long, long time to twig to the lessons we're imparting.'

John laughed. 'Are you talking about me?'

'No comment,' said Grey.

John and Paul made their way across the park that was sprawled next to the flats where they lived, over the footpath, and crossed the quiet road. Upon reaching the other side, they met a low mesh fence. John hopped over, then reached down, lifted Paul up and popped him down on the other side. He brushed some stray debris from his son, then pointed down towards a very small clearing. 'These trees,' he said in a whisper, 'are very old.'

Paul looked at John, a little confused. 'Why are we here?' he said, the hint of a whine creeping into his voice. He reached for the bright red briefcase.

'Don't worry, mate,' John said kindly. 'I'll explain when we get there.'

'What are we looking for?' Paul asked, matching his dad's whisper and following in his huge footsteps.

'Evidence,' John said, suddenly aware just how much he felt like Grey, talking as his mentor had talked to him when *he* first joined Forensics. 'Footsteps. We need to take casts of footsteps.' He waved the briefcase again and they continued on in silence, moving deeper and deeper into the undergrowth.

Then, John stopped. He waved Paul over, leaned down and pointed. There, in a muddy puddle, was a smattering of bird prints, tiny but distinct. He grinned back at Paul, but rather than the rapt look of a fellow investigator, he was met with the deadpan stare of a sweaty, slightly impatient child who was looking around the place, distracted by a mosquito.

John placed his hand on Paul's shoulder, smiled, and waited for his son to drift back to the present. Eventually, Paul looked back at his dad and returned the smile. John put the briefcase down, opened it, and handed his son a small dish. He then tore open two small sachets and tapped a liberal quantity of white powder into the dish. He handed Paul a small flask, nodded, and watched as his son poured the water into the dish, mixing it with a tiny copper spoon. The mixture eventually smoothed.

'Plaster of Paris,' said John, delighted. He extended a finger towards the first bird print.

Paul poured the mixture in, watching it fill the shape. 'When can we take it out? Is this going to take long?' he asked, a little more surly than normal.

John looked over at his son, a little disappointed but trying to hide it. 'It'll take as long as it takes, mate,' he said. 'Be patient.'

The two Verhoeven boys squatted there, watching the thick white guck drying. After about three minutes of near-silence, a dumpy little mosquito landed on the surface, and, frustrated and impatient and overcome with petulance, Paul did the unthinkable. He swatted it. Hard. The plaster of Paris mixture went flying, spraying John and Paul with clotting ivory goo.

John looked furious, but before he could defuse the situation, Paul stood up and stormed off. John got up from his squat, grunting with exertion as he clambered to his feet. 'Paul!' he called, sounding a little sad now. 'Paul!'

Mum and Dad finish telling the story, and I stand there, a little numb, holding the phone.

'So . . . you were trying to show me what you did for a living.'

'I guess so,' Dad replies.

'And you got me a book . . . about being a detective.'

'Yes. Yes, I did.'

I mull over this for a minute. 'So I guess . . . I guess maybe you *did* get me, after all.'

I can almost hear Dad smile down the phone. 'I tried, mate,' he says tiredly. 'But I'll tell you what.'

'What?'

'Being a cop, doing forensics, high-speed chases. Coming across headless bodies. People on fire. Electrocutions. Necklaces made from severed penises. Cramming thermometers into dead people's arses. All of that, absolutely all of it . . . is ten times easier than having kids.'

Mum cackles so loudly I almost drop the phone.

My parents, ladies and gentlemen.

And I wouldn't trade them for the world.

ACKNOWLEDGEMENTS

Electric Blue is the book I always wanted to write – hell, it's about ten books in one – and as such there are a lot of wonderful people to thank.

First of all, I owe a tremendous thank you to Jane Novak, my literary agent, who on our first phone call together swore so emphatically I almost dropped my phone. I knew I liked her then. I adore her now. My ardent and eternal thanks go to Sophie at Penguin Random House, who took a chance on this frankly bonkers premise, and to Tom, the genius who patiently and lovingly edited *Electric Blue*. Thanks to everyone at Penguin Random House: you're all superstars.

I know I started this book with an idiotic Borat joke, so let me clarify: Tegan, my wife, is my entire world. Anyone who knows her can attest to the fact that she's always the smartest, fastest, sharpest and best person in the room. She pushes me, and makes me better, and she turned the *Loose Units* brand into a well-oiled machine. I love her so much it makes my teeth hurt.

My dad and mum deserve thanks, partially because they're heroic and wonderful, but mostly because they're incredible human beings. Thanks to Dad for letting me turn things that he lived through into bizarre metatextual adventures, and for letting me show the world how I see you, and thanks to Mum for being a constant, unending source of humility. And thanks, Mum, for teaching me to laugh more.

I'd like to thank my parents-in-law, Kevin and Carolyn Higginbotham. They're wonderful people, and they let me stay at their house to edit *Loose Units* for several arduous weeks. They're very patient, very kind, and are so physically small that they can conveniently be stowed in any overhead baggage compartments.

Thanks to the Two Jons for seizing *Loose Units* by the waist and holding it up on a railing like Kate bloody Winslet. Thanks to Josh and Liz for being a port in a storm, and to Bec and Jonathon and their mighty steed, Whiskey, for being incredible friends with lovely glossy coats. Thanks to Adam McKenzie and Rama Nicholas, whose love and support is the wind beneath my bloody wings. Thanks to all my beautiful friends at Roadshow, whose god-level tolerance for my shenanigans has changed my life. Thanks to Matt Lucas, who is a topnotch human.

And finally, thanks to all the *Loose Units* fans out there. You've turned some stories I told about things that happened to my dad into something very big, and very lovely, and very odd, and you've altered the course of my career in ways I'll be forever grateful for.

ABOUT THE AUTHOR

Paul F. Verhoeven is an author, broadcaster and entertainer. His first book, *Loose Units*, inspired the acclaimed spin-off *Loose Units* podcast, which he hosts with his father John. A mainstay on the Australian media landscape, Paul has spent years working extensively as a games and pop culture journalist across print, radio and TV. After starting his career hosting *Weekend Breakfast* on Triple J, he went on to host and write *Steam Punks* on ABC TV. Paul enjoys city pop, David Lynch's *Dune* and literally anything with meringue in it.

Discover a new favourite

Visit **penguin.com.au/readmore**